THE LETTER OF
JAMES

AN INTRODUCTION AND COMMENTARY

by

DOUGLAS J. MOO, B.A., M.Div., Ph.D.

Associate Professor of New Testament,
Trinity Evangelical Divinity School, Deerfield, Illinois

Inter-Varsity Press
Leicester, England

William B. Eerdmans Publishing Company
Grand Rapids, Michigan

Inter-Varsity Press
38 De Montfort Street, Leicester LE1 7GP, England

Wm. B. Eerdmans Publishing Company
255 Jefferson S.E., Grand Rapids, MI 49503

Published and sold only in the USA and Canada by Wm. B. Eerdmans Publishing Co.

British Library Cataloguing in Publication Data

Moo, Douglas J.
   The letter of James: an introduction and
   commentary.—(The Tyndale New Testament
   commentaries)
   1. Bible. N.T. James—Commentaries
   I. Title II. Series
   227'.9107   BS2785.3

IVP PAPERBACK EDITION 0-85111-885-2
EERDMANS EDITION 0-8028-0079-3

Set in Palatino
Typeset in Great Britain by Parker Typesetting Service, Leicester
Printed in USA by Eerdmans Printing Company, Grand Rapids, Michigan

Inter-Varsity Press is the publishing division of the Universities and Colleges Christian Fellowship (formerly the Inter-Varsity Fellowship), a student movement linking Christian Unions in universities and colleges throughout the United Kingdom and the Republic of Ireland, and a member movement of the International Fellowship of Evangelical Students. For information about local and national activities write to UCCF, 38 De Montfort Street, Leicester LE1 7GP.

GENERAL PREFACE

The original *Tyndale Commentaries* aimed at providing help for the general reader of the Bible. They concentrated on the meaning of the text without going into scholarly technicalities. They sought to avoid 'the extremes of being unduly technical or unhelpfully brief'. Most who have used the books agree that there has been a fair measure of success in reaching that aim.

Times, however, change. A series that has served so well for so long is perhaps not quite as relevant as it was when it was first launched. New knowledge has come to light. The discussion of critical questions has moved on. Bible-reading habits have changed. When the original series was commenced it could be presumed that most readers used the Authorized Version and one could make one's comments accordingly, but this situation no longer obtains.

The decision to revise and up-date the whole series was not reached lightly, but in the end it was thought that this is what is required in the present situation. There are new needs, and they will be better served by new books or by a thorough up-dating of the old books. The aims of the original series remain. The new commentaries are neither minuscule nor unduly long. They are exegetical rather than homiletic. They do not discuss all the critical questions, but none is written without an awareness of the problems that engage the attention of New Testament scholars. Where it is felt that formal consideration should be given to such questions, they are discussed in the Introduction and sometimes in Additional Notes.

But the main thrust of these commentaries is not critical. These books are written to help the non-technical reader to understand his Bible better. They do not presume a knowledge of Greek, and all Greek words discussed are transliterated; but the authors have the Greek text before them and their comments are made on the basis of the originals. The authors are free to choose their own modern translation, but are asked to bear in mind the variety of translations in current use.

The new series of *Tyndale Commentaries* goes forth, as the former series did, in the hope that God will graciously use these books to help the general reader to understand as fully and clearly as possible the meaning of the New Testament.

LEON MORRIS

CONTENTS

AUTHOR'S PREFACE

My first sermon, delivered to a long-suffering professor and four fellow novice preachers, was on James 1:22–25. I thought that James' emphasis on the need to do the Word was important in a seminary context, where all too easily the Scripture becomes a book to be analysed rather than a message to be obeyed. That the message was needed then is certain; that it is still urgently required is equally certain – and not only in seminaries. All across the world, people are awakening to biblical Christianity. Third world churches are burgeoning, American 'evangelicalism' continues to attract much attention, and European Christians are seeing renewal and a new evangelistic concern. Yet the personal and social transformations that should accompany such revival are, very often, sadly lacking. Why is this? Surely one of the main reasons is that the simple plea of James – 'do the Word' – is not being heeded. The Bible is being translated, commented on, read, studied, preached and analysed as never before. But it is questionable whether it is being obeyed to a comparable degree.

All this suggests that the message of James is one that we all need to hear – and obey. No profound theologian, James' genius lies in his profound moral earnestness; in his powerfully simple call for repentance, for action, for a consistent Christian lifestyle. His words need to thrust through our theological debates, our personal preconceptions, our spiritual malaise and set us back on the road to a biblical, invigorating, transforming Christianity.

I owe thanks to many people who helped in making this commentary possible. Dr Leon Morris has been an encouraging yet eagle-eyed editor. Trinity Evangelical Divinity School, where I teach, has graciously provided secretarial time – and Luann Kuehl has had the perplexing (and sometimes amusing) job of deciphering my handwriting. Students here at Trinity and in several churches have, with their papers, questions and comments, greatly influenced my understanding of the letter. My five children have been a source of diversion (not always wanted!), personal renewal and joy. Most of all, my wife Jenny has both encouraged me in the work and, by commenting on the whole manuscript carefully, immeasurably improved both its style and content. It is to her I dedicate the book.

DOUGLAS J. MOO

CHIEF ABBREVIATIONS

Adamson J. B. Adamson, *The Epistle of James* (*The New International Commentary on the New Testament*, Eerdmans, 1976).

Ant. Josephus, *Antiquities*.

AV The Authorized (or King James') Version, 1611.

BAGD *A Greek-English Lexicon of the New Testament and Other Early Christian Literature* (trans. of W. Bauer, *Griechisch-Deutsches Wörterbuch*), ed. by William F. Arndt and F. Wilbur Gingrich; second ed. revised and augmented by F. Wilbur Gingrich and F. W. Danker (University of Chicago Press, 1979).

BDF *A Greek Grammar of the New Testament and Other Early Christian Literature* by F. Blass and A. Debrunner; trans. and revised by Robert W. Funk (Cambridge University Press, 1961).

BibSac *Bibliotheca Sacra*.

Burdick D. W. Burdick, 'James' in *The Expositor's Bible Commentary, vol. 12* (Zondervan, 1981).

Calvin J. Calvin, *Commentaries on the Catholic Epistles*, trans. by John Owen (Edinburgh, 1855; Eerdmans, 1948).

Cantinat J. Cantinat, *Les Epitres de Saint Jacques et de Saint Jude* (Gabalda, 1973).

CBQ *Catholic Biblical Quarterly*.

Davids P. B. Davids, *The Epistle of James* (*The New International Greek Testament Commentary*, Paternoster Press/Eerdmans, 1982).

Dibelius M. Dibelius, *A Commentary on the Epistle of James*,

11

	revised by H. Greeven (*Kritisch-exegetischer Kommentar*; Eng. trans. Fortress Press, 1976).
EQ	*Evangelical Quarterly.*
ExpT	*Expository Times.*
GNB	Good News Bible: Today's English Version, 1976.
H.E.	Eusebius, *Historia Ecclesiastica.*
Hort	F. J. A. Hort, *The Epistle of St. James* (The Greek Text with commentary, as far as 4:7) (Macmillan, 1909).
HTR	*Harvard Theological Review.*
ISBE	*The International Standard Bible Encyclopaedia*, revised ed. edited by G. W. Bromiley (Eerdmans, 1979–).
JB	The Jerusalem Bible, 1966.
JBL	*Journal of Biblical Literature.*
JR	*Journal of Religion.*
Knowling	R. J. Knowling, *The Epistle of St. James* (*Westminster Commentaries*, Methuen, ²1910).
Laws	Sophie Laws, *A Commentary on the Epistle of James* (A. & C. Black/Harper & Row, 1980).
LW	Luther's Works.
LXX	The Septuagint (pre-Christian Greek version of the Old Testament).
Mayor	J. B. Mayor, *The Epistle of St. James* (Macmillan, ³1913).
Mitton	C. L. Mitton, *The Epistle of James* (Marshall, Morgan & Scott/Eerdmans, 1966).
MM	J. H. Moulton and G. Milligan, *The Vocabulary of the Greek New Testament* (Hodder & Stoughton, 1914–29; Eerdmans, 1930).
Moule	C. F. D. Moule, *An Idiom Book of New Testament Greek* (Cambridge University Press, 1971).
Mussner	F. Mussner, *Der Jakobusbrief* (Herder, ⁴1981).
NASB	The New American Standard Bible, 1963.
NEB	The New English Bible, Old Testament, 1970; New Testament, ²1970.
NIDNTT	*New International Dictionary of New Testament Theology*, edited by C. Brown. 3 vols. (Zondervan, 1975–78).
NIV	The Holy Bible: New International Version, Old

	Testament, 1978; New Testament, ^{2}1978.
NovT	*Novum Testamentum.*
NTS	*New Testament Studies.*
Phillips	J. B. Phillips, *The New Testament in Modern English*, 1958.
Reicke	B. Reicke, *The Epistles of James, Peter and Jude* (Doubleday, 1964).
Ropes	J. H. Ropes, *A Critical and Exegetical Commentary on the Epistle of St. James* (*International Critical Commentaries*, T. & T. Clark, 1916).
Ross	A. Ross, *The Epistles of James and John* (Marshall, Morgan and Scott, 1954).
RSV	The Holy Bible, Revised Standard Version, Old Testament, 1952; New Testament, ^{2}1971.
Tasker	R. V. G. Tasker, *The General Epistle of James* (*Tyndale New Testament Commentaries*, Inter-Varsity Press/ Eerdmans, 1956).
TDNT	*Theological Dictionary of the New Testament*, edited by G. Kittel and G. Friedrich, trans. by G. W. Bromiley. 10 Vols. (Eerdmans, 1964–76).
Turner	N. Turner, *Syntax*. Vol. 3 of *A Grammar of New Testament Greek* by J. H. Moulton (T & T. Clark, 1963).
WTJ	*Westminster Theological Journal.*
ZNW	*Zeitschrift für die neutestamentliche Wissenschaft.*

Quotations from Philo are taken from the Loeb Classical Library edition of the Works of Philo. The Apocrypha is cited from the RSV translation. The Pseudepigrapha is cited in the translation edited by J. H. Charlesworth, *The Old Testament Pseudepigrapha*, vol. 1 (Doubleday, 1983).

INTRODUCTION

I. THE LETTER IN THE CHURCH

The epistle of James has had a controversial history. Along with
1 and 2 Peter, 1, 2 and 3 John, and Jude, it belongs to that
category of New Testament epistles called 'general' or 'catholic'
(in the sense of 'universal'). This designation was given to these
seven letters early in the history of the church because each
appears to be addressed to the church at large rather than to a
single congregation. These letters also shared an uncertain
status in many areas of the early church. Along with Hebrews
and Revelation, several of them were the last to achieve
generally recognized canonical status. In the case of James, it
was not until the end of the fourth century that both eastern and
western Christendom acknowledged it as Scripture.

The first mention of the epistle of James by name comes early
in the third century. But since ancient authors did not always
cite their sources, it is possible that earlier writings made use of
James without acknowledgment. Mayor discerned allusions to
James in most of the New Testament epistles and in many late
first and early second century non-canonical Christian writings.[1] In many of these cases, however, dependence on James
cannot be confirmed. The difficulty is that most of these parallels involve widespread traditional teaching. Very often, then,
the relationship between James and these other books is
indirect: both have made use of this traditional body of teaching.
This is almost certainly the case for the two New Testament

---

[1]Mayor. pp. lxix–lxxi, lxxxviii–cix.

books that have the most in common with James – Matthew and 1 Peter. Among non-canonical early Christian writings, the Shepherd of Hermas (early or middle second century) has the greatest number of parallels to James. In the section of that book called the 'Mandates', several of James' characteristic themes are found; the encouragement to pray with faith and without 'double-mindedness' in Mandate 9 is particularly close in wording and emphasis to James 1:6–8. Probably this section of Hermas is dependent on James. It is also possible that 1 Clement (AD 95) and the Epistle of Barnabas (written some time between AD 70 and 132) show dependence on James, but this is not certain.

Clement, head of the important catechetical school in Alexandria, is said to have written a commentary on James, but no such commentary has ever been discovered, and Clement never shows dependence on James in his extant writings.[1] Clement's successor in Alexandria, Origen, is the first to refer to the letter of James by name. He cites the letter as Scripture (*Select. in Ps.* 30:6) and attributes the letter to James, 'the apostle' (*Commentary on John*, frag. 126).[2] The Latin translation of Origen's works, made by Rufinus, explicitly identifies the author of the letter as the brother of the Lord, but the reliability of Rufinus' work is open to question.

Other third-century writings show acquaintance with James, and the pseudo-Clementine tractate *Ad Virgines* seems to quote James as Scripture. Eusebius (d. AD 339) uses James frequently in his writings and apparently accords it canonical status. However, he also includes it among the 'disputed books' (*antilegomena*), signifying that he was aware of some Christians who questioned its scriptural authority (*H.E.* III. 25.3; II.23.25). Probably he has in mind the Syrian church, where many of the

---

[1]B. F. Westcott (*A General Survey of the History of the Canon of the New Testament* [Macmillan, ⁶1889], pp. 357–358) theorizes that 'Jude' should be read for 'James' in the statement of Cassiodorus that attributes the commentary to Clement. See, on the other hand, Mayor, p. lxxx and Tasker, p. 18.

[2]In *Comm. in John* XIX, 6 (*Patrologia Graeca* XIV, 569), Origen quotes from James 2 and asserts that the words are found in *tē pheromenē Iakobou epistolē* (the epistle bearing [the name of] James). The word *pheromenē* ('bear, carry') has been taken as an indication of Origen's doubts about the epistle's origins, but the word simply means 'current' and does not qualify Origen's acceptance of the letter (*cf.* Ropes, p. 93; Mussner, p. 39).

general epistles had a difficult time finding acceptance – Theodore of Mopsuestia (d. 428) rejected all the general epistles. James was, however, included in the fifth-century Syriac translation, the Peshitta, and is quoted approvingly by Chrysostom (d. 407) and Theodoret (d. 458). With some exceptions, then, the eastern church readily accepted James as a canonical book.

The situation in the west was similar, although acceptance of James came a bit later there. Neither the Muratorian canon (late second century) nor the Mommsen catalogue (giving the African canon *c.* 360) mentions James.[1] The earliest clear references to James in the west come in the middle of the fourth century, when Hilary of Poitiers (writing in 356–358) and Ambrosiaster (d. 382) each quote James once. Jerome's influence was important in leading to the final acceptance of James in the western church. He included the epistle in his Latin translation, the Vulgate, and cited it often in his writings. And, in an argument which was to have considerable importance, Jerome identified the author as the 'brother' of the Lord mentioned in Galatians 1:19. At about the same time, Augustine added his weight of authority, and no questions about James were again raised in the western church until the Reformation.

Thus James came to be recognized as canonical in all segments of the early church – and this without the benefit of a single authority imposing a decision. To be sure, James' status was not immediately recognized. But it is important to stress that James was not *rejected*, but *neglected*. How may this neglect be explained? One factor may have been uncertainty about the apostolic origin of the book, since the author identifies himself only by name and James was a common name in the ancient world. Another factor could have been the traditional character of much of James' teaching – the letter contains little fuel for the fiery theological debates in the early church.[2] More importantly, perhaps, was the nature and destination of the epistle. The letter betrays a strong Jewish orientation and was probably

---

[1] It is possible, however, that the omission from the Muratorian Canon is accidental, since the text of the canon is mutilated. *Cf.* Westcott, *History of the Canon*, pp. 219–220; Mayor, p. lxvii; on the other hand, Mussner, p. 41.

[2] Dibelius, pp. 53–54; D. Guthrie, *New Testament Introduction* (Inter-Varsity Press, 1970), pp. 736–739.

written to Jewish churches in Palestine or Syria. The early demise of the Jewish church in Palestine as a result of the Jewish revolts of AD 66–70 and 132–135 may have resulted in a serious slow-down in the circulation of the letter. It may be significant in this regard that Origen makes reference to James only after coming into contact with the church in Palestine.[1]

It was at the time of the Reformation that doubts about James were again expressed. Erasmus, impressed by the good quality of James' Greek, questioned the traditional view that the letter was written by the Lord's brother. Luther, too, questioned the apostolic authorship of James, but his criticism went much deeper than Erasmus'. For Luther, the sticking-point was the theological tension that he perceived between James and the 'chief' New Testament books over the matter of justification by faith. James, said Luther, 'mangles the Scriptures and thereby opposes Paul and all Scripture' (*LW* 35:397), and he characterized the letter as 'an epistle of straw' (*LW* 35:362). Along with Jude, Hebrews and Revelation, therefore, Luther consigned James to the end of his German translation of the New Testament. But, while Luther obviously had difficulties with James and came close to giving the letter a secondary status, his criticism should not be overdrawn. He did not exclude James from the canon and, it has been estimated, cites over half the verses of James as authoritative in his writings.[2] Even the 'epistle of straw' reference must be understood in its context: Luther is not dismissing James as worthless, but contrasting it unfavourably with the 'chief books' (John's Gospel, 1 John, Paul's epistles [especially Romans, Galatians and Ephesians] and 1 Peter), 'which show you Christ and teach you all that is necessary and salutary for you to know, even if you were never to see or hear any other book or doctrine'. Therefore, Luther says of James elsewhere, 'I cannot include him among the chief books, though I would not prevent anyone from including or extolling him as he pleases, for there are otherwise many good sayings in him' (*LW* 35:397).

Few of the other reformers followed Luther in his criticism of

[1] *Cf.* Laws, p. 24.
[2] D. Stoutenberg, 'Martin Luther's Exegetical Use of the Epistle of St. James' (M.A. Thesis, Trinity Evangelical Divinity School, Deerfield, Illinois, 1982), p. 51.

James. Calvin, for instance, while admitting that James 'seems more sparing in proclaiming the grace of Christ than it behooved an Apostle to be', notes that 'it is not surely required of all to handle the same arguments'.[1] He accepted the apostolic authority of James and argued for a harmonization between James and Paul on the issue of justification. Calvin's approach is surely the correct one. In hindsight, we can see that Luther's excitement over his 'discovery' of the doctrine of justification by faith and his polemical context prevented him from taking a balanced approach to James and some other New Testament books. With greater knowledge of the Jewish background of James, and at a distance of several centuries from the battles Luther was fighting, we can appreciate the way James and Paul complement one another. Their opponents are different, and their arguments accordingly different, but each makes an important contribution to our understanding of our faith.

II. AUTHORSHIP

The author of the letter identifies himself simply as 'James' (Gk. *Iakōbos*). Who is this individual? The New Testament knows of at least four different men named James:

1. James the son of Zebedee. Called to be a follower of Jesus early in the ministry (Mk. 1:19), James, along with his brother John and Peter, became one of the apostles closest to Jesus (*cf.* Mk. 5:37; 9:2; 10:35; 14:33).

2. James the son of Alphaeus. Also one of the twelve, he is mentioned only in the lists of the apostles and (possibly) in Mark 15:40 as 'James the younger', or 'lesser' (simply 'James' in the parallel, Mt. 27:56).[2]

3. James the father[3] of Judas. This Judas, who is distinguished from Judas Iscariot (see Jn. 14:22), is identified as one of the twelve in Luke 6:16 (and see Acts 1:13) and is probably to be

---

[1]Calvin, p. 277.

[2]Alternatively, it is possible to regard this James as a fifth individual with that name (as does W. G. Kümmel, *Introduction to the New Testament* [Westminster, 1976], p. 411).

[3]The phrase in Lk. 6:16 and Acts 1:13 could also be rendered 'Judas *the brother* of James' (as in AV), in which case James the Lord's brother might be intended (*cf.* Jude 1). But the translation 'son of' for the 'genitive of relationship' is more likely.

identified with Thaddaeus in Matthew 10:3 and Mark 3:18.

4. James, 'the Lord's brother' (Gal. 1:19). Jesus' brothers did not believe in him during his earthly ministry (Jn. 7:5; *cf.* Mk. 6:3), but James quickly attained a position of prominence in the Jerusalem church (Acts 12:17; 15:13; 21:18; Gal. 2:9).

The James of the epistle need not, of course, be identified with a James mentioned in the New Testament. But the use of the name by itself in a letter written with such authority implies that the author was a well-known figure and it is improbable that such an individual would have gone unmentioned in the New Testament. Of the four New Testament James, only the son of Zebedee and the Lord's brother stand out as prominent. James the son of Zebedee, however, died a martyr's death in AD 44 (Acts 12:2) and it is unlikely that the epistle was written as early as this. We are left, therefore, with James, the Lord's brother, as the most likely author of the epistle.

This James became a popular and respected figure in the early church, especially among Jewish Christians. He was venerated as the first 'bishop' of Jerusalem and was given the title 'the righteous' or 'the just' because of his faithfulness to the law and constancy in prayer. Much of our information about James comes from Hegesippus' account of James' death as recorded by Eusebius (*H.E.* II.23). He tells us that James was stoned by the scribes and Pharisees for refusing to renounce his commitment to Jesus. This account of James' death is independently confirmed by Josephus (*Ant.* xx.9.1), who also enables us to date it in AD 62. However, much of the rest of Hegesippus' account, which portrays James as a zealot for the law, is legendary.[1] It may be that Hegesippus derived his information from a strict sect of Jewish Christians, called Ebionites, who regarded Paul with considerable disfavour and extolled James as the true heir to Jesus' teaching.[2] Therefore, while all our sources agree that

---

[1] *Cf.* J. B. Lightfoot, *The Epistle of St. Paul to the Galatians* (Macmillan, [10]1890), p. 366; Ropes, p. 66.

[2] In the pseudo-Clementine *Epistle of Clement* 1:1, James is named as the 'bishop of bishops'; according to the Gospel of the Hebrews (quoted in Jerome, *De vir. ill.* 2) the Lord appears first to James after his resurrection; in *The Gospel of Thomas*, Logion 12, the disciples ask Jesus, 'Who is to be our leader?' and Jesus replies, 'Wherever you are you are to go to James the righteous, for whose sake heaven and earth came into being' (the quotation is

James was a pious, devoted Jewish Christian, anxious to maintain good relationships with Judaism, the picture of a legalistic, anti-Paul James must be rejected as a tendentious caricature.

James has figured importantly in church history on another score also. As ascetic tendencies became ever more influential in the early church, the description of James, along with others, as a 'brother of the Lord' became a controversial issue. For, taken straightforwardly, this designation contradicts the notion that Mary remained a virgin after the birth of Jesus. Jerome popularized the view (often called the Hieronymian view, after that church father) that James and the other 'brothers' of Jesus were in fact his cousins. He identified Mary of Clopas, a sister of Mary (Jn. 19:25), with the Mary who is said to be the mother of James and Joses (Mk. 15:40), both of whom are identified as 'brothers' of Jesus (Mk. 6:3). Thus James and Joses would be cousins, not brothers of Jesus. The interpretation of the relationship among the different Marys and Jameses mentioned in these texts is a vexing question that we will not pursue further here;[1] suffice to say that Jerome's interpretation is by no means the only one. Most damaging to the Hieronymian position is the fact that *adelphos* always means 'brother' when blood relationship is denoted in the New Testament. James, then, must either be an older brother of Jesus, borne to Joseph by a wife before Mary (the 'Ephiphanian' view),[2] or a younger brother of Jesus, borne to Joseph and Mary (the 'Helvidian' view). Of these, the Helvidian better explains the close association suggested in the New Testament between Mary, the mother of Jesus, and the brothers of Jesus (*cf.* Mk. 3:31; 6:3).[3]

It is this James, then, a younger brother of Jesus and respected

---

taken from *The Nag Hammadi Library*, ed. J. M. Robinson [Harper & Row, 1977], p. 119). Mussner (pp. 4–7) cites much of the literature and provides a helpful discussion.

[1]See especially the discussion between J. J. Gunter, 'The Family of Jesus', *EQ* 46, 1974, pp. 25–41, and J. W. Wenham, 'The Relatives of Jesus', *EQ* 47, 1975, pp. 6–15.

[2]This view is defended at length by Lightfoot in his excursus on 'The Brethren of the Lord' in *The Epistle of St. Paul to the Galatians*. Lightfoot claims that this view offers the best explanation for the authority Jesus' brothers have over him (Jn. 7:1–5), and for Jesus' committing the care of his mother to a disciple rather than to one of his brothers (Jn. 19:25–27). But it is not clear that Jesus' brothers have any more authority over him than any relative might possess, and his brothers' opposition to his message suffices to explain his passing them over as caretakers of his mother.

[3]For an extended defence of the Helvidian position, see especially Mayor, pp. vi-lv.

leader of the Jewish-Christian church in Jerusalem, who is most naturally identified as the author of the letter bearing his name. Is there other evidence to confirm this identification? The testimony of the ancient church, as we have seen, is in agreement with this conclusion. This testimony, though not very early, is consistent in maintaining that James, the Lord's brother, wrote this epistle. It was only very late, and then rarely, that the epistle was assigned to James the son of Zebedee or to James the son of Alphaeus.[1]

The Greek of the epistle contains some striking similarities to the Greek of the brief speech attributed to James, the Lord's brother, in Acts 15:13–21, and to the letter sent under his authority, recorded in Acts 15:23–29. The epistolary 'greeting' (*chairein*) occurs in James 1:1 and Acts 15:23, but only one other time in the New Testament; the use of 'name' (*onoma*) as the subject of the passive verb 'call' (*kaleō*) is peculiar, yet occurs both in James 2:7 and Acts 15:17; the appeal 'listen, my brothers' is found in both James 2:5 and Acts 15:13; and there are other slight similarities.[2] These parallels are certainly not numerous enough to provide proof of common origin, yet they are suggestive when taken in conjunction with the first two points.

Finally, there are several features of the letter that do not point directly to James the Lord's brother, but would be quite in keeping with his authorship. The Jewish atmosphere of the book is very marked: Old Testament and Jewish teachings are frequently alluded to; the style reflects in places both the 'proverbial' nature of Jewish wisdom traditions and the denunciatory preaching of the prophets; the meeting-place of the church is called a synagogue (2:2); and a central Jewish tenet, the oneness of God, is specifically mentioned (2:19). On the other hand, the epistle shows little evidence of a developed or self-consciously Christian theology. All this suggests an author who was writing at an early date, in a Jewish context, and who sought to maintain good relationships with Judaism. The way in which the teaching of Jesus thoroughly permeates the letter,

---

[1]Some Spanish writers, from the seventh century on, claimed that their patron, the son of Zebedee, was the author; the tenth-century Corbey MS makes the same ascription. Calvin (p. 277) suggests that James the son of Alphaeus may be the author.
[2]See Mayor, pp. iii–iv, for a full list and discussion.

without being directly cited, would also be entirely natural for someone with James' background. And, finally, James' position as the leader of the 'mother' church of Jewish Christians in Jerusalem would eminently qualify him to address an authoritative admonition to 'the twelve tribes in the Dispersion'.

These considerations together give us excellent reason to adopt the traditional view that James, the brother of the Lord, wrote this letter. But many scholars have felt otherwise and a number of alternative theories of authorship have been propounded. One of the more extreme views denies that James is basically a Christian book. According to this proposal, James was originally a Jewish tractate that was 'christianized' with a couple of references to Jesus (see 1:1 and 2:1).[1] This theory has many weaknesses, but the decisive objection to it is the degree to which the letter is permeated with references to the teaching of Jesus.[2] A few scholars have attributed the book to an unknown James.[3] But the view that has attained the most popularity assigns the epistle to an unknown Christian leader. The name James in 1:1 – which is usually taken to refer to the Lord's brother – was either added at a later date (so that the book was originally anonymous) or was used by the author himself in order to lend greater authority to the book (in which case the book is pseudonymous). Advocates of these alternative theories are convinced that the letter itself contains features incompatible with authorship by the Lord's brother. Four such features are most often cited. We will examine each in turn.

1. First, it is held to be inconceivable that a brother of the Lord could have written such a document without some reference to his special relationship to the Lord, or to the resurrection appearance which may well have led to his conversion (cf. 1 Cor.

---

[1] Cf. L. Massebieau, 'L'épitre de Jacques – est-elle l'oeuvre d'un Chrétien?', Revue de l'Histoire des Religions, 32, 1895, pp. 249–283; F. Spitta, 'Der Brief des Jakobus', Zur Geschichte und Literatur des Urchristentums, 2 (Vandenhoeck und Ruprecht, 1896), pp. 1–239. A. Meyer (Das Rätsel des Jacobusbriefes [Töpelmann, 1930]) suggested that this original Jewish document was based on the 'testament' of Jacob to his twelve sons in Genesis 49.

[2] G. Kittel, 'Der geschichtliche Ort des Jacobusbriefes', ZNW 41, 1942, pp. 84–91.

[3] Erasmus; Luther; A. M. Hunter, Introducing the New Testament (Westminster, 1957), pp. 164–165 (although Hunter is more cautious in the third edition [1972]; cf. pp. 168–169). J. Moffatt (The General Epistles: James, Peter and Judas [Hodder & Stoughton, 1928], p. 2) thinks that an unknown James was the author and that the name of the more famous James of Jerusalem was later linked with it.

15:7).[1] However, special interest in physical ties to Jesus emerged only after the time of James' death; therefore the author's failure to include the title 'brother of the Lord' stands against pseudonymity and in favour of authenticity.[2] Moreover, James' physical relationship to Jesus did not spill over into a spiritual relationship. He remained estranged from Jesus and his true 'family' – those who do the will of God (Mk. 3:35) – until after the resurrection. If, then, being a brother of the Lord gave James no special insight into the person and mission of Jesus and carried with it no special status, his failure to mention the relationship should occasion no surprise. Nor should it occasion surprise that James does not describe his special confrontation with the resurrected Christ. Paul, whose vision of the resurrected Christ decisively changed the course of his life, refers to it in only two of his thirteen letters. Tasker has pointed out the capriciousness of this sort of argument by noting that 2 Peter is often considered pseudonymous because its author *does* emphasize his relationship to Jesus.[3] In fact, without considerably more information about the circumstances in which New Testament letters were written, and the degree of intimacy between the author and his readers, arguments based on what a particular individual was likely to have written or not are of little value.

2. A second factor which is said to weigh heavily against the traditional view of authorship is the language and the cultural background of the letter. James is written in idiomatic Hellenistic Greek, with some literary flourishes (*cf.* the incomplete hexameter in 1:17), and occasionally employs language derived from Greek philosophy and religion (*e.g.* 'the cycle of nature' in 3:6). This Greek, it is alleged, can hardly be attributed to the son of a Galilean carpenter who was known in tradition as a conservative Jewish Christian and who, as far as we know, never left the confines of Palestine. Three responses may be made to this argument. First, while the Greek of James is undeniably more polished and closer to the 'higher *koinē*' than most New Testament Greek, its quality should not be exaggerated. While exhibi-

---

[1]*Cf., e.g.*, Laws, p. 40.   [2]Kittel, *art. cit.*, pp. 73–75.
[3]Tasker, p. 20. Dibelius, who thinks that James is pseudepigraphic, also notes the subjectivity of this argument (p. 17).

ting some literary skill, the author does not use long words and elaborate grammatical structures. As Ropes says, '. . . there is nothing to suggest acquaintance with the higher styles of Greek literature'.[1]

Secondly, the degree to which any particular Palestinian Jew could have written idiomatic Greek is impossible to determine. Certainly Greek was widely used in Palestine (particularly in Galilee) and many Palestinians, even from poor families, would grow up with fluency in the language.[2] The real question is: would James have been exposed to the kind of influences that would have enabled him to write the semi-literary Greek of this letter? Without knowing the details of James' education, the extent of his travels or the people with whom he associated, this question is impossible to answer. We may certainly suspect that a man elevated to the head of the Jerusalem church had the capacity to learn Greek well; and the 'Hellenistic' element of that church (cf. Acts 6:1) would have given him both the opportunity and perhaps the motivation to acquire facility in the language. J. N. Sevenster, who uses James as a test case in his investigation of the use of Greek in Palestine, concludes that the Lord's brother could have written this letter.[3] This, of course, does not prove that he did; but the language is no obstacle to the view.

Thirdly, the philosophical and religious concepts that are found in James are all in the nature of widespread, popular concepts that would have been familiar to decently educated people in Palestine, where Hellenistic ideas were very widespread.[4] It is quite arbitrary to argue that James could not have been familiar with them. One may as well argue that a 'man in the street' has a degree in philosophy because he uses the word 'existentialism'.

3. The approach to the Old Testament law exhibited in the

[1]Ropes, p. 25. T. Zahn (Introduction to the New Testament, 1 [Kregel, 1906], p. 112) minimizes the quality of the Greek even further: 'how limited is his [author of James] command of this foreign language.'

[2]This has been demonstrated by, among others, J. N. Sevenster, Do You Know Greek? How much Greek could the first Jewish Christians have known? (Brill, 1968).

[3]Do You Know Greek?, p. 191. Cf. also N. Turner, Style, Vol. 4 of A Grammar of New Testament Greek by J. H. Moulton (T. & T. Clark, 1976), p. 114.

[4]M. Hengel's already classic work, Judaism and Hellenism (2 vols. Fortress, 1974) has documented the evidence of a thorough penetration of 'Hellenistic' ideas in first-century Palestine.

epistle is the third reason why many critics think James 'the Just' could not have written it. The author characterizes the law (*nomos*: the Jewish *torah*) as 'the law of liberty' (1:25; 2:12) and 'the royal law' (2:8) and focuses exclusively on moral commandments (2:11), ignoring the ritual law (see the silence in 1:27). This 'liberal' approach to the law, it is claimed, is in complete contrast to what we know of the attitude of James, who sought to impose the ritual law on Paul in Acts (21:20–25) and who is known in both Jewish and Christian tradition as an exemplar of 'torah-piety'.[1] Again, there are two things to be said about this argument. First, the picture of James as 'an advocate of hidebound Jewish-Christian piety'[2] requires considerable modification. As we have seen, much of the evidence for this picture comes from Hegesippus, whose historical veracity is more than a little questionable. The New Testament certainly portrays James as one who was concerned to maintain the best possible relationships between Jews and Christians and who accordingly advocated the legitimacy of Jewish tradition and customs for Jewish-Christians (Acts 21:20–25; perhaps Gal. 2:12). But it also makes clear that he opposed the attempt to impose the Mosaic law on Gentile Christians (Act 15:13–21); and nowhere does he argue that Christians, Jewish or not, *must* continue observing the ritual law. The point is, then, that the ritually legalistic James, with whom the author of the epistle is sometimes contrasted, is little more than an unhistorical fabrication. We must also keep in mind that an author's silence about an issue does not necessarily indicate his lack of concern about it. Thus, if James is writing to a group of Christians among whom the observance of the ritual law is not an issue, there may be no reason for him to mention it.[3] We will say more about James' attitude towards the law in our summary of his theology and in our comments on the relevant verses. Suffice to say here that the attitude towards the law found in the epistle is by no means incompatible with the view which James of Jerusalem is likely to have held.

4. The fourth main reason for denying that James, the Lord's

---

[1]Dibelius calls this the 'decisive argument' against the traditional view (p. 18). *Cf.* also Laws, pp. 40–41.

[2]The description is Dibelius' (p. 17).   [3]Guthrie, *New Testament Introduction*, p. 751.

brother, could have written this epistle involves the vexing problem of the relationship between James and Paul in their teaching on justification. As is well known, James' insistence that works are taken into account in justification (2:14–26) is often seen as a direct contradiction of Paul's proclamation of justification by faith 'alone'. Most scholars now agree, however, that the two cannot be said to be in direct contradiction on this issue. Their use of key terms with different meanings and the different problems with which they are concerned result in their arguments passing each other's by, like ships in the night. Either each is unaware of what the other is saying, or one of them is responding to a misunderstood form of the other's teaching. Most scholars think the latter situation is the case, and that James is reacting to a misunderstood Pauline theology. This is because the slogan 'justification by faith' which James deals with is difficult to trace to any other source than the preaching of Paul, who made it a distinctive part of his message. On this basis, then, it is claimed that the letter of James could not have been written by James of Jerusalem, because this James must have been very well acquainted with the teaching of Paul – the two were key participants in the first 'council' of the church (Acts 15), and met at a later date also, when some of these basic theological issues must have been discussed (Acts 21:18–25). The letter of James must have been written late in the first century, when Paul's theology was no longer understood in its proper context. Kümmel gives succinct expression to this argument: 'The debate in 2:14ff. with a misunderstood secondary stage of Pauline theology not only presupposes a considerable chronological distance from Paul – whereas James died in the year 62 – but also betrays a complete ignorance of the polemical intent of Pauline theology, which lapse can scarcely be attributed to James, who as late as 55/56 met with Paul in Jerusalem (Acts 21:18ff.).'[1]

The issue touched on here is one of the most difficult in the epistle of James. We shall devote a full discussion to it in the section on James' theology and in the commentary on 2:14–26. For the present, however, it is sufficient to point out that the

---

[1]Kümmel, *Introduction to the New Testament*, p. 413.

situation we have described – assuming, for the moment, its accuracy – is capable of a very different explanation. Could it not be that the perverted form of Paul's teaching contested in James 2 is very *early* and that James is not yet aware of Paul's true intent because they have not yet met? Paul undoubtedly began preaching very shortly after his conversion (to be dated about AD 33). How soon Paul seized on and proclaimed his distinctive emphasis on justification 'apart from works of the law' is impossible to know for certain; but the earliest Pauline letters presume the full development of the concept. We know also that already during Paul's ministry his preaching on justification by faith was being misunderstood (*cf.* Rom. 3:5–8). It is not at all improbable, then, that some Christians who had been exposed to Paul's preaching may have – intentionally or not – perverted Paul's doctrine into an excuse for spiritual passivity. James' attack on this perversion would then betray 'a complete ignorance of the polemical intent of Pauline theology' because James was not yet directly acquainted with Paul's teaching.[1] Indeed, it is perhaps more probable that a 'complete ignorance' of the thrust of Paul's teaching would exist before his letters were widely circulated than long afterward. The possibility we suggest would imply an early date for James; but we hope to show in the next section that an early date has much to commend it. At least we can conclude that an early date is as capable of explaining James 2 as a late one. This means, then, that the argument of James 2 presents no difficulty in ascribing the letter to James, the Lord's brother.

We conclude, therefore, that the epistle contains nothing that James, the Lord's brother, could not have written. The way is then open to accept the epistle's own apparent claim that James was the author. Still, there are some who, while accepting this claim, are impressed by one or more of the arguments just examined. These scholars suggest some sort of compromise solution, according to which someone besides James had a hand in the composition of the letter. Some attempt to explain the quality of the Greek by supposing that a scribe was responsible

---

[1]Kittel, *art. cit.*, ZNW 41, 1942, pp. 96–97; W. Wessel, *ISBE*, 2, p. 765.

for the actual composition.[1] This hypothesis cannot *a priori* be ruled out, for we know that scribes (or *amanuenses*, as they were called) were frequently used in the drafting of ancient letters. In the case of James, however, the exact wording is so often crucial to the flow of the letter (see, *e.g.*, the word-plays: *chairein*, 'greeting', 1:1/*charan*, 'joy', 1:2; *leipomenoi*, 'lacking', 1:4/*leipetai*, 'lacks', 1:5) that the final compositor must almost be identified as the author.[2] Another suggestion is that our epistle is a free translation of an Aramaic discourse or series of sermons originally given by James.[3] It cannot be argued against this view that James' Greek does not betray evidence of translation from a Semitic language. For, if the translation is 'paraphrastic' enough, little evidence of the original language will be present (would it be obvious to the uninformed reader that J. B. Phillips' paraphrase is based on Greek?). But while, in the nature of the case, it is impossible to disprove the theory, there remains little in favour of it.

A third 'compromise' position is ably defended by P. Davids. He is impressed by some of the apparent anomalies of the letter – good Greek alongside Semitisms, curious divergences in vocabulary, disjointedness in the treatment of various topics – and concludes that these are best explained if we posit a two-stage process of origin for the letter. The first stage would have consisted of a series of Jewish-Christian homilies (some translated from Aramaic, others original Greek compositions); the second stage the 'redactional' process by which these were moulded into a single composition. Davids allows that James may have been the author of the first stage, or of both stages.[4] Again, this theory is difficult to prove or disprove. But in so far as it rests on anomalies in James, we may question whether it is necessary. The inconsistencies that Davids cites are not of a type that require the hypothesis of two different stages of composition. An author who was fluent in both Aramaic and Greek

---

[1]A. Robert and A. Feuillet, *Introduction to the New Testament* (Desclée, 1965), p. 564. Mussner (p. 8) suggests the participation of a *Mitarbeiter*.

[2]Sevenster, *Do You Know Greek?*, pp. 10–14.

[3]F. C. Burkitt, *Christian Beginnings* (University of London, 1924), pp. 65–71; *cf.* also F. F. Bruce, *Peter, Stephen, James and John: Studies in non-Pauline Christianity* (Eerdmans, 1979), p. 113.

[4]Davids, pp. 12–13.

would naturally betray some influence from Aramaic when writing in Greek. And while Semitic ways of putting things can often be discerned in James, the Greek, as Dibelius says, is 'relatively homogenous'.[1] Similarly, the 'disjointedness' of topics seems to be a product of the genre in which the letter is written; and would not an editor, as much as an author, seek to 'smoothe out' the composition? That James may have utilized his own sermons in writing the letter is not improbable in itself. But evidence for an earlier literary stage is not compelling.

While none of these 'compromise' positions can be definitely ruled out, they are, in the end, unnecessary. It is more natural to take the reference to James as an indicator of the epistle's sole author.

III. CIRCUMSTANCES OF THE LETTER

From the content of the letter itself we are able to learn something about the people to whom it was written. First, it is almost certain that the readers were Jews. The letter is thoroughly imbued with the spirit and imagery of the Old Testament and Judaism – so thoroughly that it must reflect the readers' background as well as the author's. For instance, James' use of the feminine 'adulteresses' (*moichalides*) in 4:4 would make no sense to anyone who was not well acquainted with the Old Testament tradition likening the Lord's covenant with his people to a marriage relationship. Similarly, the simple and unexplained way in which James refers to the 'law' presumes that his readers are familiar with this law and have no questions about its relevance to them. Also indicative of a Jewish audience is the use of the monotheistic confession to summarize 'doctrine' (2:19) and the use of the word 'synagogue' in 2:2. The implied Jewish audience of the letter is in keeping with the New Testament and early Christian portrayal of James as one who ministered among 'the circumcised' (Gal. 2:9).

The letter implies that these Jewish believers were mainly poor people who were caught in a situation of considerable

[1]Dibelius, p. 34.

social tension. Oppressed and taken advantage of by wealthy landlords (5:4–6), hauled into court by rich people (2:6) who also scorn their Christian faith (2:7), the readers are exhorted to be patient and reminded that the coming of their Lord, the judge and deliverer, is at hand (5:7–11). In the meantime, the trials they are suffering are to be met with steadfast endurance, so that their Christian character might reach full maturity and their reward, 'the crown of life', be secured (1:2–4, 12).

But while the situation of the church in the world provides the background for the letter, James' concern is with the world getting into the church. He warns his readers that 'friendship with the world is enmity with God' (4:4) and highlights as one key ingredient of 'pure and undefiled religion' 'keeping oneself unstained from the world' (1:27). The worldliness in the church has manifested itself in a number of ways: a fawning deference to the rich and callous indifference of the poor (2:1–4); uncontrolled, critical speech (3:1–12; 4:11–12; 5:9); 'earthly, unspiritual, devilish' wisdom with its envy and selfish ambition that in turn produce dissensions and violent quarrels (3:13 – 4:3); arrogance (4:13–17); and, most of all, an essential 'double-mindedness' with respect to God that short-circuits the effectiveness of prayer (1:5–8) and manifests itself in a failure to put faith into practice (1:22–27; 2:14–26). James calls on his readers to repent from this worldliness; to humble themselves before the Lord so that he might exalt them (4:7–10); and to work diligently to bring other sinners back from the error of their ways (5:19–20).

Described in these terms, the circumstances of the readers do not help us a great deal in narrowing down the specific audience. Unfortunately, the address of the letter does not get us much farther. 'The twelve tribes in the Dispersion' is a rather ambiguous designation. After the exile of many Jews to Assyria and Babylonia, Israel's historical twelve tribes no longer existed in a physical sense. The term became a popular way of describing the regathered and spiritually renewed Israel that would be brought into being in the last days (Is. 49:6; Ezk. 47:13, 21–23; 48:29; Ecclus. 36:11; 2 Esdras 13:39–40). Given this background, James may have chosen the designation 'twelve tribes' in order to signify his intention to address the Jewish people as a whole, non-Christians as well as Christians. Had James envisaged such a broad readership, we could understand why he has so few references to specifically Christian doctrines.[1] But one would surely have expected more of an evangelistic thrust if non-Christian Jews had been among the intended readers. Moreover, the title 'twelve tribes' was used by Jews only in an eschatological context, to describe the regathered people of the last days[2] – and it is impossible that James would think of *all* Jews as belonging to this group.

Almost certainly, then, James uses 'the twelve tribes' to describe Christians. Again, the background of the phrase may suggest that James has only Jewish-Christians in mind.[3] But there is considerable New Testament evidence for a broadened sense of the term, according to which the church, the new people of God, is pictured as the fulfilment of the Old Testament and Jewish expectation of a regathered and renewed Israel (Mt. 19:28; Rev. 7:4–8; 21:12; *cf.* Gal. 6:16). Thus, while the content and tone of the letter strongly imply that the readers are Jewish-Christians, the designation 'twelve tribes' in itself does not require this restriction.

The second element of the address, the word *diaspora* ('the Dispersion'), is also capable of several interpretations. Taken from the Greek verb that means 'to scatter' or 'disperse', the word was used to describe Jews who were living outside of Palestine among Gentiles (Ps. 147:2; Is. 49:6; 2 Macc. 1:27; Jn. 7:35) and, by extension, the place where those who had been dispersed lived. If James uses the word with this literal sense, then he would be designating his readers as Jews or Jewish-Christians who lived outside of Palestine.[4] As with 'twelve tribes', however, the New Testament clearly uses *diaspora* with a metaphorical meaning, to characterize Christians as those who live, on this earth, away from their true heavenly 'homeland'

---

[1] A. T. Cadoux, *The Thought of St. James* (James Clarke, 1944), pp. 10–18; A. Schlatter, *Der Brief des Jakobus* (Calwer, 1932), pp. 90–98; G. R. Beasley-Murray, *The General Epistles* (Lutterworth, 1965), pp. 12–21.

[2] C. Maurer, *TDNT*, 9, p. 250.

[3] J. E. Huther, *Critical and Exegetical Handbook to the General Epistles of James, Peter, John, and Jude* (Funk & Wagnall, ²1887), pp. 11–13; A. S. Geyser, 'The Letter of James and the Social Condition of his Addressees', *General Epistles of the New Testament* (*Neotestamentica* 9, 1975), pp. 27–28.

[4] Mayor, pp. 30–31; Hort, pp. xxiii–xxiv; Adamson, pp. 49–50.

(see 1 Pet. 1:1). Thus the term may give us little help in locating James' readers. But it may be that we can be more specific. Tasker makes the attractive suggestion that Acts 11:19 may provide the specific background against which we should understand James' use of *diaspora*. Here Luke tells us that, as a result of the persecution connected with the stoning of Stephen, many Jewish Christians were 'scattered' (*diaspeirō*, the verb used here, is cognate to *diaspora*) and travelled as far as Phoenicia, Cyprus and Antioch, where they preached the gospel 'to none except Jews'. If James were the head of the Jerusalem church by this time, it is entirely natural that he would address a pastoral admonition to these believers from his 'home' church who had been scattered abroad because of persecution.[1] This theory cannot be proven, but it does fit remarkably well with the nature and circumstances of the letter, as well as with the date we will suggest for the letter.

Date

If James, the brother of the Lord, wrote the letter, as we have argued, it must be dated sometime before AD 62, when James was martyred. Some scholars argue for a date close to 62 on the grounds that James shows many similarities to 1 Peter. But James contains parallels with many writings, dating all the way from 100 BC to AD 150, so this is hardly significant. Others claim that the 'settled' condition of the churches addressed in James, with the typical 'second generation' problem of worldliness, favours a date around 60.[2] But worldliness is no monopoly of the second generation (see 1 Corinthians) and the letter does not enable us to say whether the churches had been in existence for ten or fifty years.

On the other hand, two indications favour an earlier date, around 45–47. First, and most important, is the most probable reconstruction of the relationship between James 2 and the preaching of Paul. As we argued in the section on authorship, James 2 implies awareness of Paul's slogan 'justification by faith', but also shows that Paul's teaching was not understood

[1]Tasker, p. 39; *cf.* also Burdick, pp. 162–163.
[2]Hort, p. xxv; Tasker, pp. 31–33; Mitton, p. 233.

correctly. This state of affairs was likely to have existed only in the early days of Paul's preaching, before James had met Paul and had an opportunity to understand, from Paul, just what he meant by 'justification by faith'. This makes a date after the Jerusalem Council (AD 48 or 49) very difficult. We can surmise that Paul's preaching in Antioch, beginning in around 45 (Acts 11:25–26), was heard and misunderstood by some Jewish Christians in the same area (see Acts 11:19). Since these Jewish Christians may well have looked on the Jerusalem church as their 'home' church, it is entirely feasible that the head of that church, James, would have got wind of this perverted form of Paul's teaching and responded accordingly.

A second indication of an early date is the absence of any reference to the controversy between Jews and Gentiles, particularly with respect to the 'ritual law'. Again, it was shortly before the Jerusalem Council that this issue first surfaced forcibly in the early church. 'Men from Judea' had come to the Antiochene church, teaching that Gentile Christians had to be circumcised and take on themselves 'the yoke of the law' (Acts 15:1). James himself, of course, was instrumental in preventing these restrictions from being applied to Gentile converts. But the point here is that it is difficult to think that James could have written to Jewish-Christians, some of whom probably lived in or near Antioch, without making any allusion to the problem or the decision of the council.

These two considerations point to a date in the middle to late forties (45–48) for the writing of James.[1] This period witnessed some severe economic disturbances (there was a famine in Judea in about 46; cf. Acts 11:28) and the beginning of the serious social-political-religious upheavals that would culminate in the Jewish war of 66–70. Both circumstances fit the background implied in James.

---

[1]Kittel provides a particularly strong case for this dating (art. cit., ZNW 41, 1942, pp. 71–102). See also Zahn, Introduction, 1, pp. 125–128; G. H. Rendall, The Epistle of St. James and Judaistic Christianity (Cambridge University Press, 1927), p. 78; Mayor, pp. cxliv–clxxvi; Knowling, pp. xxxiv–xxxviii; Guthrie, New Testament Introduction, pp. 761–764; D. E. Hiebert, The Epistle of James (Moody Press, 1979), p. 41; Burdick, pp. 162–163; Wessel, ISBE, 2, p. 965.

Place of writing

The conclusions we have reached on the authorship and dating of the letter virtually determine the place of writing. James lived in Jerusalem during this period and his readers are probably to be found in the regions just outside of Palestine along the coastline to the north, in Syria and perhaps southern Asia Minor. Several allusions in the letter, most notably the reference to the 'earlier and latter rains' (5:7), seem to confirm this location; for only along the eastern coast of the Mediterranean Sea do the rains come in this sequence.[1] Laws has recently suggested Rome as the provenance of the letter,[2] but the only reasons she gives are the literary resemblances between James and several works of Roman origin: 1 Peter, Hermas and 1 Clement.

The general social conditions in the Near East in the middle of the first century also correspond with the situation presupposed in James. The merchants who ranged far and wide in search of profits (4:13–17) and the wealthy, often 'absentee' landlords who exploited an increasingly large and impoverished labour force (5:1–6) were familiar figures. Familiar also were the heated and often violent religious debates that seem to have infected the churches under James' care (see 3:13 – 4:3). The Zealot movement, which sought to win freedom for Israel by violent means, was becoming more and more influential. Some scholars, in fact, think that James 4:2 – 'you desire and do not have; so you kill' – may refer to zealot partisans who had brought their violent ideology into the church.[3] Whether this is so or not, the social conditions of first-century Palestine and Syria certainly provide an appropriate backdrop for the letter of James.

[1] See D. Y. Hadidian, 'Palestinian Pictures in the Epistle of James', *ExpT* 18, 1951–1952, pp. 227–228.

[2] Laws, pp. 25–26.

[3] R. P. Martin, 'The Life-setting of the Epistle of James in the Light of Jewish History', *Biblical and Near-Eastern Studies*, ed. G. A. Tuttle (Eerdmans, 1978), p. 100; M. J. Townsend, 'James 4:1–4: A Warning against Zealotry?' *ExpT* 87, 1976, pp. 212–213.

IV. THE NATURE OF THE LETTER

In form, James is a 'literary' letter. The book begins with a typical epistolary introduction – identification of the author, address and greeting – but lacks the personal reminiscences, references to specific problems and situations, and closing remarks that characterize 'real' letters. Like a modern church official or bishop addressing an 'open letter' to his parishioners, James has used the epistolary form to bring spiritual exhortations and comfort to Christians living in a broad area. The letter of James therefore differs both from Paul's letters to individuals (Philemon, Timothy, Titus) and to specific churches (Rome, Corinth, *etc.*) and resembles most closely 1 Peter and 1 John, both of which are also directed to wide audiences.

When we look more closely at the specific nature of the material in James, four outstanding features emerge. First and most prominent is the strong tone of pastoral exhortation. James has a greater frequency of imperatives than any other New Testament book. His purpose is clearly not so much to inform, but to command, exhort and encourage. Yet James issues his commands, for the most part, in a tone of tender pastoral concern, addressing his readers fifteen times as 'my brothers' or 'my beloved brothers'. A second well-known feature of James is the looseness of its structure. Several sections develop a single issue at some length (2:1–13; 2:14–16; 3:1–12), but most of the book is made up of short, seemingly independent, sayings or short paragraphs. Moreover, it is often difficult to discern any logical relationship between one section and another.

James' extensive use of metaphors and illustrations is another feature that arrests the attention of the reader. These images – the billowing sea, the withered flower, the mirror, the horse, the ship, the brush fire, the taming of animals, the water spring, the arrogant businessman, the corroded metal and moth-eaten clothes, the patient farmer – are universal in their appeal and go a long way towards accounting for the popularity of James among ordinary readers. A fourth feature of the letter is not so evident to the modern reader, although the original recipients would undoubtedly have been struck by it: James' penchant for borrowing from other sources. We have already commented on the extent to which James is permeated with allusions to the teaching of Jesus, and the Old Testament also figures prominently in James – both by way of explicit quotation and by way of allusion. But particularly interesting are the number of parallels between James and several early Jewish and Christian books. To be mentioned above all in this regard are 1 Peter, Ecclesiasticus (Sirach), the Testaments of the Twelve Patriarchs, The Shepherd of Hermas (particularly the 'Mandates' section) and 1 Clement (significant, but fewer parallels are found with Wisdom of Solomon, Philo, the Didache, and the letters of Ignatius). In most cases, these parallels involve language or motifs that are found in more than one of these works, and direct dependence of one book on another is almost impossible to prove. It would appear that these books use a widespread tradition of ethical teaching, probably Hellenistic-Jewish in origin. James shows familiarity with this tradition and appropriates some elements from it to exhort his readers.

Taking these features, and others, into account, scholars have sought to give a specific classification to the material in James. Ropes argued that James was a diatribe, a colloquial genre used to instruct general audiences and which featured short sentences, rhetorical questions, conditional sentences and repetition of material.[1] However, while some sections of James could perhaps be classified as diatribe, the letter as a whole resists the designation. Much more popular has been the suggestion that James is paraenesis (exhortation). Martin Dibelius, whose commentary has been responsible for the widespread acceptance of this classification, identified four crucial elements in paraenesis: eclecticism, or the use of traditional material; the unstructured stringing together of moral exhortations; repetition of key ideas; and the general applicability of the material. Such paraenesis, it is argued, can be found in a wide variety of ancient sources, including many New Testament epistles (cf. Rom. 12 – 13; Heb. 13).[2]

[1] Ropes, pp. 10–16.
[2] Dibelius, pp. 5–11. See also the article by L. G. Perdue, 'Paraenesis and the Epistle of

In a general way, there is no doubt that James displays these four characteristics, although much more continuity of thought is to be found than Dibelius allowed. But the description itself is so vague that it could apply to an extraordinary variety of material and loses much of its helpfulness as a classification. Without necessarily denying the designation to James, then, we might go further and suggest a more specific literary context for the background of James: the early Christian sermon or homily. Many of the features of James enumerated above can be paralleled in the Jewish synagogue homily, and it would be perfectly natural for James to have adopted this form for use in the church. And what would be more natural than for James to summarize his preaching to his flock in Jerusalem in a letter sent to those who could not be there to hear it in person?[1] James is best understood, then, as a brief, perhaps condensed, sermon or homily, or extraction drawn from a series of sermons, sent to James' dispersed parishioners in the form of a letter.

A good sermon, we are told, must have structure. Does James display this all-important homiletical characteristic? Many would agree with Luther, who accused the author of the letter of 'throwing things together . . . chaotically'.[2] Dibelius resolutely denied that individual sayings and paragraphs in James could be related to one another, and this viewpoint has been dominant in commentaries on James for decades. Recently, however, a reassessment has been made. Adamson argues that James displays a 'sustained unity',[3] while Davids, applying to James the epistolary structure identified by F. O. Francis,[4] discerns a carefully constructed literary structure in the letter. He divides the letter into three major sections: a 'double opening statement' (1:2–27), the body (2:1 – 5:6) and the 'closing statement' (5:7–20), and finds repeated in each section the three basic themes of the

---

James', ZNW 72, 1981, pp. 241–256, which gives a slightly different set of criteria. Indeed, a major difficulty with the designation 'paraenesis' is the looseness of its definition.

[1]The synagogue homily or sermon is suggested as the background to James by G. H. Rendall, The Epistle of St. James, p. 33; Davids, p. 23; and especially Wessel, ISBE, 2, p. 962, who builds on the results of his doctoral dissertation.

[2]Luther, 'Preface to the New Testament' (1522), in LW, 35, p. 397.   [3]Adamson, p. 20.

[4]F. O. Francis, 'The Form and Function of the Opening and Closing Paragraphs of James and 1 John', ZNW 61, 1970, pp. 110–126.

letter: testing, wisdom/pure speech and poverty/wealth.[1] While Davids is to be credited with especially helpful insights into the structure of James, he goes perhaps too far in subordinating all of the letter under these themes. For example, he fits 2:14–26 under the theme of poverty/wealth, suggesting its theme to be 'generosity' – a description whose accuracy could be questioned.

In reacting against the extreme atomizing approach of Dibelius, then, Davids and others have found more structure than the diverse material in James can justify. His various exhortations cannot be categorized into a few topics or put into a coherent, logically developed structure without imposing artificial and sometimes misleading headings on the material. We shall not be able to credit James with the kind of comprehensive structure and focus that would be expected in a modern sermon. Rather, we should view James as a homily in which the author takes up one subject after another, sometimes relating it to the previous one, sometimes picking up an idea or theme mentioned earlier in the letter, sometimes abruptly introducing a wholly new topic. Several key motifs continually crop up, like musical motifs in a symphony or opera, but these are not dominant enough to serve as organizing heads.

James' exhortations can be grouped into five general sections. The first and last are little more than miscellaneous collections of material, but the middle three display more unity around a common theme. 1:2–18, the 'opening statement', introduces several basic concerns of James': the need for endurance in testing, the importance of unwavering faith, the problems of poverty and wealth. The second section, 1:19 – 2:26, has as its theme the need to put the word of God into practice. Christians are to be 'doers of the word', for 'true religion' involves practical obedience, such as showing love to the poor by not discriminating against them. A faith that has no works is a gross parody of true Christian faith. Community strife and its antidote is the general topic of the third main section, 3:1 – 4:12. 'Wisdom from below', with its envy and selfishness, leads to harsh, critical speech and is the root of the quarrels plaguing the

---

[1]Davids, pp. 22–29.

church. These sins can be overcome through humble repentance before God. The fourth section, 4:13 – 5:11, deals with the kind of attitudes and behaviour that should characterize life 'in the last days'. Because life is so uncertain, human arrogance is to be renounced; and believers should look patiently to the Lord's return as they struggle with the oppression brought on them by wealthy persecutors. The final section (5:12–20) takes up the issues of oaths and prayer and concludes with an encouragement to bring sinners to repentance.

V. THEOLOGICAL EMPHASES OF THE LETTER

It is a commonplace to claim that James has no theology. The truth or falsity of that claim depends entirely on what is meant by 'theology'. On the one hand, it is obvious that James says little about many basic Christian doctrines. James say nothing about the ministry of the Holy Spirit, the theological significance of the church, the fulfilment of the Old Testament in Christ, the atoning death of Christ, or the resurrection. It can hardly be expected, however, that a letter the length of James will include teaching on every major point of theology. More serious is the charge that James fails to orient his teaching around the person of Christ. Jesus Christ is named only twice (1:1; 2:1), only once is he made the object of belief (2:1), and the ethical appeals of the letter are not explicitly based on the work or significance of Christ. If by 'theology', then, one means a system of beliefs that explicitly refers to the person and work of Christ as a major focal point, then the letter of James does indeed lack a theology.

On the other hand, however, it is grossly unfair to accuse James of being 'untheological'. What we must remember is that James' purposes in the letter dictated the amount of explicit theological teaching that he included. He was writing to believers who were already well acquainted with fundamental Christian teachings; and, especially if his readers were former parishioners, there was little reason for him to rehearse these teachings again. His readers were not perplexed over any major doctrinal issues (with the possible exception of the place of works in salvation). Their problem was a failure to put their faith into practice. Naturally, therefore, it is here, at the level of practical daily living, that James concentrates.

His letter is a practical homily, designed to encourage believers to show the reality of their theological commitment in practice. The purpose of the letter, then, explains why James does not include a great deal of theological teaching. As G. E. Ladd says, 'It is impossible to conclude from the contents of the epistle that he was not interested in theology; a theologian can write practical homilies'.[1] Furthermore, while the letter may not feature much explicit doctrinal teaching, we must not assume that it lacks theological underpinnings. Indeed, numerous references in the letter reveal the existence of this theological foundation. For example, in dealing with the problem created for his readers by evil rich people, James assumes that the 'last days' have begun (5:3,5), yet also looks to the future for the judgment associated with the coming of the Lord (5:7–9). These references reveal that James is building his exhortation on the characteristically Christian view of eschatology according to which the Messianic Age had broken into history without immediately bringing the consummation of history also.

Finally, in addition to these theological assumptions, we should not overlook the specific theological teaching that *is* found in James. His letter makes an important contribution to our understanding of faith and works, prayer, the nature of God, the origin of sin, and wisdom. True, these are all given a 'practical' context, but it will be a sad day for the church when such 'practical divinity' is not considered 'theology'. Therefore, while the occasional and homiletical nature of the letter prevents us from sketching 'a theology of James', we are able to survey James' contribution to several important areas of theology.

God

If we use 'theology' in its strictest sense – the doctrine of God – then James can be said to contain a considerable amount of theology. For he is very concerned to relate the kind of conduct he expects of his readers to the nature of God. Christians, James

[1]G. E. Ladd, *A Theology of the New Testament* (Eerdmans, 1974), p. 589.

implies, are to live and act in full consciousness of the character of the God they serve. It is because God gives 'generously and without reproaching' that Christians should not hesitate to ask him for wisdom (1:5). James' invitation is similar to, and perhaps dependent on, Jesus' encouragement of his disciples to ask God for what they needed – an encouragement that is also anchored in the nature of God, the Father who gives his children good things (Mt. 7:7–11). The goodness of God's gifts is emphasized in 1:17 also, where James also stresses the invariability of God's character. This emphasis is needed as a counter to those who would attribute to God the evil of temptation. Not only does God give everything that is perfect, James asserts, but he is not even capable of being enticed by evil. How foolish, then, to think that God could be the author of temptation (1:13). He may test his servants for their own good, but he must never be associated with the enticement to evil that is a product of man's own sinfulness (1:14–15). Never can we excuse sin by trying to shift the blame on to God.

Theology proper is also at the heart of one of the key texts in the letter, 4:4–10. This passage contains a stinging indictment of the readers for their worldliness, along with a strongly worded summons to repentance. Both the indictment and the invitation are based on God's character. 4:5 is a difficult verse to interpret, but it is best taken as a reminder of the 'holy jealousy' of God for his people (see further, the commentary *in loc.*). As such, it provides the perfect foundation for James' accusation that his readers are spiritual 'adulterers', who are tarnishing their relationship with God through entanglement with the world (4:4). But, James reminds his readers, God's grace is able to meet fully the demands of God's jealous holiness. Only those who humbly submit to God will experience that grace, however (4:6). Thus the gracious character of God becomes the basis for James' earnest plea to his readers to humble themselves before the Lord (4:7–10).

That James is a monotheist goes without saying, but the emphasis he places on this point is interesting. We have not only the confession of the oneness of God used for illustrative purposes (2:19), but also the reminder that 'there is *one* lawgiver and judge' (4:12). Although not strictly related to monotheism,

James' interest in the idea of 'oneness' may also be seen in the description of God as giving 'generously' (*haplōs*, 1:5), since the word may have the connotation of 'simple', 'undivided'. The oneness of God also underlines James' reminder that *all* the commandments must be obeyed (2:11). The question may well be raised about the relationship between these statements and what James says about Jesus. How does James' emphasis on the 'one judge' square with the plain implication of 5:7–9 that Christ, the coming one, is the 'Judge standing at the doors'? And while James uses 'Lord' as a designation of Jesus in three verses (2:1; 5:7, 8), the other seven occurrences of the title (3:9; 4:10, 15; 5:4, 10, 11, 15) all pretty clearly refer to God the Father. These circumstances suggest two conclusions. First, by designating Jesus 'Lord' (and perhaps 'the glory', if the word is taken in 2:1 as a separate title reflecting the idea of the 'Shekinah') and attributing to him the function of eschatological judge, James plainly implies that Jesus is God. Secondly, James is apparently unaware of any difficulty in asserting within the same letter that 'there is one lawgiver and judge' and that Jesus Christ, at his return, will act as the judge. We can see here the way in which the very early church naturally and almost unconsciously began viewing Jesus as God.

Eschatology

While many of James' ethical admonitions are similar to those found in Jewish and even pagan Greek literature, the eschatological context in which he sets them gives them a new and different focus. The coming judgment receives great emphasis. 'The Judge is standing at the doors', James reminds his readers (5:9). The fact and basis of this judgment function repeatedly as a means of motivating believers to holy living, pleasing to the Lord (1:10–11; 2:12–13; 3:1; 5:1–6, 9, 12). On the other hand, James also reminds his readers of the reward to be bestowed on those who have proved faithful and fruitful in service (1:12; 2:5; 4:10; 5:20). James is convinced that this climactic time of judgment and salvation is imminent: 'the coming of the Lord is at hand'; 'the Judge is standing at the doors' (5:8–9). Many scholars have interpreted these statements to mean that James was sure the Lord would return immediately, in his own lifetime. But James' language need not mean that at all. He is clearly convinced that the Lord *could* return within a very short time, but nothing he says suggests that he was sure that the Lord *would* return within a specific period of time.

If the prospect of judgment or deliverance at the future coming of the Lord is an important motivating factor in James, the present 'eschatological' dimension of Christian existence is not neglected: Christians are 'heirs of the kingdom' (2:5) and 'a kind of first fruits of his creatures' by virtue of spiritual rebirth (1:18). 5:3 probably attests to James' conviction that 'the last days' had already dawned (translating 'in the last days' rather than 'for the last days' as in RSV). In other words, James gives evidence of holding to the same kind of 'inaugurated eschatology' that is found in the teaching of Jesus, in Paul and throughout the New Testament: the days when God's promises are to be fulfilled have begun, but a climax to that period is still expected. It is in the eschatological tension of that 'already . . . not yet' that James' ethics are to be understood.[1]

Faith, works and justification

The most famous, controversial and important contribution of James to theology comes in his teaching about the relationship of faith, works and justification in 2:14–26. Indeed, many theologies mention James only for the negative purpose of showing that his argument in this section is not irreconcilable with the Pauline teaching on justification. But James has his own point to make, and we should give positive appreciation to this point. He is resolutely opposing any form of Christianity that drifts into a sterile, action-less 'orthodoxy'. As important and necessary as is 'right belief', it is much less than true *Christian* belief if it is not accompanied by works. That this is James' overriding concern in this section cannot be mistaken: for he states the point three times (2:17, 20, 26). Some of his readers, apparently through a misunderstanding of Paul, were confining 'faith' to a verbal profession (2:19) and empty, insincere good wishes

---

[1]Mussner, pp. 207–210, particularly emphasizes this point.

(2:15–16). This 'faith' that a person may claim to have (v.14) is 'dead' (vv.17, 26) and 'barren' (v.20) and will be of no avail in the day of judgment (v.14).

It is important to recognize that this 'faith' of which James speaks, the faith that a person 'claims' to have (v.14), does not correspond to James' own understanding of faith. He sees faith as a firm, unwavering commitment to God and Christ (see 2:1) that is tested and refined in trial (1:2, 4), and grasps hold of the blessings of God in prayer (1:5–8; 5:14–18). These texts demonstrate how wrong it is to accuse James of having a 'sub-Christian' or 'sub-Pauline' conception of faith. On this point, James and Paul are in complete agreement. As Paul says in Galatians 5:6, it is 'faith working through love' that counts before God; so James: 'faith without works is dead'.

On another point, however, it is frequently claimed that James and Paul do represent contrasting positions. This point has to do with the place of works in justification. Paul, as is well known, strongly emphasized the complete sufficiency of faith as the basis for justification: 'We hold that a man is justified by faith apart from works of the law' (Rom. 3:28). James, on the other hand, claims that 'a man is justified by works and not by faith alone' (2:24). Furthermore, each cites Abraham to illustrate his own point, Paul arguing that God's pronouncement of Abraham's righteousness (Gn. 15:6) came solely on the basis of faith, before he was circumcised (Rom. 4:1–12), and James claiming that Abraham's justification came as a result of his obedience in being willing to sacrifice Isaac and that in this act Genesis 15:6 was 'fulfilled'. These viewpoints are often singled out as representative of two different, even conflicting, tendencies in the early church: the law-free Gentile mission (Paul) and law-affirming Jewish-Christianity (James).[1] If this were true, we would be faced with a disturbing situation. On an issue as vital as the question 'What must I do to be saved?' the New Testament would seem to speak with two different voices. Thankfully, we are not forced to this conclusion. Understood in their own contexts, and with careful attention to the way each is using certain key words, it can be seen that James and Paul are

[1]See, for example, J. D. G. Dunn, *Unity and Diversity in the New Testament* (Westminster, 1977), pp. 251–252.

making complementary, not contradictory, points.

The first thing to be noticed is that Paul and James are combating opposite problems. In Paul's statements about justification in Galatians and Romans, he is countering a Jewish tendency to rely on obedience to the law ('works of the law') for salvation. Against an over-emphasis on works, Paul highlights faith as the sole instrument of justification. James, on the other hand, is combating an *under*-emphasis on works, a 'quietistic' attitude that turned faith into mere doctrinal orthodoxy. Against this perversion of faith, James is forced to assert the importance of works.

The second point to be mentioned is the different context in which Paul and James are speaking of 'works'. When Paul claims that a person cannot be justified on the basis of works of the law, he is clearly referring to works that *precede* conversion. The works in James 2, however, are the works that stem from and are produced by faith: works that *follow* conversion. It is obvious that works done before a person has faith in Christ and works done as a result of faith in Christ would not have the same role in salvation.[1]

This leads us to the third, and most important, consideration. If Paul has in mind works that precede conversion and James works that follow conversion, it follows that the 'justification' for which these respective works are the basis must be something different in Paul than in James. Indeed, this seems to be the case. Paul uses the Greek verb *dikaioō* ('justify') to describe the dynamic activity whereby the sinner is graciously given a new status. This status, this righteous standing before God, the Judge of all the world, is based on the sinner's union with Christ and is secured through faith. For Paul, in other words, *dikaioō* is a term that denotes the initial *transfer* of a person from the realm of sin and death into the realm of holiness and life. Because it is precisely the sinner, the 'ungodly' (Rom. 4:5), the one with no righteousness of his own to offer, who is justified, 'works' can have no place in effecting this transfer.

In James, however, *dikaioō* has a different meaning, a meaning

---

[1] Other scholars find a greater difference between Paul and James on this matter, suggesting that 'works of law' in Paul refer to ritualistic or legalistic works only. This is doubtful, however; see the Additional Note, 'Works' in Paul and James, p.101, below.

that is well attested in the Old Testament, in the Gospel of Matthew and in many Jewish sources. In these sources *dikaioō* usually describes a verdict that is based on the actual facts of the case; a judge declares a person 'righteous' because that person can be proven, in fact, to *be* 'righteous' or innocent (see the Additional Note, 'Justification' in the Old Testament and Judaism, p.110, below). Furthermore, this verdict of justification is often associated with the last judgment. Since James is so clearly oriented to a Jewish context and shows so many parallels with the teaching of Jesus in Matthew, it would be expected that he would use 'justify' with this meaning. Confirmation that this is so comes from the link between justification in 2:21–25 and salvation in 2:14, where the salvation is to be related to the verdict pronounced at the last judgment (see 2:12–13). What James is saying, then, is that ultimate, or 'final justification', the verdict pronounced over our lives in the last day, takes into account the works that must inevitably be produced by true faith. On the fact and basis of this ultimate verdict, James and Paul are at one. For Paul also reminds us that 'we must all appear before the judgment seat of Christ, so that each one may receive good or evil, according to what he has done in the body' (2 Cor. 5:10). Where they differ is on the terminology used to describe this verdict.

It is true that 'Paul and James move in this matter in different circles of thought, and the attempt to superimpose one circle on the other in order to determine their agreement or disagreement in detail is futile'.[1] But what can be done is to understand the point each is making from within his own sphere of thought and word usage, and *then* to bring them together. When this is done a unified, theologically coherent picture emerges. Paul fervently maintains that faith is the only human condition for the transfer of the sinner into the sphere of God's grace. James says little about this initial transfer – although we should not overlook his statement that Christians have been 'brought forth by the word of truth' and that this process is due to the will of God (1:18). What James is concerned about is the attempt to eliminate works from having any role in the verdict rendered over our lives.

[1]Ropes, p. 36.

While our union with Christ by faith is the sole basis for justification in God's sight, the works necessarily produced as a result of that union are taken into account in God's ultimate judgment over us. In theological terminology, Paul is speaking of the *imputation* of righteousness, James of the *declaration* of righteousness.[1]

The law

Discussions about the relationship between James and Paul usually focus on the matter of justification, but another issue, the function of the law in the Christian life, presents its own problem. Indeed, Cadoux maintains that James and Paul are farther apart over this question than over justification.[2] Luther's critique of James made mention of this issue also; in his preface to James and Jude, he notes that James 'calls the law a "law of liberty" though Paul calls it a law of slavery, of wrath, of death, and of sin'. The difficulty touched on here by Luther is that Paul appears to absolve Christians from any obligation to the law; they have 'died to the law' (Rom. 7:4), are no longer 'under the law' (Rom. 6:14–15), but are 'led by the Spirit' (Gal. 5:18). James, however, implies that Christians must still be 'doers of the law' (4:11) and insists that 'the whole law' will be the standard of judgment (2:9–12). Without exploring here the question as to whether Paul completely eliminates the law as an authority for Christians – and passages such as 1 Corinthians 14:34, Ephesians 6:2–3 and Romans 8:7 should give us pause at this point – James' perspective deserves further attention.

First, it is evident that James does not include the ceremonial commandments in his conception of the law. Never does he mention this aspect of the law, even when it would be natural for him to do so. Thus, in 2:10–11, where he argues that failure to obey 'one point' of the law is to be guilty of all of it, he cites as examples two commandments from the Decalogue, where the

---

[1] See Calvin, *Institutes*, III.17.12. John Wesley takes a similar approach in his explanation of the difference between Paul and James. He contends that James is speaking of 'final justification' and that, while works are not the causal basis of this justification, it does take into account 'the evidence of works' (Minutes of 1744; Wesley's *Works*, VIII, p. 277, Q. 14).

[2] A. T. Cadoux, *The Thought of St. James*, p. 81.

typical Jewish argument would have mentioned a minor ritual commandment to highlight the need to obey even seemingly inconsequential commands. We see already, then, that James is very far from a conservative Jewish attitude towards the law, for the ritual commandments were an inseparable and important part of the law in Judaism.

Secondly, the way James qualifies the law in three places is significant. In 2:12 he calls the law a 'law of liberty', in 1:25 the 'perfect law, the law of liberty' and in 2:8, citing Leviticus 19:18, the 'royal law'.[1] Now the designation 'perfect' for the Old Testament law was customary among Jews, and descriptions of the liberating effect of law were common among both pagans (especially the Stoics; *cf.* Epictetus, *Diss.* IV. 1. 158; Seneca, *De vita beata* 15.7) and Jews (Philo, *Every Good Man Is Free* 45; b. Abot. 6, 2b). But the context in which James uses the description suggests that he intends more than this. Crucial here is the fact that 'the perfect law . . . of liberty' in 1:25 seems to be equivalent to 'the word of truth' by which Christians are 'born again' (1:18), the 'implanted word' that brings salvation (1:21). Since this 'word' is clearly the gospel, 'the law of liberty' must have some relationship to the gospel also. The description of the law as 'royal' (*basilikos*) in 2:8 suggests something similar; for while, again, the Old Testament law could be described by Jews as 'royal' (Philo, *Posterity of Cain* 102), the word here must be seen in the light of James' mention of the kingdom of God in 2:5. Thus the law is 'royal' because it pertains to those in the kingdom, or perhaps because it was promulgated by the King. Since it is the 'love command' of Leviticus 19:18, the command which Jesus singled out as the summary of the law, that is quoted here, the reference is probably to the command as taught by Jesus.

We find, then, that James' use of the word 'law' (*nomos*) cannot be separated from the gospel associated with Jesus.

---

[1] L. T. Johnson has pointed out that Leviticus 19 plays a prominent role in James, and suggests that James viewed the royal law by which Christians are to live 'as explicated concretely and specifically not only by the Decalogue (2:11) but by the immediate context of the Law of Love, the commands found in Lev 19:12–18' ('The Use of Leviticus 19 in the Letter of James', *JBL* 101, 1982, pp. 391–401 [399]). While James certainly seems to have Leviticus 19 in mind in the immediate context of 2:8, some of the parallels discerned by Johnson elsewhere in the letter are not so clear.

Many scholars, in fact, would suggest that James identifies law and gospel; that, in a manner similar to some of the early fathers (see Barnabas 2:6), he views Jesus' teaching as a 'new law'.[1] But while there is much evidence to suggest that James puts Jesus' teaching on a par with the Old Testament law, it is impossible to eliminate the Old Testament law from James' conception of *nomos* (see 2:9–11). Mitton helpfully suggests a relationship between James' 'implanted word' (1:18) and the law that Jeremiah predicted would be written on the heart in the administration of the new covenant (Je. 31:31–34).[2]

What this suggests is that James upholds the authority of the Old Testament law, but only as it has been 'fulfilled' in Jesus' teaching and work. He does not consciously separate the teaching of Jesus from the Old Testament law, because these have become intermingled under the authority of Jesus, the inaugurator of the kingdom of God. As Wessel says, ' "law of freedom" is a Palestinian Jew's way of describing the Christian standard of conduct found in the *didache*'.[3] This teaching is still 'law' because it expresses the authoritative will of God for our conduct; but it is a law 'of liberty' inasmuch as it is the teaching of one whose 'yoke is easy' and whose 'burden is light' (Mt. 11:30).

Viewed in this light, the alleged conflict between Paul and James over the law vanishes. For, as was the case with justification, the two are using the crucial term differently. Paul uses 'law', *nomos*, to denote the law given through Moses and contests the continuing validity of that law, *as part of the Mosaic covenant*. But even he can speak of a 'law of Christ' (Gal. 6:2; *cf.* 1 Cor. 9:21) to which Christians are subject. This 'law of Christ' does not differ from James' 'royal law of liberty'.

The Christian life

It is in this area that James makes his most important contribution; 'no other book of the New Testament concentrates so

---

[1]Mayor, p. 74; W. Gutbrod, *TDNT*, 4, pp. 1081–1082.   [2]Mitton, p. 72.
[3]Wessel, *ISBE*, 2, p. 960; *Cf.* also L. Goppelt, *A Theology of the New Testament* (Eerdmans, 1982), 2, pp. 203–206; D. Guthrie, *New Testament Theology* (Inter-Varsity Press, 1981), p. 699.

exclusively on ethical questions'.[1] A full treatment of this topic would accordingly demand virtually a repetition of the commentary itself: but a few general topics deserve consideration here.

As we emphasized earlier, it is important that James' ethics be seen in the context of his eschatology. His advice, while often having the quality of timeless, 'wisdom' teaching, is nevertheless always oriented to the 'saved but not yet glorified' situation of his readers. Accordingly, he recognizes that his readers will not be able to escape entirely from their tendency to sin ('we will make many mistakes', 3:2), but he encourages them to work strenuously towards the goal of 'perfection' or 'completeness' (teleios, 1:4). It is the condition of 'doubleness', man's condition of being divided between his loyalty to God and the attractive lure of the world, that bothers James more than anything. He condemns his readers as 'double-souled' people (dipsychos, 4:8), and uses the same term to describe the doubter, who is like 'a wave of the sea that is driven and tossed by the wind' (1:6). This 'divided' condition manifests itself in speech, as when the same tongue both blesses God and curses men (3:9–10), and, in a different way, when we fail to live out our faith in practice (the theme of 1:19 – 2:26). James' earnest desire, that Christians leave behind this unstable and inconsistent 'halfway faith' and progress towards a whole-hearted, unvarying commitment to God in thought, word and deed, is at the heart of his homily. John Wesley's description of Christian perfection captures it very well: 'In one view it is purity of intention, dedicating all the life to God. It is the giving God all our heart, it is one desire and design ruling all our tempers. It is the devoting, not a part, but all our soul, body, and substance to God.'[2]

James' insistence that Christians do, not just listen to, the word of God, and his demand for works as integral to faith, are part and parcel of this emphasis. Obedience to the 'law of liberty', the demand of God summarized by Jesus, must be

This is in contrast to the view of O. J. F. Seitz, 'James and the Law', Studia Evangelica 2, 1964, pp. 472–486.
[1] W. Schrage, Ethik des Neuen Testaments, Grundrisse zum Neuen Testament, 4 (Vandenhoeck & Ruprecht, 1982), p. 266; cf. also Laws, p. 27.
[2] J. Wesley, A Plain Account of Christian Perfection (1766; Wesley's Works, II, p. 444).

heartfelt and consistent. And this obedience has an important *social* aspect. The command to 'love our neighbours as ourselves' is 'the royal law' (2:8). James is insistent that 'pure and undefiled religion' must manifest itself in concern for the under-privileged and disadvantaged ('visiting orphans and widows in their affliction', 1:27) and in a meek and unselfish attitude towards others (3:13–18). Favouritism towards the rich violates this 'royal law' (2:1–7), as does speaking evil of others (4:11–12).

Prayer is another part of the Christian life that James illuminates for us. As we have seen, he encourages prayer by reminding us that God generously and without reproach gives good gifts to those who ask him. But James is especially concerned to ensure that prayers be offered in the right spirit. Faith, an unvarying, whole-hearted commitment of ourselves to God, is the basic requirement (1:6–8); it is 'the prayer *of faith*' that will bring deliverance from physical disease (5:15). If faith is the condition for God's response to us, selfishness is that attitude which will often frustrate the effectiveness of our prayers: 'You ask and do not receive, because you ask wrongly, to spend it on your passions' (4:3). It is the 'righteous person' who experiences the full power of prayer; for him, prayer 'has great power in its effects' (5:16).

Wisdom

James mentions 'wisdom' in two passages: 1:5 and 3:13–18. In the former, James encourages his readers to ask God for wisdom if they lack it. It may be that James mentions wisdom here because it is the quality needed if his readers are going to persevere in their trials (vv. 2–4), but this is not clear. In 3:13–18 James castigates some jealous, divisive people in the church who were apparently claiming to be wise by contrasting the kind of wisdom they possess – 'earthly, unspiritual, devilish' – with the true wisdom that 'comes down from above'. The latter is characterized by good deeds and a humble attitude and produces virtues that are conducive to harmonious relations with others. James' use of the term is very much in keeping with the Old Testament emphasis, where wisdom is said to be the gift of God (Pr. 2:6) and is prized so highly because it helps its possessor to understand the will of the Lord and, more importantly, to obey it.

In Jewish writings, wisdom was sometimes identified with the law, the *torah*, and took on more metaphysical connotations. James shows no contact with this background.[1] More interesting is the possible connection between James' wisdom and the Spirit. A close relationship between these two is suggested in the Old Testament (Is. 11:2), and it is pointed out that James' description of the virtues produced by wisdom (3:17) is closely parallel to Paul's description of the 'fruit of the Spirit' (Gal. 5:22–23). 'Wisdom in James', suggests Davids, 'functions as the Spirit does in Paul.'[2] This may be true, but James has not given us enough material to enable us to decide about whether he himself intended the parallel. And, in general, it cannot be said that wisdom has a prominent role in James; he uses it in only two texts and does not seek to develop the idea beyond what was already well established in the tradition.[3]

Poverty and wealth

'There is hardly a single element of the OT-late Jewish piety-poverty tradition which is not also encountered in the letter of James.'[4] This being so, it is necessary to know something of this tradition in order to understand James' important contribution.

In the Old Testament, this tradition can be summarized in four points. First, God has a particular concern for the poor, the downtrodden, the outcasts. God is the 'Father of the fatherless and protector of widows' (Ps. 68:5); 'he executes justice for the fatherless and the widow, and loves the sojourner, giving him food and clothing' (Dt. 10:18). Accordingly, secondly, God's people must manifest a similar concern for helpless people. The

---

[1]R. Hoppe considers wisdom to be a powerful theological concept in James, related to the regenerating word of God (1:18) and possessing the power to produce those works needed for Christian living (*Der Theologische Hintergrund des Jakobusbriefes* [*Forschung zur Bibel* 28; Echter, 1977], pp. 51–71). But Hoppe is able to draw these conclusions only by making some unlikely connections within James and by reading into James the Jewish dualistic wisdom tradition.

[2]Davids, p. 56; *cf.* also J. A. Kirk, 'The Meaning of Wisdom in James: Examination of a Hypothesis', *NTS* 16, 1969–1970, pp. 24–38.

[3]Mussner, p. 249.   [4]Mussner, p. 80.

Deuteronomy passage continues, 'Love the sojourner therefore', and one of the most frequent denunciations that the prophets brought against Israel was that they failed to care for the poor (*cf.* Am. 2:6–7). A third Old Testament tradition, particularly prominent in the Psalms, is the tendency to identify 'the poor' (*'ānî*) with the pious, the righteous (see especially Pss. 10; 37:8–17; 72:2,4; Is. 29:19). Here there is a mingling of social and religious concepts that is the source of much confusion. Economic lack and social persecution become closely related to religious piety. In their oppression, 'the poor' put forth their oppressed condition as a basis for their plea to God for deliverance: 'As for me, I am poor and needy; but the Lord takes thought for me. Thou art my help and my deliverer; do not tarry, O my God!' (Ps. 40:17). In the situation in which these psalms were written, it is clear that many of the righteous were also suffering oppression at the hands of the wealthy. This leads to the fourth aspect of the tradition, more prominent in later Jewish writings than in the Old Testament: wealthy and powerful people tend to become identified with the wicked.[1]

The teaching of Jesus is strongly influenced by this background and James undoubtedly draws from that teaching as well as from the Old Testament. He reminds his readers that 'God has chosen those who are poor in the world to be rich in faith' (2:5), where we are reminded of our Lord's beatitude, 'Blessed are you poor, for yours is the kingdom of God' (Lk. 6:20). Picking up directly the Old Testament theme, James sets forth care of the orphan and widow as a basic part of true religion (1:27). In a text that closely resembles the prophets' denunciations, James' pronounces judgment on the rich (5:1–6). And like the 'poor' in the Psalms, James' readers need to look to the Lord with patience and endurance for deliverance (5:7–11). Neither James nor the prophets, however, condemn the wealthy just because they are wealthy. James, for instance, enumerates the specific sins for which 'the rich' will be judged: selfish hoarding of money (5:2–3), senseless luxury (5:5), defrauding the worker (5:4) and persecuting the righteous (5:6). That James does not condemn the rich as such is probably also

[1]See E. Bammel, *TDNT*, 6, pp. 888–902; Davids, pp. 41–44.

demonstrated from 1:10–11, where 'the rich man' is probably a Christian 'brother' (see the commentary). Nevertheless, it is clear that most of James' readers were poor, and that many were experiencing oppression from wealthy and powerful people. In this situation, the rich biblical tradition we have described provides James with a fruitful source of imagery and content.

ANALYSIS

I. ADDRESS AND SALUTATION (1:1)

II. TRIALS AND CHRISTIAN MATURITY (1:2–18)
   a. *Letting trials accomplish their purpose* (1:2–4)
   b. *Wisdom, prayer and faith* (1:5–8)
   c. *Poverty and wealth* (1:9–11)
   d. *Trials and temptations* (1:12–18)

III. TRUE CHRISTIANITY SEEN IN ITS WORKS (1:19 – 2:26)
   a. *An exhortation regarding speech and anger* (1:19–20)
   b. *'Be doers of the word'* (1:21–27)
   c. *Impartiality and the law of love* (2:1–13)
   d. *The faith that saves* (2:14–26)

IV. DISSENSIONS WITHIN THE COMMUNITY (3:1 – 4:12)
   a. *The harmful effects of the uncontrolled tongue* (3:1–12)
   b. *True wisdom brings peace* (3:13–18)
   c. *Evil passions are the source of dissensions* (4:1–3)
   d. *A summons to repentance* (4:4–10)
   e. *A prohibition of critical speech* (4:11–12)

V. IMPLICATIONS OF A CHRISTIAN WORLD-VIEW (4:13 – 5:11)
   a. *A condemnation of arrogance* (4:13–17)
   b. *A condemnation of those who misuse wealth* (5:1–6)
   c. *An encouragement to endure patiently* (5:7–11)

VI. CONCLUDING EXHORTATIONS (5:12–20)
   a. *Oaths* (5:12)
   b. *Prayer and healing* (5:13–18)
   c. *A closing summons to action* (5:19–20)

COMMENTARY

I. ADDRESS AND SALUTATION (1:1)

1. The author of the letter introduces himself simply as *James*, or 'Jacob' (Gk. *Iakōbos*; Heb. *ya"qōb*; our English 'James' is derived from the Italian 'Giacomo'). The simplicity of the identification points to the well-known 'James the Just', half-brother of the Lord (Gal. 1:19) and leader of the early Jerusalem church (*cf.* Acts 12:17; 15:13–21; 21:18–25). James does not claim apostolic authority, although Paul calls him an 'apostle' in Galatians 1:19. Rather, James chooses to characterize himself simply as *a servant of God and of the Lord Jesus Christ*. By calling himself *servant* (*doulos*, which could also be translated 'slave'), James shows that he considers his position to be one of humble service to his master, the Lord Jesus. But there is also a certain authority that comes from representing so majestic a master. Similarly, in the Old Testament the titles 'servant of God', 'servant of the LORD', 'my servant', *etc.*, are used particularly often of Moses (see Dt. 34:5; Dn. 9:11), David (Je. 33:21; Ezk. 37:25), Israel (Is. 41:8; *passim*) and others who are given a particular commission to carry out on behalf of God.

In the New Testament, the title is often given to the apostles and their associates (Acts 16:17; Rom. 1:1; Gal. 1:10; Phil. 1:1; Col. 4:12; Tit. 1:1; 2 Pet. 1:1; Jude 1). This is the only place in the New Testament where an individual is called a servant *of God and of the Lord Jesus Christ*. Some think that 'Christ' is not used as a title here, but is almost a proper name. But it is more likely that James intends both qualifications of Jesus to carry theological weight: Jesus is both the promised Messiah of Israel and the Lord to

57

whom service is due. Interestingly, the only other time James refers to Jesus, he describes him with the same two titles (2:1).

James addresses his letter to *the twelve tribes in the Dispersion*. 'The twelve tribes' no longer existed physically, but the title had become a way of describing the regathered and spiritually renewed Israel that God would create in 'the last days' (see Ezk. 47:13; Mt. 19:28; Rev. 7:4–8; 21:12). *Diaspora* (*Dispersion*) was the technical name for the Jewish community that lived 'dispersed' among the nations outside of Palestine (see 2 Macc. 1:27; Jn. 7:35). Whether these terms retain a specifically Jewish orientation, and whether *diaspora* is to be taken literally or figuratively, is not clear. Certainly 1 Peter, which appears to be directed to Gentiles, uses *diaspora* in the latter sense: Christians are those who live as 'exiles' from their true, heavenly homeland (1:1). The early date, Jewish atmosphere and circumstances of James' position, however, favour a more literal meaning here. Perhaps we can associate James' address with the reference in Acts 11:19 to those who had been 'scattered' (*diaspeirō*, the verb used here, is cognate to *diaspora*) by persecution and were preaching the gospel to Jews 'as far as Phoenicia and Cyprus and Antioch'. These could well have been former 'parishioners' of James' whom he now addresses in a 'pastoral letter'.

James' salutation as such is very brief: *Greeting* (*chairein*). This is a typical Greek epistolary greeting (*cf.* Acts 23:26) and reflects James' familiarity with Greek style. Besides Acts 23:26 this particular greeting occurs in the New Testament only in James' letter embodying the Jerusalem Council decision (Acts 15:23) – a parallel that tends to confirm common authorship.

II. TRIALS AND CHRISTIAN MATURITY (1:2–18)

A clear and systematic progression of thought is difficult to find in James. He prefers to move from topic to topic, sometimes joining them with a loose connection in subject-matter, sometimes using a play on words to make the transition. 1:2–18 contains two of these word-plays. The 'greeting' (*chairein*) in 1:1 is picked up by 'joy' (*chara*) in 1:2, and the verb 'lack' (*leipō*) connects 1:4 and 1:5. Other verbal contacts indicate continuity in subject-matter. The words 'trial' (*peirasmos*), 'test', 'testing' (both using the root *dokim*-) and 'endurance' (*hypomonē*; *hypomenō*) join 1:12–16 to 1:2–4; the term 'mature', 'perfect' (*teleios*) occurs in both 1:4 and 1:17; and the theme of God's giving occurs in both 1:5 and 1:17. No single specific theme emerges from this section. In general, however, James appears to touch on matters that could threaten the integrity and strength of his readers' faith. He is concerned that these believers progress to a mature, stable faith (v.4), and to do so, they need to maintain a distinctively Christian attitude towards potential stumbling-blocks.

a. Letting trials accomplish their purpose (1:2–4)

2. James opens the body of his letter with two very characteristic features. He calls his readers *my brethren*, an address which he uses fourteen times (three times with the qualification 'beloved'), often to introduce a new section. This affectionate address sets a strong pastoral tone for the many exhortations of the letter. And, secondly, he issues a command: *count it all joy*. The command is categorical, suggesting the need for a definitive decision to take up a joyful attitude. The 'all' modifying 'joy' might suggest that the joy is to be unmixed with other emotions – 'count it *only* joy' or '*nothing but* joy' – but probably emphasizes rather the quality of the joy (NEB 'supremely happy'). What is remarkable about this command is that it applies to a situation in which a joyful reaction would be most unnatural: *when you meet various trials*. The word translated 'trial', *peirasmos*, has two basic meanings in the New Testament. It can refer to the inner enticement to sin, as in 1 Timothy 6:9 'That those who desire to be rich fall into temptation, into a snare, into many senseless and hurtful desires that plunge men into ruin and destruction.' At other times it denotes external afflictions, particularly persecution (*cf.* 1 Pet. 4:12). In several verses it is possible that both meanings should be included (*e.g.* Mt. 26:41 and parallels).

In the present verse, the use of *meet* (lit. 'fall into') and the replacement of *peirasmos* by 'testing' in verse 3 strongly favour the second meaning. With the qualification *various*, we should probably think both of the difficulties that are common to all people as well as the specific adversities that Christians must face as a result of their faith. Thus, illness (*cf.* 5:14), financial reverses (*cf.* 1:9) and social and economic persecution (*cf.* 2:6) would all be included in the *various trials*. Whatever they be, trials are to be considered by the believer as an occasion for rejoicing.

3. The reason that believers should react with joy when faced with various trials is that these trials are means of *testing* through which God works to perfect faith. The word translated *testing* in RSV, *dokimion*, is rare, being found elsewhere in the New Testament only in 1 Peter 1:7, and in the Septuagint in Psalm 11:7 (Eng. Ps. 12:6) and Proverbs 27:21. In 1 Peter this word appears to denote the result of the testing process: 'the genuineness of your faith' (RSV). In both Septuagint occurrences, however, the word refers to the *process* by which silver or gold is refined by fire. This is probably the meaning intended by James: suffering is a means by which faith, tested in the fires of adversity, can be purified of any dross and thereby strengthened. The idea, then, is not that trials determine whether a person has faith or not. Rather they strengthen the faith that is already present.

Steadfastness (*hypomonē*) is the intended outcome of this testing process. This word occurs frequently in the New Testament to indicate the quality required by Christians as they face adversity, temptation and persecution (*cf., e.g.,* Lk. 8:15; 2 Thes. 1:4; Rev. 2:2; 13:10). 'Fortitude' (NEB), 'staying power' (Ropes), 'heroic endurance' (Dibelius) are attempts to capture the meaning of the word. Trench helpfully distinguishes between 'patience' (*makrothymia*), which Christians are to exercise towards *people*, and *hypomonē*, with which they are to respond to external difficulties.[1] This *hypomonē* is not a meek, passive submission to circumstances, but a strong, active, challenging response in which the satisfying realities of Christianity are proven in practice.

The believer is asked to respond to trials with joy, then, because he knows that they are working to produce a deeper, stronger, more certain faith. The sequence of ideas, and of terminology also, is closely paralleled in two other New Testament passages: Romans 5:3–4 and 1 Peter 1:6–7. In the former Paul reminds the Romans that suffering (*thlipsis*) produces

[1] R. C. Trench, *Synonyms of the New Testament* (1880. Reissued Eerdmans, 1973), pp. 195–198.

endurance (*hypomonēn katergazetai*) and endurance produces character (*dokimēn*). Peter speaks of suffering as testing 'the genuineness (*dokimion*) of your faith'. Some scholars are convinced that direct borrowing is the only explanation of these similarities in thought and language (*e.g.* Mayor, p. cii). But the use of these words to express the process and outcome of the testing of faith through trials is natural and has, as we have seen, some Old Testament precedent (*cf.* also Ecclus. 2:1–6). It is probable, then, that all three authors have utilized language from a popular early Jewish and Christian tradition.

4. Both Paul and Peter imply an almost 'automatic' process by which trials lead to hope and security. James, typically, interrupts the 'process' with a command. Believers are to *let steadfastness have its full effect*. The *full effect* (lit. 'perfect' or 'complete' work – *ergon teleion*) has been variously understood as the culmination of the endurance itself (Mayor), the 'full and proper fruits' endurance should produce (Ropes), or the perfection and wholeness of Christian character as described in the last part of the verse. Probably the last of these should be accepted: mature Christians are the end-product of testing. The word *hina* ('in order that') introduces a description of the 'full effect' as well as the ultimate purpose of trials. To be *perfect and complete* is the state that should result from a genuinely *Christian* response to trials. The perfection or wholeness of the Christian is a basic concern of James. He constantly stresses the need for a whole-hearted, unreserved commitment to God and his will and highlights 'double-mindedness' as a root sin.

The word *perfect* (*teleios*) links the two parts of this verse: the 'perfect' work is the 'perfect Christian'. In what does this perfection consist? Some give the term the idea of 'maturity', or 'completeness', and suggest that this virtue is attainable in this life. It is doubtful whether the term can be 'softened' in this way, however. Elsewhere James uses the adjective of God's gift (1:17), of the 'law of liberty' (1:25) and of the man who is capable of 'bridling his tongue' (3:2). In each case 'perfection', not just 'maturity', appears to be connoted. The goal specified in verse 4b, then, is an eschatological gift – something towards which the Christian is constantly to strive with all his power, but which will not in fact be attained until the culmination of the new age of salvation. Only then will Christians *lack nothing* in their panoply of virtues.

b. Wisdom, prayer and faith (1:5-8)

5. One of the most important virtues that a Christian may *lack* is *wisdom*. *Wisdom* (*sophia*) plays a central role in the Old Testament book, Proverbs, and in many intertestamental books such as The Wisdom of Solomon and Ecclesiasticus (more commonly called today The Wisdom of Jesus the Son of Sirach, or just Sirach).[1] These books, with their terse, hortatory style and practical emphases, have exerted a significant influence on both James' style and content. In the tradition found in these works, wisdom is above all a practically-oriented virtue that gives direction for the life of the godly person. 'Insight' into the will of God and the way it is to be applied in life are both given by wisdom (see Pr. 2:10-19; 3:13-14; 9:1-6, and the section on 'Wisdom' in the Introduction, pp. 52-53). Particularly relevant to James 1:5 is the way in which wisdom is said to produce in its possessor a full-blown godly character. According to Proverbs 8:35, the one who finds wisdom 'finds life and obtains favour from the LORD'. Wisdom of Solomon 10:5 says that wisdom preserved Abraham 'blameless before God' when he obeyed the terrible command to sacrifice his son Isaac. In light of this tradition, it may well be that James introduces the subject of wisdom in verse 5 because he regards it as having the power to make the believer 'perfect and complete' (v.4b). A further connection with verses 2-4 is discerned by some commentators (*e.g.* Calvin, Mayor, Davids), who suggest that wisdom is needed so that believers can take the perspective on trials commanded in verses 2-3. The fact that wisdom is sometimes said to enable the righteous to endure testing (see the reference above and Ecclus. 4:17) lends plausibility to this hypothesis. On the other hand, James does nothing to draw attention to these connections. Therefore, while the relationship of wisdom to completeness and testing may have influenced James' order of topics, we should probably not tie

[1]See also Derek Kidner, *Wisdom to live by* (Inter-Varsity Press, 1985).

verses 5–8 too closely to verses 2–4.

In promising his readers that God will give wisdom to those who ask, James reflects Old Testament teaching (Pr. 2:6a, 'the LORD gives wisdom'). He probably also has in mind Jesus' promise: 'Ask, and it will be given you' (Mt. 7:7a). And, like Jesus, James bases his confidence in God's response on the character of God. God, James reminds us, *gives to all men generously and without reproaching*. The word translated *generously* (*haplōs*) occurs only here in the New Testament. It is from a root whose basic meaning is 'single', 'simple', a meaning retained in Paul's use of the noun *haplotēs* in Ephesians 6:5 (*cf.* Col. 3:22): 'slaves, be obedient . . . in singleness of heart'. When used to describe giving, the idea of 'singleness' suggests the notion of generosity (see 2 Cor. 8:2; 9:11, 13). This meaning is adopted by most translations of James 1:5, and many commentators defend it (see especially the full discussion in Hort). Nevertheless, the idea of 'singleness', suggesting God's undivided, unwavering intent, may be closer to James' meaning. The related adjective, *haplous*, may have this connotation in Luke 11:34 (see Mt. 6:22),[1] and we have seen that James is thoroughly familiar with Jesus' teaching. Moreover, the meaning 'single', 'without reservation', fits well with the immediately following 'without reproaching' and provides a clear, and probably intentional, contrast with the 'double-souled' person of verses 7–8. James' intent, then, would be to highlight God's unreserved, uncalculating, unwavering intent to give his gift of wisdom to those who ask.

Not only is God's giving whole-hearted; it is also unmixed with reproach. 'A fool's gift', according to Ecclesiasticus, 'will profit you nothing, for he has many eyes instead of one. He gives little and upbraids (*oneidizei*) much . . .' (20:14–15a). In contrast, God gives with 'one eye' ('singly') and *without reproaching* (*oneidizontes*) – he does not reprimand us for past failures or remind us endlessly of the value of the gifts he gives. This verse, like the teaching of Jesus to which it is related (Mt. 7:7–11), encourages us to come boldly with our requests to the unwaveringly gracious God.

---

[1]The meaning of *haplous* in Mt. 6:22 / Lk. 11:34 is debated. For the meaning 'single-minded', 'pure', see O. Bauernfeind, *TDNT*, 1, p. 386; I. H. Marshall, *The Gospel of Luke* (Eerdmans, 1978), p. 489.

6. James turns from the manner in which God gives to the manner in which we are to ask. It is not clear that James is thinking specifically of the request for wisdom in verses 6–8; rather, he attaches to the specific subject of praying for wisdom general teaching about the importance of *faith* in prayer. God's meeting of our requests, while not limited arbitrarily to a select number (he gives 'to all', v.5), *is* limited by the manner in which we ask. It is not any request, made however selfishly and foolishly, that God grants, says James (see 4:1–3), but the request that is made *in faith, with no doubting*. This same combination of words occurs in Jesus' teaching about prayer, given in response to the amazement of the disciples when, at his command, the fig tree had withered before their eyes: ' "Truly, I say to you, if you have faith and never doubt, you will not only do what has been done to the fig tree, but even if you say to this mountain, 'Be taken up and cast into the sea,' it will be done. And whatever you ask in prayer, you will receive, if you have faith" ' (Mt. 21:21–22). The key terms, *faith* and *doubting*, have similar meanings in the two passages. *Faith* means more than a belief that God will give what we ask; it also includes confident, unwavering trust in God. *Doubting* translates a word (*diakrinō*) that means basically 'to differentiate'. From this root idea it was extended to include the ideas of 'judging' (1 Cor. 14:29) and 'disputing' (Acts 11:2), and hence, in the middle voice, 'to dispute with oneself', 'to waver', 'to doubt'. James uses the same word in 2:4 to describe the 'distinctions' or 'divisions' which an undue attention to rich people can create in a church. The word suggests, then, not so much intellectual doubt as a basic conflict in loyalties – as for instance between God and 'mammon' (Mt. 6:24) or God and 'the world' (Jas. 4:4).

The *for* (*gar*) in the second part of the verse introduces the argument of verses 6b–8 as a whole. These verses provide, by a negative example, the *reason* why we must ask in faith: the one who lacks faith, the 'divided person', receives nothing from the Lord. At the end of verse 6, this person is compared to the motion of the sea. The image is not so much that of the wave rushing shoreward as of the constant, restless surging of a body of water.[1] Like the surface

---

[1]The word *klydōn* means properly a 'billowing' or 'surging' rather than 'wave' (Hort, pp. 10–11). The ceaseless, sometimes violent motion of the sea was a popular image of change and instability in ancient literature. See Ecclus. 33:2; Philo, *On the Giants*, 51; *On the Sacrifice*

of the sea, never having the same appearance from moment to moment, shifting and moving according to the direction and strength of the wind, the divided person has no fixed beliefs and direction. Having no 'anchor of the soul' (Heb. 6:19), he is a prey to every shifting wind of doctrine and contrary storm of opposition and persecution, and his loyalty to God is constantly threatened. He does not possess that unwavering confidence in God, uninfluenced by adversity and diverse opinions, that receives from the Lord what is asked.

7–8. The correct punctuation of these two verses is difficult to determine (the earliest New Testament manuscripts having no punctuation). Some English versions place the description of the 'double-minded man' in verse 8 in apposition to 'that person' of verse 7, as in NASB: 'For let not that man expect that he will receive anything from the Lord, being a double-minded man' (cf. also NIV). Others take the 'double-minded man' to be the subject of the verb 'receive' in verse 7, as RSV: 'For that person must not suppose that a double-minded man, unstable in all his ways, will receive anything from the Lord.' In the NASB rendering, 'that man' is identified with 'the doubter' of verse 6b and is criticized for thinking that his prayers will be answered. If the RSV punctuation is adopted, however, 'that person' is identified with 'the one asking' in verse 6a, and is reminded that doubters will not have their requests answered. Probably the first alternative is better, because it is natural to take 'that man' as a somewhat derogatory designation of 'the doubter' who was just introduced. 'That man', 'that doubter' must not expect that God will respond to his requests, for he is insincere and inconsistent in his allegiance to God.

The word *double-minded* (*dipsychos*) means literally 'double-souled', a suggestive indication of the depths of the division within this person. The word is used here for the first time in Greek literature, and some think James himself may have coined it. But however new the word may be, the idea is not. The Old Testament characterizes the sinner as having a 'divided heart' (Ps. 12:2; Ho. 10:2) and pronounces a blessing on those who

---

of Abel and Cain, 90; On the Eternity of the World, 125.

pursue God with 'a whole heart' (Ps. 119:2). The rabbis captured the essential sinfulness of man by depicting him as having two tendencies, good and evil, warring in the soul. And Jesus, when asked by a scribe what was the greatest commandment, quoted Deuteronomy 6:5: 'You shall love the Lord your God with all your heart, and with all your soul, and with all your mind' (Mt. 22:37). To have a fundamental cleavage in one's basic attitude towards God; to be believing now one way, now another – this is the direct opposite of the faith James urges us to exhibit in prayer (v. 6a). Certainly God does not answer prayers uttered in such unbelief. We should note that this 'double-mindedness' is the antithesis both of that 'wholeness' or 'perfection' (*teleios*) which is the goal of Christian living (v. 4) and of God's 'single', 'whole-hearted' character (v. 5). This desire for singleness and purity of intention is a leading theme in verses 2–8, and occurs throughout the letter (see especially 4:4–10).

c. Poverty and wealth (1:9–11)

9. The connection between verses 9–11 and the preceding is not entirely clear. Some think that James intended no logical progression of thought and that verses 9–11 begin an essentially separate subject. Others discern a connection to the theme of trials, introduced in verse 2 and taken up again in verse 12: poverty may be the most outstanding and difficult trial facing the readers of the letter (Hort, Mussner, Davids). Still others suggest that James' discussion of the 'double-minded' person leads him to speak about that area of life that is most often troublesome in creating divided loyalties in our attitude towards God: the conflict between God and mammon (Tasker). While admitting that either of these ideas may have influenced James in his order of topics, we must note that James makes neither explicit. It is perhaps better, then, not to tie this section too closely to either of these topics.

The description of *the brother* in verse 9 as *lowly* (*tapeinos*) suggests a Christian who is low down on the socio-economic scale – one who is relatively poor and powerless. This sense of the word *tapeinos* is warranted both because the Old Testament frequently uses the term with this meaning (*cf.* Pss. 10:18; 34:18;

102:17; Is. 11:4; Am. 2:7), and because *tapeinos* is here contrasted with *plousios*, 'rich' (v. 10). If James is writing to Jewish-Christians in Palestine and Syria, many, if not most, of his readers would have been poor. We know of a famine that struck at about this time and it is probable that Christians, ostracized by much of the populace, would have suffered particularly severely (see Acts 11:28–29). In the midst of such afflictions, the Christian, whose position in worldly terms is low indeed, is to *boast in his exaltation*. *Boast* (NEB 'be proud') means in this context not the arrogant boasting of the self-important, but the joyous pride possessed by the person who values what God values. The word *exaltation* (*hypsos*) is used elsewhere in the New Testament to describe the heavenly realm to which Christ ascended (Eph. 4:8) and from which the Holy Spirit descends (Lk. 24:49). By faith believers now belong to that heavenly realm as its citizens (Phil. 3:20) and also await from heaven the Lord Jesus who will transform our 'bodies of humility' into 'bodies of glory' (Phil. 3:21). We may suggest, then, that *exaltation* includes the believer's present enjoyment of his exalted spiritual status as well as his hope of participation in the glorious eternal kingdom inaugurated by Christ. It is just this combination of present status and future inheritance that James singles out in a verse that is almost a commentary on the meaning of *hypsos* (2:5): 'Has not God chosen those who are poor in the world to be rich in faith and heirs of the kingdom which he has promised to those who love him?'

10. The rich person, like the poor person, must look beyond his outward physical circumstances to the abiding spiritual values and circumstances of the unseen 'heavenly realm'. The antithetical contrast between 'poor' and 'rich' picks up a common biblical theme. This theme developed particularly in the later Old Testament period, when the 'poor' (Heb. *'ānî*) became closely identified with the humble, afflicted saints who trusted God for deliverance. Similarly, the 'rich' were often linked to godless oppressors who trusted in their wealth for deliverance. God promises to exalt the former group, but to judge the latter. The hope expressed by Mary in the Magnificat is typical of this tradition: 'he has put down the mighty from their thrones, and exalted those of low degree; he has filled the hungry with good things, and the rich he has sent empty away' (Lk. 1:52–53; see also the section 'Poverty and wealth' in the Introduction, pp. 53–55).

With this tradition in mind, many commentators see the 'rich person' in verse 10 as an unbeliever. They point out, further, that *rich* (*plousios*) is never used of a Christian in James (except in a spiritual sense), that James 5:1–6 pronounces judgment upon the rich generally, and that verses 10b–11 identify the 'humiliation' of the rich person with condemnation in the last judgment. Those who take this view generally suggest that the exhortation to boast in humiliation is ironic: ' "The rich man has had his day; all he can expect from the future is humiliation; that is the only thing left for him to 'boast about'." '[1] The use of irony is, however, not plainly indicated and it would seem to be somewhat out of place. A serious exhortation to boast fits much better; and in this case, the 'rich person' must be a believer. This alternative finds support in the syntax since 'brother' (*adelphos*), coming before 'the lowly one' (*tapeinos*) in verse 9, is most naturally taken as governing 'the rich one' (*plousios*) in verse 10 also.

Rather than taking verses 10b–11 as explanatory of the humiliation, then, we can understand them as providing a reason for the rich Christian to boast in humiliation: the transitory nature of this world renders confidence in riches an undependable prop. Isaiah 40: 6–8, to which James clearly alludes in verses 10b–11, makes just this point: 'all flesh' fades away, in contrast to the word of God that stands for ever (and see also the use of this text in 1 Pet. 1:23–25). Psalm 49:16–17 contains a similar warning about wealth: 'Be not afraid when one becomes rich, when the glory of his house increases. For when he dies he will carry nothing away; his glory will not go down after him.' James draws from this biblical tradition to remind the wealthy Christian that riches do not endure and that he must be constantly on guard against placing too much emphasis on what he cannot 'carry' away with him into the next world.

What, then, is the *humiliation* in which this rich Christian is to boast? Two related ideas may be suggested. First, the rich Christian should remember that, however 'exalted' he may seem in the eyes of the world, his status before God is different. He must

[1]Dibelius, p. 85.

consciously maintain this perspective on his true, spiritual position in order to experience the blessings of God's good pleasure. James may well have in mind the words of Jesus, to which he refers in 4:10, 'whoever humbles himself will be exalted' (Mt. 23:12). A second, related, idea is that *humiliation* may suggest the believer's own identification with Jesus Christ, who 'humbled himself' (Phil. 2:8) and who was considered of no account in the world.

James, then, exhorts both the poor and the rich Christian to remember that the sole basis for their confidence is their identification with Jesus Christ. The poor believer, insignificant and of no account in the eyes of the world, is to rejoice in his relationship with the Lord who has been exalted to the highest position in the universe. The rich believer, well-off and secure in his possessions, with great status in the eyes of the world, is to remember that his only lasting security comes through his relationship with the 'man of sorrows', 'despised and rejected by men'. Both Christians, in other words, must look at their lives from a heavenly, not an earthly, perspective.

11. This verse continues the allusion to Isaiah 40:6–7, describing in more detail the 'fading away' mentioned in verse 10. The RSV translates the four main verbs in the first part of the verse with present tenses, reflecting the probably gnomic, 'customary' force of the Greek aorist tenses here. The tense may, however, also suggest the suddenness of the action.[1] The image of the quickly fading flower would have been a familiar one for Middle Eastern readers who annually saw the early spring flowers wither suddenly under the sun's merciless heat. The word translated in RSV *scorching heat* (*kausōn*) should probably be translated 'scorching wind', as in NASB; the word occurs several times in the Septuagint to denote the 'east wind', the hot desert wind, and is frequent in images of judgment; *cf.* Hosea 13:15: 'Though he [Ephraim] may flourish as the reed plant, the east wind, the wind of the LORD, shall come, rising from the wilderness; and his fountain shall dry up, his spring shall be parched; it shall strip his treasury of every precious thing.'

[1] Moule, p. 12; Adamson, p. 63.

The point of the botanical comparison is explicitly summarized in verse 11b: just as the flower, seemingly flourishing one day, is dead the next, so the rich person *will fade away in the midst of his pursuits*. The verb *fade away* (*marainō*) clearly connotes death here. *Pursuits* is a particularly happy rendering of the word *poreia*. While it can mean simply 'way' in the sense 'way of life', it often has a more specific sense, a 'journey'. In this context, and in the light of James 4:13, the word probably denotes the profit-motivated business trip in the midst of which the rich Christian is suddenly 'taken away'.

d. Trials and temptations (1:12–18)

12. After these somewhat parenthetical exhortations regarding wisdom and prayer (vv. 5–8) and poverty and wealth (vv. 9–11), James returns in verse 12 to the theme of trials (vv. 2–4). The relationship of this verse to the earlier paragraph is obvious from the verbal resemblances between them. The word 'trial' occurs in both places, 'test' in verse 12 picks up the 'testing' of verse 3 (both come from the root *dokim–*) and the word 'endure' in verse 12 is simply the verbal form of the word translated 'steadfastness' in verses 3 and 4. While the earlier text presented 'steadfastness' as the product of testing, the present verse pronounces a blessing on those who endure during the trial. What James is suggesting, then, is that the Christian must practise 'steadfastness' in order to achieve a settled, steadfast character. As the athlete 'endures' bodily stress in order to achieve a high level of physical endurance, so the Christian is to endure the trials of life in order to attain the spiritual endurance that will bring perfection.

A reward is promised to the Christian who successfully meets the test: *the crown of life*. The word *crown* (*stephanos*) sometimes refers to a royal crown, but is more frequently used of the laurel wreath given to the victorious athlete (see 1 Cor. 9:25) and, figuratively, symbolizes glory and honour. It is this last meaning that fits best here. The *crown* is the emblem of spiritual success, given by the King of the universe to those who 'keep their faith' in the midst of suffering and temptation. *Life* should be taken as identifying the reward – 'the reward that is life'. This *life* is, of course, not physical life, but eternal life, the enjoyment of God's presence on into eternity. Revelation 2:10, a word of Jesus addressed to suffering Christians, closely parallels the thought here: 'Be faithful unto death, and I will give you the crown of life.' Even when enduring the trial means physical death, *life* is the reward for those who love God. This love for God is demonstrated by, and perfected in, our willingness to suffer for the cause of Christ.

There are those who react against the notion of a 'reward' for faithful Christian living. And, indeed, service of God that is motivated by a calculated desire for reward is the very antithesis of Christian spirituality. But the New Testament consistently invites the Christian to contemplate the inheritance that awaits him. The contemplation of this glorious inheritance can be a marvellous source of spiritual strength and sustenance as we realize 'that the sufferings of this present time are not worth comparing with the glory that is to be revealed to us' (Rom. 8:18). By fixing his gaze on this inheritance, the believer is able to find sustenance and strength in the trial, recognizing that the suffering of this present time is not long. This inheritance cannot be earned and it is unattainable by those who do not serve God from a heart of love and devotion. Moreover, as Mitton aptly says, 'the rewards are of a kind that only a true Christian would be able to appreciate'.[1]

13. The various hardships and afflictions that meet Christians in the world can produce spiritual perfection (v. 4) and lead to God's reward (v. 12) if they are endured in faith. However, they can have a harmful effect if met with the wrong attitude. One such wrong attitude, James suggests, is to blame God for the enticement to sin that accompanies trials. The Old Testament makes clear that God does test his people, in the sense that he brings them into situations where their willingness to obey him is tested. 'God tested Abraham' when he ordered him to sacrifice his son Isaac (Gn. 22:1), he tested Israel by leaving them surrounded by pagan nations (Jdg. 2:22) and he tested King Hezekiah by leaving him to his own devices in his reception of the Babylonian envoys (2 Ch. 32:31; *cf.* 2 Ki. 20:12–19). But while God

[1] Mitton, p.44.

may test or prove his servants in order to strengthen their faith, he never seeks to induce sin and destroy their faith. Thus, despite the fact that the same Greek root (*peira-*) is used for both the outer trial and the inner temptation, it is crucial to distinguish them. It is probably within verse 13 that James makes the transition from one to the other: 'If a person is tempted by such trials, he must not say, "This temptation comes from God" ' (GNB). The tendency to blame God for temptation, and hence excuse succumbing to it, was a familiar problem for a people who stressed the sovereignty of God – if temptation comes from God, how could one resist it? A century and a half before James, Jesus the son of Sirach was protesting against this tendency: 'Do not say, "Because of the Lord I left the right way"; for he will not do what he hates. Do not say, "It was he who led me astray"; for he has no need of a sinful man' (Ecclus. 15:11–12).

The last part of verse 13 gives two related reasons why one ought not to blame God for temptation. The first relates to the character of God: he *cannot be tempted with evil*. This rendering, which is paralleled in most English translations, understands the rare word *apeirastos* as a passive verbal adjective with the meaning 'unable to be tempted'. But two other possibilities should be mentioned. Hort compared the word to the similar, and more frequent, word *apeiratos* which has the meaning 'inexperienced'. This interpretation is reflected in the NEB, 'God is untouched by evil'. Davids, on the other hand, argues for the meaning 'ought not to be tested'. This, he suggests, makes better sense than the traditional interpretation – for how can God's inability to be tempted be an argument against thinking that God tempts others? – and would tie in nicely with the Old Testament condemnation of Israel for testing God in the wilderness.[1] Neither alternative is preferable to the traditional interpretation. Hort's suggestion ignores the probable play on the word *peirazō* (God does not 'tempt' because he cannot be 'tempted'). Davids has a point when he questions the logic involved in the traditional view, but his own interpretation gives to *apeiratos* a very poorly attested meaning.[2] If we adopt the RSV rendering, then, how does

[1]Davids, pp. 82–83, and, in greater depth, 'The Meaning of *APEIRASTOS* in James I. 13', *NTS* 24, 1977–1978, pp. 386–392.
[2]Davids argues that *apeiratos* means 'ought not to be tempted' in the NT apocryphal books

the clause contribute to James' argument? Presumably, it is to be seen as a preliminary observation leading on to the main point: *he himself tempts no one*. 'What must be understood is that temptation is an impulse to sin, and since God is not susceptible to any such desire for evil he cannot be seen as desiring that it be brought about in man' (Laws).

14. The person facing adversity must not attempt to excuse any failure to resist temptation by blaming that temptation on God. If he wants to blame someone, he has only himself to consider – temptation comes from *his own desire*. Desire (*epithymia*) does not always have a bad meaning (*cf.* Lk. 22:15; Phil. 1:23), but here, as most often in the New Testament, it refers to fleshly, selfish, illicit desire. While the word often describes specifically sexual passions, the use of the singular here suggests a broader conception. Like the rabbis, who spoke of 'the evil impulse' (*yeser hara*) that inhabits every person, James seems to think of man's innate tendency towards sin. Temptation springs from this 'evil impulse', as it *lures* and *entices* man. The former of these verbs (*exelkō*) connotes a forceful dragging out or away, while the latter (*deleazō*) suggests the attraction exerted by proffered bait. Both terms were used in a metaphorical sense to describe the attractive force of pleasure or persuasive teachers.[1] But the imagery of fishing with which the words were originally associated is probably still present: 'desire' is like the hook with its bait, that first entices its prey and then drags it away. If the superficial attractiveness of 'desire' is not strenuously resisted, a person can become 'hooked' on it, unable to escape from its all-powerful lure. James' omission of Satan as a source of temptation does not mean that he ignores the ultimate 'tempter' (*cf.* 4:7). His purpose here is to highlight individual responsibility for sin. And, as

---

Acts of John 57 and *Pseudo-Ignatius* 11, but the definition 'unable to be tempted' is preferable in both. Furthermore, his view has difficulty explaining *estin* ('is') and must give an unusual force to the genitive *kakōn*.

[1]In 2 Pet. 2:14,18, *deleazō* is used of the 'enticements' of false teachers. With Hort (pp. 25–26), we may suppose that *exelkō* is used here equivalently to its non-compounded form *helkō* ('drag'). The latter has a well-attested figurative sense. Philo uses *deleazō* and *helkō* together in a passage reminiscent of Jas. 1:14: 'There is no single thing that does not yield to the enticement [*deleasthēn*] of pleasure, and get caught [*helkō*] and dragged along in her entangling nets . . .' (*On Husbandry*, 103).

Bengel remarks, 'Even the suggestions of the devil do not occasion danger, before they are made "our own" '.[1]

15. 'Desire', in itself, is not sin. It is only when a person, by an act of the will, assents to its enticement that sin results. James vividly describes this sequence with imagery drawn from child-birth and maturation. *Desire* is pictured as the mother (*epithymia* is feminine), *giving birth to sin*, her child. And this child, if it is allowed to become *full-grown*, gives birth in turn to death. The image of 'desire' as a seductress luring the believer into an adulterous union that brings death is reminiscent of the role played by the 'loose woman' in Proverbs 5 – 9. This figure, who leads her guests into the depths of Sheol (Pr. 9:18), is contrasted with wisdom, who gives life to those who embrace her (Pr. 8:35). Since James has mentioned wisdom in verse 5, it may be that he has this Old Testament imagery in mind as he contrasts the life given to those who endure trials (v. 12) with the death produced in those who allow 'desire' to run its course (v. 15). Such are the serious consequences involved in the Christian's struggle with trials.

16. This verse serves as a transition between verses 12–15 and 17–18. The attributing to God of evil intent – tempting people – is a serious matter. James wants to make sure that his readers are not *deceived* about this. Far from enticing to evil, God is the source of every good gift (v. 17), one of the greatest of which is the new birth (v. 18).

17. The general meaning of this verse is clear: God, whose benevolent character is unchanging and unchangeable, is the source of everything that is good. Many of the details are, however, obscure. There is, first, the question as to why James mentions both *good endowment* and *perfect gift*. Tasker suggests that we understand 'good' as a predicate adjective introducing a contrast between the two terms: All giving is *good*, but every *perfect* gift comes from God (*cf.* NEB mg.) But, if this were the meaning, we would have expected an adversative conjunction,

---

[1] J. A. Bengel, *Gnomon of the New Testament*, 5 (T. & T. Clark, 1860), p. 7.

'but' (*alla* or *de*), between the two terms. Probably no real difference in meaning between the phrases should be seen; James may repeat them for stylistic effect or he may be quoting from an unknown source.[1]

A second difficulty is the punctuation of the verse. RSV, along with most translations, places a comma after 'from above', making the participial phrase 'coming down . . .' an additional, independent description. But the NEB joins together 'from above' and 'coming down': 'All good giving and every perfect gift comes from above . . .' Probably the RSV rendering is better, because the alternative leaves the prepositional phrase ('from the Father of lights') hanging somewhat awkwardly.

The description of God as *the Father of lights* is unique in Scripture. The *lights* are almost certainly to be understood as the heavenly bodies, probably including sun, moon and stars (see Ps. 136:7–9; Je. 31:35 [LXX 38:36]). Scripture often alludes to the heavenly firmament as evidence of God's creative handiwork and his continuing exercise of power (see esp. Jb. 38:4–15, 19–21, 31–33; Ps. 136:4–9; Is. 40:22, 26; and, in Jewish literature, Ecclus. 43:1–12). The description of God as *Father* can also allude to his creative work (*cf.* Jb. 38:28). Thus James' intention is to remind us of the benevolent power of God that he has manifested in his 'good' creation (*cf.* Gn. 1).

Imagery drawn from the heavenly bodies is carried on in the last phrase of the verse. As is noted in the margin of the RSV, the Greek text is uncertain. The majority of manuscripts read two nominative nouns, *variation* (*parallagē*) and *shadow* (*aposkiasma*) separated by *or* (*ē*) with a genitive noun, *turning* (*tropēs*), dependent on *shadow*. If this reading is adopted, the genitive *tropes* must presumably be construed as source or subjective, yielding the RSV translation *variation or shadow due to change*. But several early and important manuscripts make *shadow* a genitive (*aposkiasmatos*). If this reading is adopted, the word *ē* will probably have to be given a rough breathing, making it a relative pronoun dependent on *parallagē*. The phrase will then be translated 'variation that

---

[1]One reason for thinking that James may be quoting is that the first eight Greek words of the verse form an almost perfect hexameter – unique even in the fairly literary James (see Mayor, p. 57; Ropes, p. 159; Dibelius, p. 99; Davids, p. 86).

belongs to the turning of the shadow'.[1] Neither reading makes exceptionally good sense, but the former, with its breadth of support, should probably be accepted. The fact that two of the words used in this phrase (*tropē* and *parallagē*) are often used with astronomical meaning, along with the reference to the 'lights' in the previous phrase, makes it probable that a reference to some sort of astronomical phenomenon is intended. *Variation* naturally suggests the periodic movements of the heavenly bodies, but whether 'shadow due to change' refers to the phases of the moon, the shadow cast by an eclipse or the constant alternation of night and day is not clear. But James' language is not exclusively technical, so we may suspect that he intends no more than a general reference to the constant changes observed in creation. This changeableness of creation was frequently used to highlight, by contrast, the unchanging nature of God the Creator (*cf.* Philo, *Allegorical Interpretation*, 2.33: 'Every created thing must necessarily undergo change, for this is its property, even as unchangeableness is the property of God').

18. As an outstanding example of God's good gifts, James cites the fact that God has *brought us forth by the word of truth*. This he did out of his own 'gratuitous and spontaneous determination' (*boulētheis*).[2] But what 'birth' is this? The birth of humankind by the sovereign fiat of God's word? The birth of Israel, his people (*cf.* Dt. 32:18)? Or the birth of Christians through the word of the gospel? In favour of the first are the clear creation references in verse 17, Philo's use of the verb 'give birth to' (*apokyeō*) of creation and the argument that *creatures* (*ktismata*) probably refers to non-human creation.[3] The second can appeal to Old Testament references to Israel as God's *first fruits*. However, there are decisive considerations favouring the third interpretation. First, *first fruits* (*aparchē*) is a customary New Testament designation of Christians (see especially 2 Thes. 2:13; Rev. 14:4). And the idea of Christians as the *first fruits* of a redeemed creation is paralleled in

---

[1] The translation is by Ropes, who decides for this reading (p. 162). *Cf.* also NEB: 'Variation, no play of passing shadows'.

[2] Cantinat, p. 95.

[3] Hort, p. 32; L. E. Elliott-Binns, 'James I.18: Creation or Redemption?', *NTS* 3, 1956–1957, pp. 148–161; Laws, pp. 75–78 (hesitantly).

Romans 8:19–23. Secondly, the verb 'give birth to' in verse 18 clearly parallels by contrast its use in verse 15 (these are the only two occurrences in the New Testament). But this favours a reference to *spiritual* life as a contrast to spiritual death in verse 15. Thirdly, and most decisively, is the overwhelming probability that *the word of truth* refers to the gospel. The phrase means this in its four other New Testament occurrences (2 Cor. 6:7; Eph. 1:13; Col. 1:5; 2 Tim. 2:15) and is connected in James to the phrase 'which is able to save your souls' in verse 21.

We take it, then, that James appeals to the spiritual 'new birth' of Christians as a particularly striking illustration of the good things God gives. This new birth is motivated by the sovereign determination of God, whose *will*, unlike the creation he made, is unvarying. The instrument through which God accomplishes this spiritual birth is the gospel, *the word of truth*. And the purpose of this birth is that Christians should stand as the 'first instalment' (*first fruits*) in the universal redemptive plan of God – 'good gifts' that he has yet to give.

III. TRUE CHRISTIANITY SEEN IN ITS WORKS (1:19 – 2:26)

The first major section of the letter (1:2–18) has a loose coherence centred on the theme of trials/temptations. 1:19 – 2:26 is more closely focused on the command expressed in 1:22: *be doers of the word*. This command is the centrepiece of 1:21–27, which argues for 'doing' as indispensable to any genuine Christianity. 2:1–13 introduces love for poorer brethren as a specific instance in which this obedience is to be manifest. The relationship between this obedience and faith is then explored in 2:14–26. Four words are particularly characteristic of the section: 'word' (*logos*), prominent especially in 1:21–27; 'law' (*nomos*), mentioned in 1:25 and high-lighted in 2:8–13; and 'works' (*erga*) and 'faith' (*pistis*), which carry the weight of the argument throughout 2:14–26.

a. An exhortation regarding speech and anger (1:19–20)

19. James' brief admonition to avoid hasty speech and uncon-trolled anger is introduced with his familiar address, *my beloved* *brethren*. Generally in the letter this address signals the transition to a new topic. However, it is suggested that, in this instance, a close relationship between these exhortations and the context can be established. Specifically, since references to 'the word' both precede (v. 18) and follow (v. 21) these exhortations, it is argued that James is encouraging his readers to be quick to listen to God's Word but slow to become teachers of it. But it is peculiar, if this were James' intention, that he did not specify 'the word' as the object of the verbs *hear* and *speak*. Moreover, the prohibition of quick *anger* does not fit well with this idea. Probably, then, we have here another instance in which James shifts suddenly to a new topic.[1]

The RSV, as do most translations, takes the initial word of the verse as an imperative, *Know this*. By form, however, the word could also be indicative; *cf.* NEB, 'Of that you may be certain'. James' fondness for the imperative, especially when he addresses his readers, favours that form here. The importance of controlling one's speech is a popular theme in Wisdom literature (*cf.* Pr. 10:19; 15:1; 17:27–28: Ecclus. 5:9 – 6:1). Significantly, looseness in speech is often linked with unrestrained anger. According to Proverbs 17:27, 'He who restrains his words has knowledge, and he who has a cool spirit is a man of understanding'. All too often, it is uncontrolled anger at someone that leads us to speak too quickly and say too much. While James does not forbid all anger (there is a place for 'righteous indignation'), he does prohibit the thoughtless, unrestrained temper that often leads to rash, harmful and irretrievable words (*cf.* also Ec. 7:9). He will have much more to say on this subject in 3:1–12.

20. The prohibition of unrestrained anger is based on the fact that anger *does not work the righteousness of God*. Considerable difficulty is involved in rightly identifying *the righteousness of God* here. Three main possibilities should be considered. First, the phrase may refer to 'the righteous status that God confers on us' (taking the genitive *theou* as subjective). This meaning of right-

---

[1] A different contextual link is proposed by C. B. Amphoux ('Une relecture du chapître I de l'Epître Jacques', *Biblica* 59, 1978, pp. 554–561), who suggests that 'slow to speak' is related to not accusing God of responsibility for temptation (v. 13). But this context is too distant.

eousness is well attested in Paul's letters (cf. Phil. 3:9) and James appears to use 'righteousness' and the cognate verb 'justify' with this general meaning in 2:14–26. Secondly, the word 'right-eousness' might mean 'justice' (cf. NEB), in which case James would be warning his readers against thinking that man's anger can somehow be excused because it is a tool of God's own just judgment (in this case, the genitive *theou* would presumably have a loose possessive force). This meaning of 'righteousness' is well attested in the Septuagint and the phrase 'work righteousness' may have this meaning in Hebrews 11:33 (cf. RSV). A third possibility is to understand 'righteousness' as 'the righteous activity that meets God's approval' (taking the genitive *theou* as objective; cf. NIV). The phrase 'do' (*poieō*) or 'practise' (*ergazomai*) righteousness consis-tently has this meaning in biblical Greek (see with *ergazomai*, Ps. 15:2; Acts 10:35; Heb. 11:33 may also fit here). This last consider-ation seems decisive, particularly in view of the fact that James' only clear use of 'righteousness' to refer to status before God (the first alternative above) comes in a quotation (of Gn. 15:6). On this understanding, then, to 'work righteousness' would be the anti-thesis of 'working sin' (2:9). Hasty, uncontrolled anger is sin, because it violates the standard of conduct that God demands of his people. Though probably coincidental, it is striking that, in the only place where 'work' (*ergazomai*) and 'righteousness' are used together in the Septuagint (Ps. 15:2), the context has to do with sins of speech.

b. 'Be doers of the word' (1:21–27)

21. This verse is usually taken with verses 19–20. But while it is obviously connected to what comes before it with the *Therefore*, it is more intimately related to the following verses, through the topic of *the word*. Moreover, the *Therefore* (*dio*) may serve to connect the discussion in verses 21ff. with verse 18 rather than with verses 19–20. Suggesting this is the fact that 1 Peter 1:23 – 2:2 exhibits a pattern strikingly similar to James 1:18, 21: new birth through the word of God is followed by the command (introduced with *dio*) to 'put away' evil behaviour and to embrace the Word of God.[1] That

---

[1] This assumes that *to logikon adolon gala* in 1 Pet. 2:2 refers to the Word of God (cf. the AV

Peter has borrowed from James, or vice versa, is improbable. But it is likely that both authors are utilizing a common early Christian sermonic order in which a reminder of the spiritual birth God had graciously given his people through his Word was followed by exhortations to shun the kind of behaviour associated with the old life and to begin living by the standard of the Word that had saved them.

James' use of the word *put away* (*apotithemai*) further supports the idea that he is employing a common tradition. This word, which is generally used of the 'taking off' of a set of clothes (*cf.* Acts 7:58), is applied widely in the New Testament to the 'putting off' of old, pre-Christian patterns of behaviour (*cf.* Rom. 13:12; Eph. 4:22, 25; Col. 3:8; Heb. 12:1; 1 Pet. 2:1). What is to be put off, according to James, is *all filthiness and rank growth of wickedness*. The word *filthiness* (*rhyparia*) is used only here in biblical Greek, but its adjective, 'filthy', is used in 2:2 to describe the clothes of the poor man, and in Zechariah 3:3–4 of the garments that the high priest Joshua has to put off before he can be given a new, rich set of clothes by the angel of the LORD. The clothing imagery suggested by 'put off' is thus maintained with this word. *Rank growth* translates a word (*perisseia*) that means 'surplus' or 'abundance'. Tasker suggests that it has here the same meaning as the word *perisseuma* and means 'the remainder of wickedness'. But in Romans 5:17 and 2 Corinthians 8:2, the word appears to mean simply 'abundance', so it is preferable to think that the word is added to emphasize the variety and prevalence of the sin that Christians have to fight against (*cf.* NIV, 'the evil that is so prevalent').

The 'putting off' of evil is to be accompanied by a 'receiving' of something else: *the implanted word*. Hort argued that the word translated 'implanted' (*emphytos*) must mean 'inborn' (as in Wisdom 12:10, the only other occurrence of the word in 'biblical' Greek), and that James was referring to man's natural, 'inborn' capacity to receive God's revelation – 'the original capacity involved in the Creation in God's image which makes it possible for man to apprehend a revelation at all'. But this conception, besides having rather dubious biblical support, is too general for

'sincere milk of the word' and the arguments of J. N. D. Kelly, *A Commentary on the Epistles of Peter and of Jude* [Harper & Row, 1969], p. 85).

the context, where 'the word' is described as having the power to save (v. 21) and to regenerate (v. 18). These references indicate rather plainly that 'the implanted word' must depict the proclaimed Word of God, not an innate quality within man.

In this case, *emphytos* would refer to something that has *become* implanted.[1] This striking conception of the Word may be dependent on the famous 'new covenant' prophecy in Jeremiah, where God promises: 'I will put my law within them, and I will write it upon their hearts' (Je. 31:33; and *cf.* further the reference to 'the law of liberty' in 1:25 and the section in the Introduction on 'The law', pp. 48–50). What James is suggesting by describing the Word in this way is that the Christian must not think he is done with the Word of God after it has saved him. That Word becomes a permanent, inseparable part of the Christian, a commanding and guiding presence within him. The command to *receive the implanted word*, then, is not a command to be converted ('receive the word' means this elsewhere in the New Testament), but to accept its precepts as binding and to seek to live by them. Christians who have truly been 'born again' (v. 18) demonstrate that the Word has transformed them by their humble acceptance of that Word as their authority and guide for life. Or, to use the imagery our Lord used to make the same point: the believer is to prepare 'good ground' in his heart in order that the 'seed' of the Word that has been planted there might produce much fruit (*cf.* Mk. 4:3–20). James speaks of 'the salvation of your souls' as this fruit. In accordance with Old Testament usage, 'soul' here simply means 'oneself', and the salvation is regarded as future: 'receiving the word' leads to deliverance in the day of judgment.

22. Lest anyone misconceive what 'receiving the word' involves, James spells out what he means in verses 22–27. In doing so, we are taken right to the heart of James' pastoral concern. However important may be mental assent to the Word, it has not been truly received until it is put into practice. 'Hearing' the Word is, of course, necessary and important – it would be a fatal misunderstanding to think that James is against listening to the Word. But what James strenuously opposes is any hearing of the

[1]For this meaning of *emphytos*, see Herodotus 9:94, Epistle of Barnabas 1:2; 9:9 (where the reference is to the gospel), and the note in Adamson, pp. 98–100.

word that does not lead to *doing*. With this emphasis James aligns himself with a widespread Jewish belief of his day. 'Not the expounding [of the law] is the chief thing, but the doing [of it]' said a second-century rabbi (Simeon b. Gamaliel in Mishnah, *Abot.* 1:17). Paul reflects this Jewish emphasis when he writes: 'it is not the hearers of the law who are righteous before God, but the doers of the law who will be justified' (Rom. 2:13). And James' concern is once again firmly in line with Jesus' teaching: 'Blessed are those who hear the word of God and keep it!' (Lk. 11:28). Jesus' preaching is filled with the overwhelming, amazing wonder of God's sovereign grace reaching down to sinful men in the gospel. But equally prominent is Jesus' summons to radical obedience – an obedience that is the necessary human response to God's grace. Both factors, the gracious initiative of God and the grateful response of man, are part and parcel of the gospel. The Word, through which we are born into new life (v. 18) and which becomes implanted in us (v. 21), is a Word that is to be put into practice.

Those who fail to *do* the word, who are *hearers only*, are guilty of a dangerous and potentially fatal self-delusion. If the gospel, by nature, contains both saving power and summons to obedience, those who relate to only one have not truly embraced the gospel. That is why James can say that people who only *hear* the word are *deceiving* themselves. They think that they have a relationship with God because they regularly attend church, go to Bible studies or read the Bible. But if their listening is not accompanied by obedience, their true situation before God is far different. 'Obedience', says Calvin, 'is the mother of true knowledge of God.'[1]

23–25. James elaborates on the contrast between the person who only listens to the word and the one who both hears and obeys it, by means of a simile. The 'hearer only' is compared to someone who considers *his natural face in a mirror*, but quickly forgets what he has seen. The doer of the word, on the other hand, looks into *the perfect law, the law of liberty* and *perseveres*; he is *a doer that acts*. What is the point of the comparison? Some have

[1]Calvin, *Institutes*, I.6.1.

suggested that James sets up a contrast in the manner of looking: the 'hearer only' glances hastily and carelessly into the law of liberty, while the doer considers it carefully (*cf.* NEB). This would presume that the *mirror* in verse 23 is comparable to the *perfect law* of verse 25. But while the mirror was often used with this sort of figurative meaning in ancient philosophy and religion, it does not seem that James intends any such allusion. More importantly, there is no justification for giving the verb *katanoeō* (*observes*) in verses 23–24 the connotation of a hasty or cursory glance. In fact, the verb regularly connotes thoughtful, attentive consideration (as in Lk. 12:27, where Jesus invites us to 'consider the lilies'). Recognizing this, Laws suggests turning the comparison on its head. She thinks James may be contrasting the fleeting impression left by even a careful look into a mirror with the lasting effect of a momentary glance into the 'perfect law'. However, while *looks* (*parakyptō*) in verse 25 can refer to a quick glance, it often reflects its root meaning (*para*, 'beside' and *kyptō*, 'bend') and suggests the physical effort involved in stooping to look at something carefully (see 1 Pet. 1:12). It does not appear, then, that James intends any significant contrast by shifting verbs. We shall have to look elsewhere to discern James' meaning.

An obvious emphasis in the text is on the contrast between 'forgetting' in verse 24 and 'remaining' in verse 25. This emphasis reappears at the end of verse 25, where the *hearer that forgets* is contrasted with the *doer that acts*. This stress suggests that James may be using the look at the mirror to illustrate the superficial and temporary effect of the Word on those who hear it without doing it. They get no more lasting benefit from the Word than they do from looking at their faces in a mirror while combing their hair. The doer of the word, on the other hand, 'remains', or *perseveres* (*parameinas*), which may suggest that he continues to *do* the Word (*cf.* NIV), or that he continues to contemplate the Word (*cf.* GNB). In either case, the doer of the Word is commended for demonstrating in his actions the continuing impact of the Word on his life.

It will be noticed that the 'word' of verse 22 has become in verse 25 *the perfect law . . . of liberty*. The meaning of 'law' (*nomos*) in James is not easy to discern (see discussion in the section on 'Law' in the Introduction, pp.48–50). To a Jew like James, *nomos* would normally mean the Mosaic law. This law was frequently called 'perfect' (*cf.* Ps. 19:7) and to it was sometimes ascribed the power to give true freedom (*cf.* Mishnah, *Abot.* 6:2). But the context makes us pause before accepting the identification of 'law of liberty' with the Old Testament law. Because of the flow of the text, the 'perfect law' of verse 25 must be the same as the 'word' of verse 22; and the 'word', in turn, is identified as 'the word of truth' that mediates spiritual birth (v. 18) and whose reception leads to salvation (v. 21). In light of this, it is necessary to associate 'the perfect law of liberty' closely with the gospel. The pervasive influence of the teaching of Jesus on James' ethics suggests that this 'law' may particularly involve Jesus' ethical demands. James wants to stress to his hearers that the 'good news' of salvation brings with it an unavoidable, searching demand for complete obedience. The use of the word 'law' to describe this commanding aspect of the Christian 'Word' is entirely natural for someone in James' position (and anticipates in some ways the 'law/gospel' distinction in later theology). This 'law' includes Old Testament commandments, as 2:8–11 makes clear, but James' characterization of the Law as *perfect* suggests that these commandments must be seen in the light of Jesus' fulfilment of the Old Testament law (Mt. 5:17). And, while still a 'law', this summons to obedience is nevertheless 'liberating' because, in accordance with Jeremiah's new covenant prophecy (31:31–34), it has been written on the heart (*cf.* 'implanted' in v. 21). With the searching, radical demand of the gospel comes the enabling grace of God. When Jesus called people to 'come' to him and to take his 'yoke' upon them, he promised that 'my yoke is easy, and my burden is light' (Mt. 11:28–30).

Additional Note: 'His natural face' (1:23)

It is often argued that a further point of contrast between verses 23–24 and verse 25 is present. The RSV translation *natural face* renders a difficult phrase in Greek: *to prosōpon tēs geneseōs autou*; literally, 'the face of his "genesis" '. Many commentators see no particular significance in the addition of *tēs geneseōs* to *to prosōpon*. They point out that *genesis* can mean 'existence' (Wisdom of Solomon 7:5; Judith 12:8), and that the phrase accordingly refers

merely to the face the man actually sees. But *genesis* usually
carries with it the sense of 'birth' or 'creation'. Hort, noting this,
argued that the phrase referred to the face man was created with,
in the sense of 'the representation of what God made him to be'.
Verses 23–25 would then contrast the man who sees what God
intended him to be, but does nothing about it, with the man who
sees what God wants him to be and strives to attain it. However,
it is difficult to think that the *invisible* image of God in man is what
the man sees in a mirror. Another possibility is that *genesis* is
used, as often in Philo, to connote that which is creaturely and
transitory, as opposed to the divine realm of eternity. James then
may imply a contrast between the 'face' or character that a man
actually sees – his sinfulness – and the ideal face or character
which the 'perfect law' reflects. This explanation has much to be
said for it, but it may be over-subtle. Certainly nothing in verse 25
implies that 'the ideal character' is reflected by the perfect law.
Moreover, by drawing a contrast between the images that are
seen, the obviously intended contrast between 'forgetting' and
'persevering' is softened a bit. Perhaps the interpretation which
does not give particular emphasis to *genesis* is best. Verses 23–24
would then be understood as a simple illustration, with no
allegorical features. The 'hearer only' is compared with the
person glancing in the mirror at one point only: the lack of any
long-lasting effect. In contrast to that is the person who shows by
his actions that he has been changed by his encounter with the
Word.

26. James concludes this important paragraph on the practical
implications of true Christianity by singling out some specific
ways in which obedience to the Word is to be manifested. One of
these, which is apparently of great concern to James, is the whole
matter of controlling the *tongue*. He has already counselled his
readers to be 'quick to hear, slow to speak' (v. 19). In chapter 3 he
will develop the issue at some length and he returns to it again in
4:11–12. The tongue, James suggests, is like a wild animal.
Properly controlled and directed ('bridled'), it can accomplish
great good. But when left on its own, its destructive powers are
enormous. A person who fails to control his tongue *deceives his
heart* about the reality of his *religion*. He is a mere 'hearer' of the

Word, and by failing to put what he hears into practice, he shows that his religion is vain. The word *religion* captures well the meaning of the Greek *thrēskeia* (and the rare adjective *thrēskos*). The term is not specifically Christian and is used widely in Greek religion to denote the reverencing and worshipping of a god (or gods). It often connotes outward acts of worship. The true test of any religious profession, suggests James, is not the outward ritual of worship, which many go through unthinkingly and with little heart commitment. No, the real litmus test of religion is obedience – without it, religion is *vain*: empty, useless and profitless.

27. We must keep in mind that James is not attempting here to summarize all that true worship of God should involve. As Calvin says, 'he does not define generally what religion is, but reminds us that religion without the things he mentions is nothing . . .'.[1] Religious ritual, if done from a reverent heart and in a worshipful spirit, is not wrong – and God's Word cannot be 'done' unless it is first 'heard'. But James is concerned about an over-emphasis on the 'hearing' to the neglect of the 'doing'. Two other areas of life that are to reveal evidence of our reverent 'listening' to the Word are introduced in the verse: social concern and moral purity. Care for *orphans and widows* is commanded in the Old Testament as a way of imitating God's own concern for them – he is the 'Father of the fatherless and protector of widows' (Ps. 68:5). In a text that bears many similarities to this passage in James, Isaiah announces that God will no longer recognize the worship his people offer him (their 'religion'); they must 'wash themselves, . . . learn to do good; seek justice, correct oppression; defend the fatherless, plead for the widow' (Is. 1:10–17). The orphan and widow become types of those who find themselves helpless in the world. Christians whose religion is *pure* will imitate their *Father* by intervening to help the helpless. Those who suffer from want in the third world, in the inner city; those who are unemployed and penniless; those who are inadequately represented in government or in law – these are the people who should see abundant evidence of Christians' 'pure religion'.

[1] Calvin, p. 299

Moral purity is another hallmark of pure religion. *To keep oneself unstained from the world* means to avoid thinking and acting in accordance with the value-system of the society around us. This society reflects, by and large, beliefs and practices that are un-Christian, if not actively anti-Christian. The believer who lives 'in the world' is in constant danger of having the taint of that system 'rub off' on him. It is important and instructive that James includes this last area, for it penetrates beyond action to the attitudes and beliefs from which action springs. The 'pure religion' of the 'perfect Christian' (v. 4) combines purity of heart with purity of action.

c. Impartiality and the law of love (2:1–13)

This paragraph is the first in James that develops a single idea at any length. The prohibition of partiality in verse 1 clearly governs the entire section. Verses 2–4 illustrate the problem James is concerned about, with reference to discrimination against the poor. This discriminatory action is ascribed to 'evil thoughts'. Two reasons why Christians must shun this sort of favouritism are given in the rest of the paragraph. First, preferential treatment of the rich stands in stark contrast to the attitude of God, who has chosen the poor to be 'rich in faith' (vv. 5–7). Secondly, *any* manifestation of favouritism is condemned by the 'royal law' that demands love of the neighbour (vv. 8–13). The amount of space James devotes to this topic suggests that the problem was a very real one among his readers. Apparently the oppression they were experiencing at the hands of the rich (*cf.* vv. 6–7) had led not to a retaliation in kind, but to an excessive deference towards the rich and powerful that resulted in a slighting and demeaning of poorer people. Such behaviour manifests a failure to 'do' the royal law that they have heard (*cf.* 1:22–25).

1. *Partiality* translates a Greek word that means, literally, 'receiving the face'. It is first used in the New Testament as a literal rendering of the Old Testament Hebrew language for partiality. To 'receive the face' is to make judgments and distinctions based on external considerations, such as physical appearance, social status or race. This God never does, as the Old

Testament repeatedly affirms (*cf.* also Rom. 2:11; Eph. 6:9; Col. 3:25). And God's people are to imitate him in this respect. In a passage that is echoed many times in the Old Testament and which touches on many of the same issues James is concerned about in 1:21 – 2:26, Moses reminds the Israelites that 'the LORD your God is God of gods and Lord of lords, the great, the mighty, and the terrible God, who is not partial and takes no bribe. He executes justice for the fatherless and the widow, and loves the sojourner, giving him food and clothing' (Dt. 10:17–18). Even more pertinent may be Leviticus 19:15 – 'You shall do no injustice in judgment; you shall not be partial to the poor or defer to the great' – since James cites the love command of Leviticus 19:18 in verse 8. The requirement laid upon those who *hold the faith of our Lord Jesus Christ* is no different from this basic Old Testament demand. A favouritism based on external considerations is inconsistent with faith in the One who came to break down the barriers of nationality, race, class, gender and religion. As Paul says, 'Here there cannot be Greek and Jew, circumcised and uncircumcised, barbarian, Scythian, slave, free man, but Christ is all, and in all' (Col. 3:11).

James 2:1 contains one of the only two explicit references to Jesus in this epistle (*cf.* also 1:1). We have seen in the introduction that this circumstance has led some scholars to think that the letter is a Jewish document which has been 'baptized' through the addition of these two references. However, while James may not mention Jesus often, his letter, as we have seen, is deeply permeated with the spirit and teaching of Jesus. And while James may not teach a full-blown Christology, his description of Jesus here gives ample evidence of the depths of his Christological beliefs. For James, Jesus is 'the *Christ*', the Messiah promised to Israel as her deliverer and judge. He is 'the *Lord*', the one who occupies the supreme position at God's right hand and who is in the process of bringing into submission all of God's enemies (*cf.* Ps. 110:1). Moreover, the title *Lord*, used of Yahweh (Jehovah) throughout the Greek Old Testament, contains implications of the divine status of Jesus. Not only is Jesus 'the *Lord*', he is *the Lord of glory*. This translation, which takes *doxēs* as a descriptive genitive dependent on 'Lord', is probably correct. Paul describes Jesus similarly in 1 Corinthians 2:8 and James is fond of this type of genitive construction. Another possibility, however, is to take *tēs doxēs* as an independent title of Jesus (an epexegetic genitive): 'our Lord Jesus Christ who is the glory'. However, the lack of New Testament parallels for the title is against the suggestion. Describing Jesus as *the Lord of glory* suggests particularly the heavenly sphere to which he has been exalted and from which he will come at the end of history to save and to judge (*cf.* Jas. 5:9). This reminder is particularly appropriate in a situation where Christians are giving too much 'glory' to human beings.

2–3. An illustration of the attitude that James condemns follows. The situation James depicts appears to be hypothetical and may even be exaggerated for effect, but that this kind of behaviour was by no means unknown is clear from James' concern. Certainly in verses 6–7 it is clear that he is dealing with existing circumstances. The illustration pictures two people of very different external appearance coming into 'the assembly'. One bears every mark of wealth: he wears a gold ring, such as members of the upper-class Roman 'equestrian' class wore; he is dressed in *fine*, 'brightly shining' (*lampros*) clothes. The other is a poor man, dressed in *shabby* (*rhyparos*) clothes. The rich man is singled out for special attention and is conducted politely to his seat. The poor man, on the other hand, is told summarily to '*Stand there*', or, as Phillips paraphrases, 'if you must sit, sit on the floor' (*hypo to hypopodion mou* [lit. 'under my footstool'] probably means 'on the floor close to my footstool' [Mayor]). Probably both these men are visitors to the assembly, since they are described by appearance and are conducted to seats. But what is the *assembly*? *Synagōgē* elsewhere in the New Testament (with the possible exception of Rev. 2:9 and 3:9) refers to the Jewish place of worship. It is difficult to think that this is meant here, however, since Christians seem to have charge over its conduct. The word was used generally of an assembly of people for various purposes, and James is probably using it in this general sense. Recently, it has been suggested that James is thinking specifically of an occasion when Christians would gather to judge issues which had risen among them (as Paul advises Christians to do in 1 Cor. 6).[1] But the text suggests that the two men were visitors

---

[1] R. B. Ward, 'Partiality in the Assembly; James 2:2–4', *HTR* 62, 1969, pp. 87–97. He builds a solid case for the association on the basis of rabbinic statements that require equitability in

and this would be unlikely in a Christian judicial assembly. James is probably thinking of any occasion when Christians would gather and the general populace would be welcome.[1]

4. In a series of conditional clauses ('if . . . , if . . .') James has sketched the sort of behaviour he finds incompatible with Christian faith. Now he characterizes and condemns that behaviour in a twofold 'then' clause. This clause is set in the form of a question, but the Greek construction used by James (the particle *ou*) shows that he expects his readers to agree with the verdict. The first verb in the verse (*diakrinō*) presents a difficult translation problem. Most translations, with the RSV, interpret it to refer to the activity of *making distinctions*. The verb can certainly have this meaning (*cf.* Acts 11:12; 15:9) and *among yourselves* is an acceptable translation of *en heautois*. But James has already used this same verb in 1:6 to mean the divided, conflicting thoughts of the person who lacks faith, and the passive form of the verb used here usually means 'to be divided'. A reference to such inner conflict fits nicely in the present context, since 'faith' has been mentioned in verse 1. What James may be doing, then, is tracing the sinful behaviour pictured in verses 2–3 back to its sinful motives. The improper 'division' being made among visitors to the assembly is nothing more than a reflection of the improper 'divisions' harboured in the minds of the believers (*en heautois* – 'in each of you'). Consistently *Christian* conduct comes only from a consistently *Christian* heart and mind.

Leviticus 19:15, which James probably had in mind as he wrote this passage, condemns partiality in the context of judging. It is perhaps this association that leads James further to characterize those who show partiality as *judges with evil thoughts*. Not only have they arrogated to themselves the role of judges; worse, they render their decision according to un-Christian, worldly standards.

---

the clothing and treatment of litigants in court. The reference to 'judges' in v. 4 would also fit very naturally.

[1]*Synagōgē* is used of an 'assembly' of Christians ('righteous men') in Hermas, *Mandates* 11.9.

5. That these standards are completely inconsistent with God's way of viewing things is demonstrated by his gracious election of the poor to salvation. James, in keeping with the rest of the New Testament, traces the Christian's salvation back to the sovereign choice of God. Thus the many poor people who had embraced the gospel could stand as powerful testimony to God's own attitude. These people, *poor* as far as everyday, material existence went, were in fact *rich* in the sight of God. Their inheritance consists of *the kingdom which he has promised to those who love him.* The kingdom of God was the focus of Jesus' preaching. He presented himself as the one through whom God's reign was even then being realized (Mt. 12:28; Mk. 1:15; Lk. 17:21). But the fullness of its power and the riches of its blessings are still future: it is 'when the Son of man comes in his glory, and all the angels with him', that faithful servants 'inherit the kingdom prepared . . . from the foundation of the world' (Mt. 25:31, 34). Christians, however poor in material possessions they may be, both possess spiritual wealth presently and anticipate greater blessings in the future. It is from this spiritual vantage-point, not the material, that Christians should judge others. Whether believers or unbelievers, people should not be evaluated by Christians according to the standards of the world.

The one who has promised the kingdom – *he* – is most naturally identified as God, the subject of the sentence. But it is possible that James also has in mind Jesus' beatitude: 'Blessed are you poor, for yours is the kingdom of God' (Lk. 6:20; *cf.* Mt. 5:3). Neither Jesus nor James means that the poor are promised the kingdom simply because they are poor. As we pointed out earlier (see the comments on 1:9–11 and the introductory sketch of James' theology), 'the poor' became almost a technical term designating those who were both economically oppressed and spiritually inclined. It is a generalization and, as such, cannot be understood as including every single poor person, nor as excluding all rich people. While Jesus' warning about riches being a stumbling-block to discipleship must be taken with utter seriousness (*cf.* Mk. 10:23; Lk. 12:34), neither he nor James excludes rich people from the kingdom. James does not say that *only* poor people are *chosen*; his point is to remind his readers that *many* are, and that this fact implicitly condemns Christian discrimination against them.

6–7. In contrast (*de*) to God's benevolent regard, *you*, accuses James, *have dishonoured the poor man*. In addressing his readers so directly, James implies that, however hypothetical the illustration in verses 2–3, some of his readers have been guilty of unjust favouritism. This attitude is all the more surprising in that it is hardly reciprocal. Far from returning kindness for kindness, the Christians are heaping honour precisely on those who are actively engaged in oppressing and persecuting the small community of believers. The oppression involves economic exploitation: *katadynasteuō* (*oppress*) occurs frequently in the Septuagint to describe the exploitation of the poor (*cf.* Am. 4:1), and orphans and widows (*cf.* Ezk. 22:7), by the rich. Acting exactly contrary to the demands of 'pure religion' (Jas. 1:26–27), these rich people are hauling poor Christians into court for economic gain.

Presupposed in this verse is the poverty of most of the believers to whom James writes. This is not surprising. Throughout the early history of the church, those with little to hold them to this world found the spiritual promises of the gospel attractive. 'Not many of you were wise according to worldly standards, not many were powerful, not many were of noble birth', Paul reminded the Corinthians (1 Cor. 1:26). Palestinian, or at any rate Jerusalem believers seem to have been particularly afflicted: the Antioch church sent relief to them during a famine in about AD 46, and later on Paul collected money from his Gentile churches to send to the 'poor among the saints in Jerusalem' (*cf.* Rom. 15:26). The strongly marked socio–economic class distinction presupposed in James corresponds closely to what we know of conditions in first-century Palestine. A small group of wealthy landowners and merchants accumulated more and more power, while large numbers of people were forced from their land and grew even poorer. Most of James' readers probably belonged to this class of poor agricultural labourers.

But James' readers are experiencing not only economic oppression, as are many of their fellow Jews; they are also suffering from religious persecution. Probably the two were related – judicial proceedings against Christians on financial grounds may have been motivated by and combined with scorn for their faith. *Blaspheme* would suggest verbal abuse, as when Paul was opposed and 'reviled' (*blasphēmountōn*) by the Jews in Corinth (Acts 18:6). The verbal slander was directed against *the honourable* (*kalon*, 'good') *name* (*cf.* 1 Pet. 4:14) – probably 'Christ'. The phrase *which was invoked over you* translates an awkward combination of words in Greek: *to epiklēthen eph' hymas* – literally, 'which has been called on you'. This is an over-literal translation of a common Hebrew idiom and is also found, interestingly, in James' quotation of Amos 9:12 in Acts 15:17. The phrase connotes close relationship, even possession, and is frequently found in the Old Testament to describe the relationship between Yahweh and his people. Now Jesus, the Messiah, occupies this place for believers. As those who confess allegiance to him, they bear his name – in a word, they are 'Christians'. How incongruous that those who blaspheme that 'honourable name' should be accorded preferential treatment in the church!

8. Verses 8–13 provide a powerful, coherent argument against all forms of partiality. Essentially this argument is that Christians will be judged by a law that includes as one of its most fundamental demands love for all. The precise relationship between verse 8 and the preceding verses is unclear. If the Greek word *mentoi* that introduces the verse is translated *really* (RSV; 'indeed', NIV), James would be suggesting that 'the royal law' is really fulfilled only when partiality is shunned. But in its seven other New Testament occurrences, *mentoi* means 'however', and this translation should be adopted here also. Understood in this way, verse 8 introduces a contrast with the previous context, presumably with verse 6a specifically: 'you do evil in dishonouring the poor; . . . however, if you fulfil the royal law you do well' (*cf.* NEB, NASB).

What is this *royal law*? Since 'law' in verses 10–11 includes commandments from the Decalogue, the phrase may refer to the Old Testament law as a whole, called 'royal' because it was given by the King of heaven.[1] The difficulty with this identification is

[1] Philo, allegorizing the 'royal highway' of Nu. 20:17, frequently calls the way to God and his words the 'royal road' (*cf., e.g.*, *The Posterity of Cain*, 102; *The Unchangeableness of God*, 144, 145).

that this same law is described as 'the law of liberty' in verse 12, a phrase that in 1:25 has reference to the commands of the gospel and, particularly, to the teaching of Jesus. That a distinctively Christian concept is intended is suggested also by the designation 'royal' (*basilikos*), which seems to pick up the reference to 'the kingdom' (*basileia*) in verse 5. Since James quotes the 'love commandment' from Leviticus 19:18 later in verse 8, we should perhaps identify this specific commandment, singled out by Christ as the sum of the law (Mt. 22:34–40), as the 'royal law'. However, it is unusual in the New Testament for a single commandment to be designated with *nomos* (*law*), and James' use of *according to* (*kata*) to introduce the quotation suggests that the commandment is not identical with the 'royal law'. In the light of these considerations, it is best to understand *the royal law* as another characterization of the entire will of God for Christians. This will is revealed particularly in the teaching of Jesus, who demanded of his disciples a radical obedience to God, befitting those who were privileged to be 'heirs of the kingdom' (v. 5). But, like Jesus and Paul (Rom. 13:8–10; Gal. 5:14), James is concerned to show that 'the law of the kingdom' does not replace, but takes up within it the demand of God in the Old Testament.

If James says that the royal law is to be fulfilled *according to* the commandment of love, he probably intends to describe not the manner in which the law is to be kept ('fulfil it *by* loving others'), but the nature of that law itself – it is a law that has at its heart the demand that the Christian *love* his *neighbour*. In the Old Testament, the *neighbour* (*rēʾa*) means particularly the fellow-Israelite, but Jesus expands the application to include everyone that a person might come into contact with, including foreigners (Lk. 10:25–37) and enemies (Mt. 5:44). James is in line with that teaching as he argues that love for the neighbour, the heart of 'the royal law', forbids the church from discriminating against any who might enter its doors.

9. The specific citation of the love commandment enables James to accuse those who 'play favourites' of 'committing sin'. Discriminating against people, whether on the basis of their dress, nationality, social class or race, is a clear violation of the unbounded love to which Jesus calls us. And since the command to love is at the very heart of the 'royal law', we become *transgressors* of that law when we show partiality. Verses 8–9, then, stand in clear antithetical relationship. We *do well* when we obey the law, with its summons to love. but we *commit sin* when we transgress that law by showing partiality.

10. Verses 10–11 explain (*gar, For*) the last clause of verse 9, by showing that the breaking of even one commandment incurs guilt for the law as a whole. Thus these verses furnish a chain of reasoning that leads at the end of verse 11 to the same accusation James has already levelled in verse 9 – these Christians who are showing partiality are 'transgressors of the law'. True, they are breaking 'only' one commandment. But, James answers, the 'law', the will of God for his people, is an indivisible whole, and to violate one part of it is to be at odds with all of it. The unity of the law, with the corollary that it had to be observed in its entirety, was a widely held notion. In 4 Maccabees, when the pious Eleazar was required to eat meat unlawfully, he refused, replying, 'Do not suppose that it would be a petty sin if we were to eat defiling food; to transgress the law in matters either small or great is of equal seriousness, for in either case the law is equally despised' (5:19–21). Jesus made a similar point when he warned that 'Whoever then relaxes one of the least of these commandments and teaches men so, shall be called least in the kingdom of heaven' (Mt. 5:19; *cf.* also Gal. 3:10; 5:13). Such warnings were necessary because of the tendency to think that obedience to the 'heavier' commandments outweighed any failure to adhere to the 'lighter' requirements of the law. But James agrees with the standard view: Failure *in one point* renders a person guilty. To be sure, the 'one point' in which James' readers were falling short – the demand for love – could hardly be called a 'light' requirement. But the point James is making possesses all the more validity for that reason. Why this is so he explains further in verse 11.

11. This verse explains why the law must be considered a unity. As long as the law is viewed simply as a series of individual commandments, it would be possible to think that disobedience of a particular commandment incurred guilt for that commandment only. But, in fact, the individual commandments are all components of one indivisible whole, because they reflect the will of the one Lawgiver. To violate a commandment is to disobey God himself and render a person guilty before him.

The logic of these verses is thoroughly Jewish. But how 'Jewish' does James intend to be here? Pressed to its logical conclusion, James would appear to be requiring obedience to every single commandment of the law, including the requirements concerning ceremonial observances. Is this what James intends? Nothing in his letter would suggest that he holds so strict a view. And he does give us a hint within verses 10–11 that this is not the case. Generally when Jewish theologians made the point that James makes in verse 11, they cited a 'light' commandment beside a 'heavy' one. Thus Eleazar, in the 4 Maccabees text quoted above, asserts that eating defiling food (a 'small' matter) is equally as serious as disobedience of a 'great' commandment. But James cites two Decalogue commandments, of supposedly equal 'weight'. This suggests that he is thinking only of some parts of the Old Testament law in verses 10–11. It is interesting to note in this regard that the love command was closely associated with the 'fellow-man' commandments of the second table of the Decalogue in early Christianity (see Mt. 19:18–19; Rom. 13:8–10). Therefore, while employing logic drawn from the Old Testament and Jewish orthodoxy, James applies it to a new situation. It is not the Old Testament law *per se* that he urges perfect compliance with, but 'the royal law' (v. 8), 'the law of liberty' (v. 12) – a law that takes up within it the Old Testament law, but as understood through Jesus' fulfilment of it. This 'fulfilment' underlies Jesus' words in Matthew 5:19 also; his demand that even the 'least' of the commandments of the law must be obeyed assumes his 'fulfilment' of that law which he has just enunciated in verse 17.

Is it possible that James might have a particular reason for citing the commandment *'Do not kill'* in verse 11? Jesus taught that this prohibition of murder could be extended to include anger (Mt. 5:21–26) and John says bluntly that 'anyone who hates his brother is a murderer' (1 Jn. 3:15). In the light of this teaching, James may be suggesting that the attitude of partiality also can be included within the scope of this commandment. James' readers should not think that they can plead innocence because they are not violating some commandments, such as the prohibition of adultery – they are violating the prohibition of murder by showing partiality. While this interpretation is plausible and suggestive, we should be cautious about placing too much weight on it. James may cite these two commands simply because they were customarily used to illustrate the demands of God in his law (cf. Mt. 19:18; Rom. 13:9).

12. Verses 10–11 are something of a parenthesis in James' argument. He is now in a position to draw a conclusion from the main point established in verses 8–9. He has argued that partiality is a sin against the love commandment and that this commandment is a touchstone of the 'royal law' that governs those who profess faith in Jesus Christ. As such this law will serve as a standard by which believers' speech and actions will be judged. James lays particular stress on each of the verbs, *speak* and *act*, by using the correlative adverb *houtōs* (*so*) before each of them. The verbs are in the present tense, emphasizing that this manner of 'speaking' and 'doing' is to be a way of life. While this verse applies generally to all conduct, James undoubtedly thinks especially of the need to exhibit love through an impartial attitude towards all.

The emphasis on judgment according to the law in this verse creates difficulties for some. Hort, for example, says: '. . . the sense would seem to be not that the law of liberty is the standard or the instrument by which they are to be judged, but that they are to be judged as men who have lived in an atmosphere as it were, of a law of liberty . . .'[1] But the suggestion that the preposition *dia* (translated *under* in RSV) denotes merely the 'atmosphere' of the law of liberty is not acceptable. *Dia* normally has an instrumental sense ('by') and this meaning fits perfectly in this verse: it is by means of the standard set forth in the law of liberty that believers' behaviour will be assessed (cf. Rom. 2:12 for a close parallel). That Christians will be *judged* on the basis of conformity to the will of God expressed in the gospel is asserted throughout the New Testament. Jesus warned that he would judge 'all the nations' at his return and reward only those who showed com-

---

[1] Hort, p. 56.

passion to others (Mt. 25:31–46). Paul affirmed that 'we must all appear before the judgment seat of Christ, so that each one may receive good or evil, according to what he has done in the body' (2 Cor. 5:10). And John says, 'All who keep his commandments abide in him' (1 Jn. 3:24). God's gracious acceptance of us does not end our obligation to obey him; it sets it on a new footing. No longer is God's law a threatening, confining burden. For the will of God now confronts us as a *law of liberty* – an obligation that is discharged in the joyful knowledge that God has both 'liberated' us from the penalty of sin and given us, in his Spirit, the power to obey his will. To use James' own description, this law is an 'implanted word', 'written on the heart', that has the power to save us (Jas. 1:21).

13. A warning reinforces the commands of verse 12: the person *who has shown no mercy* cannot expect to receive mercy at the judgment. James suggests that 'showing mercy' is one particular aspect of the law of liberty that is important for his readers to recognize. 'Showing mercy' is, in fact, just what the love command requires (v. 8) and what James' readers are failing to do when they 'dishonour the poor man'. This relationship between mercy and concern for the poor is explicit in Zechariah 7:9–10: 'Thus says the LORD of hosts, Render true judgments, show kindness and mercy each to his brother, do not oppress the widow, the fatherless, the sojourner, or the poor. . . .' If James' readers continue to discriminate, they place themselves in danger of facing a harsh judgment. The reciprocal relationship between man's mercy and God's is brought out repeatedly by Jesus, most strikingly in the parable of the unmerciful servant (Mt. 18:21–35; *cf.* also Mt. 6:14–15).

If failure to show mercy receives a severe penalty, the opposite is also true: *mercy triumphs over judgment.* This can be interpreted as a statement about the relative weight of two attributes of God, the point being that God rejoices in being able to overcome his judgment with his mercy. But it is better to take the *mercy* as man's: our showing mercy *triumphs over* God's judgment in that it defends us before God's judgment seat. As Hort describes the image, 'κρίσις [judgment] comes so to speak as the accuser before the tribunal of God, and ἔλεος [mercy] stands up fearlessly and as it were defiantly to resist the claim'.[1] The believer, in himself, will always deserve God's judgment: our conformity to the 'royal law' is never perfect, as it must be (vv. 10–11). But our merciful attitude and actions will count as evidence of the presence of Christ within us. And it is on the basis of this union with the One who perfectly fulfilled the law for us that we can have confidence for vindication at the judgment.

d. The faith that saves (2:14–26)

This passage is the climax of James' plea for a 'pure religion' that vindicates itself in action. It is a text that sustains a single, theological argument throughout.

Clearly we have here a passage that lies at the very heart of James' concern. He is deeply troubled by an attitude towards 'faith' that sees it mainly as a verbal profession – such as the confession that 'God is one' (v. 19). This is a faith that is 'apart from' works (vv. 20, 26), and James views *this* faith as 'dead' (vv. 17, 26), 'barren' (v. 20); it does not have the power to save (v. 14) or to justify (v. 24). James assumes the necessity of faith. He claims to have faith (v. 18). But the faith *he* has, '*real* faith', 'has works' (vv. 14, 17), is 'completed by' works (v. 22), is 'active along with works' (v. 22). It is the kind of faith exhibited both by the revered 'father' of faith, Abraham (vv. 21–23), and Rahab, the immoral outcast (v. 25). It is absolutely vital to understand that the main point of this argument, expressed three times (in vv. 17, 20 and 26), is not that works must be *added to* faith but that genuine faith includes works. That is its very nature.

James writes this part of his letter in an 'argumentative' style, sometimes called a 'diatribe'. He introduces an 'imaginary objector' who states his own viewpoint as a foil for James' argument (v. 18). He attacks those holding the teaching he combats as if they were present ('you foolish fellow', v. 20); and he appeals directly to his readers to judge the cogency of what he is saying ('you see', vv. 22, 24). This style strongly suggests that James is combating some false teachers who were setting forth an incorrect view of faith. Almost certainly, these teachers were familiar with Paul's

[1]Hort, p. 57.

insistence on 'justification by faith alone'. But it is equally clear
that their understanding of Paul's view is tragically flawed; the
view James contests in this passage is certainly not Paul's.
Properly interpreted, Paul and James are united in their understanding of faith and works and their relationship to justification.
The *appearance* of a conflict is created because they give two key
words, 'faith' and 'justify', different meanings and because their
arguments are advanced against different errors.

14. James' emphasis on 'showing mercy' and its consequence
for the day of judgment (vv. 12–13) leads naturally to such
questions as, 'How can deeds of mercy help in the judgment?'
and, 'Is not faith all that matters?' James answers these questions
by pointing to the inseparable union between faith and works.
He begins with two rhetorical questions addressed to his readers,
but directed to *a man* who is advocating a 'faith only' view. The
questions are clearly to be answered in the negative (in fact, the
Greek construction in the second question requires a negative
answer): faith that has no works brings no *profit*; that kind of faith
cannot *save*. The stress in the last statement on the specific nature
of the faith involved is important. In the AV, the clause is
translated 'Can faith save him?', which suggests that James is
denying that faith can save. But the Greek word for *faith* (*pistis*)
has the article in this clause, and shows that it is referring back to
the faith just mentioned: the faith the person claims to have.
James is not saying that faith does not save: he is saying that the
faith this person claims to have, a faith that *has not works*, cannot
save. Therefore, while James' own view of faith does not differ
from that found in Paul and the rest of the New Testament (*cf.* 1:6;
2:1,5; 5:5), in 2:14–26 'faith' often refers to 'bogus' faith that
neither Paul *nor* James would regard as genuine Christian faith.

This bogus faith, James says, does not have *works*. In this word
also, some discern a difference between Paul and James. On the
one hand, James uses *works* in a positive sense, to refer to deeds of
love and mercy that Christians do to fulfil the law of love (*cf.*
2:8–13). Paul, on the other hand, polemicizes against 'works of
the law', a phrase that is said to connote the legalistic observance
of especially the ritual aspects of the Mosaic law. But it is
questionable whether this phrase can be given so restricted a

meaning in Paul. And, in general, Paul and James mean the same thing by 'works': actions done in obedience to God. The difference between them is the context in which these works are done. Paul denies that works can have any value in bringing us into relationship with God; James is insisting that, once that relationship is established, works are essential (see further the Additional Note: 'Works' in Paul and James, following this verse).

A faith that lacks these actions cannot *save*. While *save* (*sōzō*) sometimes describes the initial entrance of a person into God's kingdom ('conversion'), it often denotes the final deliverance from sin, death and judgment in the last day. This is the meaning the word seems to have in James (*cf.* 1:21; 4:12; 5:20), and it makes good sense here, since verse 13 has spoken of the final judgment. When James says, then, that the faith some people claim to have cannot save, he probably means that it will be of no profit at the time of God's righteous judgment.

Additional Note: 'Works' in Paul and James (2:14)

As a means of lessening the apparent tension between Paul and James on the matter of justification, it is often asserted that they are giving to the word *erga*, 'works', significantly different meanings. Paul, it is alleged, excludes as a basis for justification only 'works of the law', interpreted either as specific works – the ceremonial old covenant regulations – or as works done in a 'legalistic' spirit. The 'works' that James demands, on the other hand, are clearly acts of charity that fulfil the law of love. Despite the widespread acceptance of this distinction, there is reason to question its validity. On the one hand, Paul's concept of 'works' is much broader than this interpretation would suggest. Romans 9:10–11 is the closest we get in Pauline literature to a definition of 'works': 'And not only so, but also when Rebecca had conceived children by one man, our forefather Isaac, though they were not yet born and had done nothing either good or bad, in order that God's purpose of election might continue, not because of works but because of his call. . . .' In these verses, it is clear that 'works' includes *anything* that is done, 'either good or bad'. In Romans 4, the 'works' of Abraham, in which he could not boast, must clearly

101

be 'good works'. And yet Romans 4 is closely tied to the argument in 3:20–28, where 'works of the law' is used. What seems to be the case is that Paul views 'works of the law' as a specific kind of 'works', those works that are done in obedience to the Mosaic law. This is certainly the meaning of the phrase in the only two instances of equivalent Jewish expressions (*mā'śê tōra* in 4Q Flor. 1:7; *cf.* 1QS 5:21; 6:18). Paul's purpose, then, is to exclude *all* works – not just certain works or works done in a certain spirit – as a basis for justification.[1]

On the other side of the fence, it is not clear that we can confine James' 'works' to acts of charity. To be sure, he has just been speaking about activities that fulfil the law of love and cites as an illustration acts of charity in verses 15–16. But his specific examples, drawn from the lives of Abraham and Rahab (vv. 21–25), do not clearly involve acts of charity. Particularly in Abraham's case, the focus is on his obedience to God *per se*, with no inkling of any charity shown to others. Thus it would seem that both Paul and James are operating with an understanding of 'works' that is basically similar: anything done that is in obedience to God and in the service of God. The difference between Paul and James consists in the *sequence* of works and conversion: Paul denies any efficacy to pre-conversion works, but James is pleading for the absolute necessity of post-conversion works.

15–16. That James is particularly concerned about the person whose faith consists in words only is clear from the illustration he uses in verses 15–16. He pictures one who has at least an external relationship to the church, since it is his *brother or sister* who is in need. The need is for basic, life-sustaining provisions: adequate clothing (the Greek work *gymnos*, 'naked', *ill-clad*, often refers to the lack of the outer garment, the *chitōn*) and *daily food*. How does this 'believer' respond? He dismisses the person in need with pious words: *Go in peace, be warmed and filled. Go in peace* is a familiar Jewish form of dismissal; NEB and Phillips capture the

---

[1] On this issue, see D. J. Moo, ' "Law", "Works of the Law" and Legalism in Paul', *WTJ*, 1983, pp. 73–100. Observing that Pelagius had sought to confine 'the works of the Law' in Rom. 3:28 to the ceremonial law, O. Weber responds: 'By limiting the antithesis of Romans 3:28 to the ceremonies, the door is opened wide for moral "works-righteousness": This "by faith alone" ("of the cross") is by no means what the Reformers were talking about' (*Christian Dogmatics*, 2 [Eerdmans, 1983], p. 311).

sense well: 'Good luck to you'. The verbs *thermainesthe* (*be warmed*) and *chortazesthe* (*be filled*) could be either middle or passive. If the former, the 'believer' would be encouraging his needy fellow-Christians to provide for themselves, 'to make their own way': 'keep yourselves warm, and have plenty to eat' (NEB). If the verbs are passive, the dismissal would take the form of a prayer: 'May you be warmed and well fed'. In either case, the point is the same: confronted with a need among his own brothers and sisters, this 'believer' does nothing but express his good wishes. *What does it profit?* James asks. Within the sense of the illustration, this 'profit' refers primarily to the situation of need that has gone unprovided for: words, however well meant, have not profited these needy people much. But the attentive reader cannot miss the way these words reproduce the phrase with which James introduced verse 14. Not only do the empty words of this 'believer' do no good for these others; they bring no spiritual 'profit' to himself either.

This illustration, like the one in 2:2–3, is clearly hypothetical; James is not referring to a specific incident. On the other hand it is clear that the illustration reflects a real and deeply felt concern of James. Providing for the poor is one of those deeds of mercy that will 'triumph over' the judgment of God (v. 13). In this, James stands in a long and well-represented biblical tradition. Isaiah called the people of his day to put real meaning into their religious rituals by 'sharing bread with the hungry', 'bringing the homeless into their houses' and 'covering the naked' – *then* God will answer when they call (Is. 58:7–9). Jesus promised the kingdom to those who feed and clothe 'the least of these my brethren' (Mt 25:31–46). And John denies that anyone who fails to provide for a brother in need can have real love; for love is found not 'in word or speech but in deed and in truth' (1 Jn. 3:17–18). The warning is one that the church needs constantly to hear. Too often we have been content to offer mere words, when God may have been calling us to action. Words – sermons, prayers, confessions of faith, wise advice, encouragement – are indispensable to true Christianity. But they are shown to have real meaning, James reminds us, when people can see actions that correspond to those words.

17. James draws the conclusion from the illustration: *faith by itself, if it has no works, is dead*. The phrase *by itself* (*kath' heautēn*) suggests, as Mayor says, that the faith is '. . . not merely outwardly inoperative but inwardly dead'.[1] This kind of faith is 'in and of itself' useless, inactive, inert (the meaning of *nekros* in a context like this; *cf.* Rom. 7:8; Heb. 6:1; 9:14). The contrast is not, then, between faith and works, but between a faith that 'has works' and a faith that does *not* have works. The latter is, like a body without a spirit (*cf.* 2:26), lifeless, and profits one nothing on the day of judgment.

18. James moves on to a new stage of his argument by interjecting the opinion of another person: *But some one will say*. The identity of this person and the content of his opinion are not easy to determine. A major reason for the difficulty is that ancient manuscripts lacked punctuation, so that we must decide for ourselves how far this other person's comments extend. There are three main possibilities.

a. The other person is an 'ally' of James, who carries on James' argument by throwing further doubt on the reality of the faith of the person who has been mentioned in verses 14–17: 'You (the 'false' believer of the illustration) say that you have faith; and I have works. But you cannot show me your faith because you do not have works; I, on the other hand, can show you my faith by my works.'[2] The great advantage of this interpretation is that it handles the pronouns consistently throughout. 'You' is always the person who claims to have faith, yet has no works; 'I' is always James or his ally, who claims to have works. But there is an even greater objection to this view: it must take the opening phrase of the verse, 'But some one will say', as introducing a viewpoint similar to James: The word *alla* ('but') certainly can have an emphatic force ('yes', 'indeed'), but the phrase as a whole is consistently used in Greek literature to introduce an objection to or disagreement with the view being presented (see 1 Cor. 15:35 and numerous examples from the 'diatribe' style). Moreover, this introduction requires that the opening words be read

---

[1]Mayor, p. 99. Josephus uses the same phrase to speak of the law's 'inherent merits' by which it has attracted so many to its study and observance (*Contra Apion* 2.284). This parallel is closer to James' use than places in which the phrase seems to mean 'by itself alone' (*cf.* Acts 28:16).

[2]Mayor, pp. 99–100; Adamson, pp. 124–125, 135–137; Mussner, pp. 136–138.

'you *claim* to have faith', a nuance that James does not at all make explicit.

 b. The other person is an objector who is casting doubt on the reality of James' faith. On this view, the objector's words can be confined to the first three words after the introduction and put in the form of a question: 'Do you, [James], really have faith?' James then responds: 'I do have works; and while you cannot show me your faith at all, since you lack works, I can show you my faith *by* those works.'[1] Others who also think the objector is doubting James' faith go to the opposite extreme and understand all of verses 18–19 to be the objector's words: 'You [James] claim to have faith, and I can just as well claim to have works. But you cannot show me your faith apart from works, whereas I, if I wanted, could show you my faith from my works. Your [James'] faith is no better than that of the demons!' James' response would then begin in verse 20.[2] This view retains the natural force of the opening phrase, but suffers from a strained interpretation of the phrase 'and I have works'. Hort takes this as James' reply to the objector's question, but *kagō* ('and I') is a very unusual way to introduce an answer to a question and the entire phrase seems redundant. The other alternative, according to which all of verses 18–19 contains the objection, suffers from an even more strained interpretation of the last part of verse 18.

 c. Largely because these first two views suffer from so many difficulties, a third interpretation is probably to be preferred. According to this approach, 'you' and 'I' in the first part of verse 18 do not refer to specific parties in the dispute, but are used simply to distinguish two different individuals. NEB adopts this interpretation in its translation: 'But someone may object: "Here is one who claims to have faith and another who points to his deeds" ' (*cf*. also GNB). The 'other person' would then be objecting to James' argument by claiming that different people may have different 'gifts': one may have faith and another may have works. Did not Paul say that the Spirit sovereignly distributed such gifts

[1]Hort, pp. 60–61.
[2]*Cf*. C. E. Donker, 'Der Verfasser der Jak. und sein Gegner. Zum Problem der Einwandes in Jak. 2:18–19', *ZNW*, 72, 1981, pp. 227–240; Z. C. Hodges, 'Light on James Two from Textual Criticism,' *BibSac* 120, 1963, pp. 341–350, who argues for a slightly supported variant reading to bolster his interpretation.

(1 Cor. 12)? And did he not say that faith itself was one such gift (1 Cor. 12:9; *cf.* Rom. 12:3)? How can James then demand that all Christians possess *both* faith and works? To this reasoning James responds that faith and works are not special gifts that a Christian may or may not have – neither is an 'option' for any Christian. Only where works are seen is genuine, saving faith present. The difficulty with this view is that 'you' and 'I' in the beginning of the verse cannot be applied to specific individuals, as they seem to be in the rest of the verse. In reply, Ropes points to a similar shift in the force of pronouns in an argument from the Cynic philosopher Teles. In the final analysis, this interpretation has fewer difficulties than the others and should probably be adopted.[1]

James, then, uses the device of the imaginary objector to further his argument for the inseparability of faith and works. Any division between the two is unthinkable, indeed impossible. Genuine faith cannot exist without works. When James says to the objector, *Show me your faith apart from your works*, he is not simply challenging him to give evidence for his faith – he is suggesting that the faith the objector claims to have is not faith at all.

19. What does this kind of 'faith', this 'faith without works', amount to? James portrays the essential poverty of this faith by comparing it to the 'faith' that demons have. They believe that *God is one*, just as does any professing Jew or Christian. The confession of the oneness of God, taken from Deuteronomy 6:4, was part of the *Shema*, a confession of basic doctrine that the Jew recited twice daily. Christians also asserted the oneness of God in the face of the polytheistic religious beliefs of many Gentiles (*cf.* 1 Cor. 8:4–6; Gal. 3:20; Eph. 4:6; 1 Tim. 2:5). It is not at all unusual, then, that James should commend assent to this doctrine: *You do well*. But the fact that James goes on immediately to ascribe the same belief to *demons* suggests that more than a little irony is intended in the commendation. James may also intend irony by mentioning the demons' reaction to their belief. The word *shudder* (*phrissō*) was used in some ancient magical texts 'of the effect that the sorcerer wishes to bring about by means of his magic' (MM). It

---

[1]Most scholars now adopt this view, although most with some reluctance. *Cf.* especially Ropes, pp. 208–214.

is, says Hort, 'at once more distant and more prostrate than worship'. But at least it is a response – which is more, apparently, then can be said of some professing Christians who make the same confession!

This verse indicates quite plainly that the faith that James speaks about in these verses is very far from the full Christian faith that both he and Paul proclaimed. As important as correct doctrine is, no-one in the early church considered it sufficient for salvation. Genuine faith must go beyond the intellect to the will; it must affect our attitudes and actions as well as our 'beliefs'. As Mitton says, 'It is a good thing to possess an accurate theology, but it is unsatisfactory unless that good theology also possesses us.'

20. This verse introduces a new stage in James' response to the suggestion that faith can exist without accompanying works. In verse 19 he has shown that this kind of 'bare' faith is nothing more than knowledge *about* God, such as demons have, and that it leads to nothing better than abject fear before God. Now he will show from the Old Testament that *real* faith always has works and that it is this 'working faith' that leads to acceptance before God. James addresses the person who has advocated a separation of faith and works as *you shallow man*. *Shallow* (*kenos*, literally 'empty') is rarely applied to people, but probably suggests deficiency in understanding as well as moral perversity. We need not assume that James has a specific person in mind (some scholars who were anxious to find dissent between James and Paul even thought that James had Paul in mind here!). The rebuke of an imaginary opponent was a customary feature of ancient argument (*cf.* also Rom. 2:1; 9:20). James asks his imaginary opponent if he would like to be *shown* (the force of *ginōskō*, 'know', here) that faith without works is *barren* (AV has 'dead' here, reflecting an inferior variant reading). The word translated *barren* is *agros*, which means, literally, 'not-working', or 'idle' – Jesus used it to describe workers who had not been hired for the day (Mt. 20:3, 6). James' choice of the word here creates a pointed play on words: 'faith that has no works does not work'! The verse re-states the main point of the entire section: faith without works does not 'save' (v. 14), does not 'profit' (v.

16): it is 'dead' (vv. 17, 26) and useless.

21. Furthermore, faith without works does not 'justify'. This is the thesis of verses 21–25, stated theologically for James' readers in verse 24 and demonstrated from the lives of Abraham and Rahab in verses 21-23 and 25. It is possible that James adduces Abraham as an example because his opponents have already used Genesis 15:6 as a proof text for the importance of faith. Abraham, one of the most revered figures in Israel's history, was referred to frequently by Jews in support of all sorts of views. As might be expected, Abraham's amazing obedience to the Lord's 'hard' command to sacrifice his son Isaac was a particularly popular source of theological and devotional comment. Philo calls this 'offering of Isaac' the greatest of Abraham's 'works' (*On Abraham*, 167); and 1 Maccabees 2:52 links Abraham's faithfulness 'in the test' to the pronouncement of Genesis 15:6 'and it was reckoned to him for righteousness'. James argues that Abraham's willingness to kill his son in obedience to the Lord's command is evidence of 'the works' on the basis of which Abraham was 'justified'.

It is at this point that James' argument becomes problematic. For in claiming that Abraham was *justified by works* he appears to be in contradiction with Paul, who claims equally clearly that Abraham was justified by faith and *not* by works (Rom. 4:1–3). While many scholars claim that the contradiction cannot be resolved, a careful examination of the way in which the crucial term *dikaioō* (*justify*) is being used will show that Paul and James are not in conflict. This term is associated above all with Paul, who makes 'justification by faith' the centrepiece of his argument in Galatians and Romans. But what is important to recognize is that Paul gives to the term justification a very distinct meaning, one that is closely related to his whole theological perspective. He designates with this language the initial transfer of a person from the realm of sin and death to the realm of holiness and life. This transfer takes place by virtue of the sinner's identification, by faith, with Jesus Christ, 'the righteous one'. For Paul, then, justification is a sovereign, judicial act in which God, apart from any human 'work', declares the sinner to be innocent before him (Rom. 4:5).[1]

[1] See, on this and the whole subject, especially L. Morris, *The Apostolic Preaching of the Cross*

There is some difference of opinion over the precise meaning James gives to *dikaioō*. A significant number of scholars think that James is using the word in a demonstrative sense. Abraham and Rahab 'were justified by works' in the sense that they demonstrated their righteous status by performing good works. Any conflict with Paul would then be removed, because, while he stresses that faith is the only condition for the *declaration* of righteousness, James would be arguing that works are the only way in which that righteous status can be *demonstrated*. However, while there is some precedent for this meaning of *dikaioō* (*cf.* Gn. 44:16; Lk. 7:29, 35 and the references in G. Schrenk, *TDNT*, 2, pp. 213–214), it is not its usual meaning. More importantly, this meaning does not fit very well in James 2, where the question is not, 'How can righteousness be demonstrated?' but, 'What kind of faith secures righteousness?' Therefore James is probably using *dikaioō* in a declarative sense, but he differs from Paul in applying the word to God's ultimate declaration of a person's righteousness rather than to the initial securing of that righteousness by faith. In other words, James uses 'justify' where Paul speaks of the judgment. It is this distinction, between what Wesley called 'initial justification' and 'final justification', that explains the apparent discrepancy between Paul and James.[1]

The use of *dikaioō* in this sense has ample precedent in the Old Testament, Judaism and the teaching of Jesus. In the Old Testament, *dikaioō* (Heb. *ṣādaq*) generally denotes a verdict of innocence which is rendered on the basis of demonstrated 'righteousness', or 'covenant loyalty' (see the Additional Note, 'Justification' in the Old Testament and Judaism, below.) This verdict is naturally associated with the last judgment. In the teaching of Jesus, this meaning of *dikaioō* is also clearly found. He warned his listeners on one occasion: 'by your words you will be justified, and by your words you will be condemned' (Mt. 12:37). James' frequent dependence on Jesus' teaching, particularly as found in Matthew, makes this reference all the more important. One important objection to this interpretation of James 2 is that, according to the RSV, Abraham was justified *when* he offered

---

(Inter-Varsity Press, 1955), pp. 251–298; also his *The Atonement: Its Meaning and Significance* (Inter-Varsity Press, 1983), pp. 177–202.

[1]Minutes of 1744 (J. Wesley, *Works*, VIII, p. 277).

Isaac. But the aorist participle *anenegkas* could equally well be translated simply 'having offered' and can be taken to specify one of those works that was instrumental in Abraham's 'final justification'.

If we understand James' teaching in this way, he cannot be said to contradict the teaching of Paul. James asserts that Abraham did works and that these works were used as criteria in God's ultimate judgment over Abraham's life. He assumes that Abraham had faith and that this faith was basic to Abraham's acceptance by God (vv. 22–23). But he stresses that the life of the one who has been so accepted by God must show the fruit of that relationship in good works. It was what precedes and enables these works that Paul concentrates on. Paul wants to make clear that one 'gets into' God's kingdom only by faith; James insists that God requires works from those who *are* 'in'.

Additional Note: 'Justification' in the Old Testament and Judaism (2:21)

The verb *dikaioō* occurs forty-four times in the LXX. Of the twenty-eight times there is a Hebrew original, twenty-two involve a form of the verb *ṣāḏaq*. The word is associated above all with the 'law court', and describes the verdict of innocence rendered by the judge. *Ṣāḏaq* is often used without direct reference to a legal setting, but the forensic connotations are maintained (Gn. 38:26; 44:16; Je. 3:11; Ezk. 16:51–52). Very often God is pictured as the judge before whom one pleads one's case (1 Sa. 12:7; Is. 43:26; Mi. 7:9) and who passes judgment on the lives of men and women. What is particularly important is that this divine verdict is usually rendered with respect to actual conduct. For example, in Micah 6:11, the Lord warns that he will not acquit (*dikaioō*) the man 'with wicked scales'. In 1 Kings 8:31–32 Solomon prays: 'If a man sins against his neighbour and is made to take an oath, and comes and swears his oath before thine altar in this house, then hear thou in heaven, and act, and judge thy servants, condemning the guilty by bringing his conduct upon his own head, and vindicating (*dikaiōsai*) the righteous (*dikaion*) by rewarding him according to his righteousness (*dikaiosynēn*).' In such cases, righteousness designates not sinless behaviour, but loyalty to the covenant;

God declares innocent those who conform to the standards expressed in the covenant. With this comes also the recognition that, in himself, man can never merit God's acquittal: 'Enter not into judgment with thy servant; for no man living is righteous before thee' (Ps. 143:2). Here there is a clear precedent for Paul's emphasis on the entirely gracious nature of justification (Rom. 3:20 and Gal. 2:16). Nevertheless the general thrust of the Old Testament is that 'men are declared to be in the right *on the facts*, *i.e.* because in general or in a specific matter they *are* upright, and innocent'.[1] This declaration is naturally closely related to the final judgment (Is. 43:9; 45:25; 50:8; 53:11?).

Judaism maintained the same basic viewpoint: 'righteousness' related to correct conduct, as defined by God's law, and the verdict of justification was pronounced over those who faithfully observed the covenant stipulations.[2] Matthew's Gospel reflects this Jewish usage. While entrance into the kingdom is dependent on commitment to Jesus ('following Jesus'), 'righteousness' is mainly, if not exclusively, the conduct expected of the disciple (Mt. 5:20) and *dikaioō* is used of the last judgment, at which time 'works', *i.e.* things we say and do, are taken into account (Mt. 12:37).

22. Still addressing himself to the 'objector' of verse 18 (the Greek verb for *You see* is in the singular), James now asserts that Abraham's *faith was active along with his works*. If verse 21 has given the impression that James is interested only in Abraham's works, this verse shows that James has presumed Abraham's *faith* all along. We should recall that it is the nature of Abraham's faith, a faith that is not 'barren' (v. 20), that James wants to illustrate. Moreover, Genesis 15:6, with its stress on Abraham's faith, has probably been in James' mind all along. He begins with Abraham's works because it was this element in the patriarch's life that he needed to highlight. Perhaps some of his readers had seized on Genesis 15:6 in order to stress Abraham's faith and had

[1] J. A. Ziesler, *The Meaning of Righteousness in Paul: A Linguistic and Theological Inquiry* (Cambridge University Press, 1972), p. 18. Ziesler's discussion of the Old Testament and Jewish conception of righteousness is particularly valuable (see pp. 17–127).

[2] B. Pryzybylski, *Righteousness in Matthew and His World of Thought* (Cambridge University Press, 1980), pp. 37–76.

111

interpreted this faith in accordance with some Jewish traditions, as his turning from idolatry 'to the worship of one god'.[1] But this kind of faith, of course, would be no better than that of the demons (v. 19), and James wants to show that Abraham's faith was much more than that.

James uses another word-play to stress the intimate relationship between Abraham's faith and his works: faith 'worked with' (*synergei*) his works (*ergois*). Abraham's faith was a 'working' faith, an active faith, a faith that was not so much the source as the constant partner of his works. This constant co-operation of faith and works is highlighted with the use of the imperfect tense of the verb, a tense that connotes continual or repeated action. 'Faith' was not something that Abraham exercised on one occasion; it stimulated, directed and co-operated with his works. But Abraham's faith not only did something to, or with, his works; his works also did something to his faith: they *completed* it. The verb used here, *teleioō*, means 'to perfect' or 'bring to maturity'. Just as the 'perfect' Christian is produced through faithful endurance of trials (1:3–4), so 'perfect' faith is produced through successive acts of obedience. Abraham's faith was strengthened, matured and deepened by the successive 'trials' through which he was called to go. By this James does not mean that faith cannot exist without works (for a dying person may truly believe without ever performing a 'work'), nor that faith is simply shown to be 'perfect' through works, but that works are the necessary, inevitable product of true saving faith, and hence bring faith itself to 'maturity'.[2] If I swing a sledge-hammer in an arc that moves through a glass table, the necessary outcome is a shattered glass table. The shattering itself is not the swing of the sledge-hammer, but it is the inevitable result. In a similar manner, faith is the decisive 'action' that leads to justification. But that 'action' leaves evidence of its occurring – 'works'. Faith must not be confused with works, but neither can faith be separated from works.

23. As a result of the active co-operation of faith and works in Abraham's life, manifested especially in his obedience to God

[1]*Cf., e.g.,* Philo, *The Virtues,* 216; Josephus, *Antiquities,* 1.154–157; Jubilees 11–12; and Davids, pp. 128–129.
[2]A parallel to James' language is found in Philo, *On Husbandry,* 42, where he says that

when asked to sacrifice his son, he received God's approval: he received *righteousness* and was called God's friend. Genesis 15:6, which has been behind James' discussion of Abraham all along, is now cited. But what does James mean when he asserts that this *scripture* was *fulfilled* as a result of Abraham's obedience? Certainly Genesis 15:6 is not a prophecy. It straightforwardly asserts that God 'reckoned', or 'considered', Abraham's faith – in this context, specifically his belief in God's promise to give him a natural son and many descendants – for 'righteousness'. 'Righteousness' should be taken in a forensic or judicial sense, as meaning that God considered him as 'being right' before him, and this is probably the meaning of the original.[1] How, then, could this pronouncement be *fulfilled*?

One important key is to recognize that the verb *plēroō* need not be given the strict meaning 'fulfil'. The word means, basically, 'to fill' or 'fill up' and can be used of fishing-nets (Mt. 13:48) and houses (Jn. 12:3). More typically in the New Testament, it is used to designate the 'filling up' or 'culmination' of the Old Testament through the advent of Jesus. This can take the form of a 'fulfilment' of a prophecy, the bringing out of the ultimate significance of a historical event (Mt. 2:15) or the climactic interpretation and application of the Old Testament law (Mt. 5:17). There is no need, then, to think that James views Genesis 15:6 as a prophecy that was 'fulfilled' later in Abraham's career. What he is suggesting, rather, is that this verse found its ultimate significance and meaning in Abraham's life of obedience. When Abraham 'put faith in' the Lord, God gave him, then and there, the status of a right relationship with him, *before* he had done works, *before* he was circumcised. This Paul brings out forcefully (Rom. 4:1–17). But the faith of Abraham and God's verdict of acquittal were 'filled up', given their ultimate significance, when Abraham 'perfected' his faith with works and the angel of the Lord reasserted God's verdict: 'now I know that you fear God' (Gn. 22:12). James does not deny that Abraham was given a righteous standing with God on the basis of his faith, long before he offered Isaac in obedience to God. But he wants to emphasize that Abraham's

---

Jacob was 'one who was perfected as a result of discipline' (*to teleiōthenti ex askeseōs*; *Confusion of Tongues*, 181 is parallel).

[1]*Cf.* L. Morris, *The Apostolic Preaching of the Cross*, p. 263; also *The Atonement*, p. 187.

faith was a vital, active faith and that God's verdict was recon-
firmed on the basis of that activity. The initial declaration of
righteousness on the basis of faith is given its ultimate meaning
and validity through the final declaration of righteousness on the
basis of a 'faith that works'. Thus Paul focuses on the chronological placement of Genesis 15:6, and cites it as evidence of the
initial declaration of righteousness that Abraham attained from
God solely on the basis of faith. James cites the same verse more
as a 'motto', standing over all of Abraham's life, and applies it to
God's ultimate declaration of Abraham's righteousness.

James introduces a second result of Abraham's active faith: *he
was called the friend of God*. RSV separates this statement from the
quotation of Genesis 15:6, implying that it is not a second scriptural text. This is appropriate, since the phrase is nowhere found
in the Old Testament. However, two Old Testament verses call
Abraham 'the one loved by God' (2 Ch. 20:7; Is. 41:8; *cf.* also Is.
51:2 and Dn. 3:35 LXX, *cf.* JB) and the title was a popular one for
Abraham in intertestamental literature.[1] James cites it as an
indication of the privileged status Abraham was given on account
of his deep faith and practical obedience.

24. James now addresses his readers directly (*You see [hōrate]* is
plural) and formulates a theological principle drawn from the life
of Abraham: *a man is justified by works and not by faith alone*. With
this statement we reach the climax of the tension between James
and Paul. For does not Paul say almost exactly the opposite? 'We
hold that a man is justified by faith apart from works of law'
(Rom. 3:28). In our comments on verses 14 and 21 we have
already dealt with the crucial points, but it will help to repeat
them here. First, we must recognize that Paul's 'faith' and James'
'faith alone' are entirely different concepts. Paul has a strongly
dynamic concept of faith, by which the believer is intimately
united with Christ, his Lord, and which includes a commitment
of obedience to that Lord. Thus Paul can speak of 'the obedience
of faith' (Rom. 1:5) and say that it is 'faith working through love'
that avails in Christ (Gal. 5:6). In other words, faith for Paul
includes the commitment to obedience; it is confessing that Jesus

---

[1] *Cf.* Philo, *On Sobriety*, 5b; *On Abraham*, 273; Jubilees 19:9.

is Lord that is the true content of faith and that brings salvation and justification (Rom. 10:9–10).[1] While James' own concept of faith may not be entirely different from this, he has spoken throughout verses 14–26 of a 'faith' that certain people claim to have (v. 14). This 'faith' is a matter of speech without action (vv. 15–16); verbal profession without trust and commitment (vv. 18–19). It is this dead, barren faith that James designates by 'faith alone' in verse 24. Paul himself would have been second to none in condemning anyone who thought that this faith could justify.

On the other hand, it is impossible to imagine Paul saying that 'a man is justified by works'. As Romans 4:2–8 (and cf. Rom. 9:10–12) shows, Paul excluded 'works' as a basis for justification. But what is important here is to remember that Paul is thinking of justification as the initial granting to the believer of a righteous status. James, as we have argued, operates with a different meaning of dikaioō, using it to refer to the ultimate verdict of God over our lives. If a man's initial relationship to God can be established only on the basis of faith (Paul), the ultimate recognition of that relationship takes into account the works that true faith must inevitably produce (James). As Calvin puts it: '. . . as Paul contends that we are justified apart from the help of works, so James does not allow those who lack good works to be reckoned righteous.'[2] That little word 'only' that James adds to 'faith' makes all the difference: it shows that James has no intention of excluding faith from the process of justification. He was deeply disturbed, however, by a faith that had no consequences for life – what we may call 'cheap faith'. Faced with this tendency, James had to place great stress on the active nature of faith and to assert that actions did matter in the long run. Paul was faced with a very different problem. His Jewish and judaizing opponents considered works done in obedience to God as a sufficient basis to maintain their place in God's covenant. Against them, Paul asserted that the covenant on which they relied was, in effect, broken and that faith in Christ was the only way that one could now be made right with God.

[1]See on this especially G. Eichholz, *Glaube und Werke bei Paulus und Jakobus* (Kaiser, 1961), pp. 24–37.
[2]Calvin, *Institutes*, III. xxvii. 12.

Whenever people rely on their religious activities for salvation, Paul's powerful plea for a radical commitment of the whole person to Christ must be vigorously proclaimed. But when 'faith' has been turned into nothing more than a verbal commitment to certain doctrines, James' understanding of faith as an active, vigorous obedience must be forcefully reasserted.[1]

25. Just in case his readers have missed the point, James adds one final illustration. If it might be objected that Abraham's works were no more than what might be expected from one who had so richly experienced God's grace, the same is certainly not true of *Rahab*. With little basis for her belief, she had become convinced that 'the LORD your God is he who is God in heaven above and on earth beneath' (Jos. 2:11). And on the basis of this 'faith' she *received the messengers and sent them out another way*. To be sure, James does not specifically mention her faith, but it is clear from his entire argument that he assumes it. Significantly, Hebrews 11:31 singles her out as an example of faith. James' point here, then, is the same as he has made in the similarly worded verse 21: God's final judgment takes into consideration the actual righteousness that a person exhibits through works. The participles *received* (*hypodexamenē*) and *sent out* (*ekbalousa*) are aorists, specifying the *works* which were the basis for God's ultimate verdict.

Why has James chosen Rahab as an example of justification by works? Perhaps he has been influenced by the traditional association of Abraham and Rahab, attested in 1 Clement 10, 12. In this text both Abraham and Rahab are extolled for their 'faith and hospitality'. The reference to Abraham is to the welcome he gave to the three 'men' in Genesis 18, an incident that was frequently mentioned in Jewish tradition. Some think that this hospitality motif explains why James mentions both Abraham and Rahab; the 'works' they did are precisely those which people with a sham

---

[1]Luther himself may well have stressed the message of James much more had he been living in a different age. Faced with an excessive preoccupation with works, he sought to right the balance by an insistence on the Pauline message of faith. See, on this, D. O. Via, 'The Right Strawy Epistle Reconsidered: A Study in Biblical Ethics and Hermeneutic', *JR* 49, 1968, pp. 253–267; J. Reumann, *Righteousness in the New Testament* (Fortress, 1982), pp. 156–157; Dibelius, pp. 179–180.

faith do not have (vv. 15–16).[1] A serious problem with this theory, however, is James' failure to mention the Genesis 18 incident. Another possibility is that Abraham and Rahab are both mentioned because they were both considered to be proselytes (converts) who acted on the basis of their faith in the 'one God'. But what James seems to emphasize more clearly, by pointedly calling Rahab a *harlot*, is the difference between Abraham and Rahab; Abraham, the widely heralded hero and 'father' of Israel, is juxtaposed with the pagan woman of loose reputation. But both the patriarch and the prostitute are declared righteous on the basis of works that issued from their faith.

26. James concludes the passage by restating its central theme: *faith apart from works is dead*. Just as the body without its invigorating spirit, or 'breath' of life (*cf.* Gn. 2:7), is nothing more than a corpse, so faith without the works that give it vitality is dead. Again we see that James is concerned not that works be 'added' to faith, but that one possess the right kind of faith, 'faith that works'. Without that kind of faith Christianity becomes a barren orthodoxy and loses any right to be called faith.

Somewhat ironically, no-one has captured the basic message of James 2:14–26 more forcefully than Luther (from his preface to Romans):

> O it is a living, busy active mighty thing, this faith. It is impossible for it not to be doing good things incessantly. It does not ask whether good works are to be done, but before the question is asked, it has already done this, and is constantly doing them. Whoever does not do such works, however, is an unbeliever. He gropes and looks around for faith and good works, but knows neither what faith is nor what good works are. Yet he talks and talks, with many words, about faith and good works.

[1] See particularly R. B. Ward, 'The Works of Abraham: James 2:14–26', *HTR* 61, 1968, pp. 283–290.

IV. DISSENSIONS WITHIN THE COMMUNITY (3:1 – 4:12)

The series of paragraphs following 1:19 – 2:26 – which, as we have seen, is relatively unified around the theme of doing the word – do not, at first sight, appear to have much in common. Nevertheless a closer scrutiny reveals some measure of cohesiveness in the material in 3:1 – 4:12. This section begins and ends with warnings about the sin of impure speech (3:1–12; 4:11–12). Between these paragraphs, James focuses on the problem of dissensions and disputes within the community. These two issues are naturally related, since impure, especially critical, speech almost always accompanies quarrels and arguments. Another unifying factor within the section dealing with community dissension (3:13 – 4:10) is the theme of envy, or selfishness, the sinful attitude that James holds responsible for the contentious, arrogant behaviour of his readers.[1] The cure for this selfish envy is radical repentance, a humbling of oneself before God (4:4–10), an embracing of 'the wisdom from above', with its fruits of humility and peace (3:13–18). Only through such a transformation in the attitude of individual Christians will it be possible to avoid sinful speech and bring healing to the community's divisions.

a. The harmful effects of the uncontrolled tongue (3:1–12)

James has already mentioned his concern about sins of speech. In 1:19 he encouraged his readers to be 'slow to speak', while the bridling of the tongue is picked out as one of the main ingredients of a 'pure religion' in 1:26. Now he attacks the problem at some length. Perhaps the general issue of 'works' in 2:14–26 has stimulated this section: 'words are also works' (Tasker). These verses, more than any others in the epistle, reveal the breadth of James' background. The problem of uncontrolled speech is a frequent theme in Proverbs and other Old Testament and Jewish Wisdom literature. But James illuminates this problem of the tongue with a series of illustrations popular among Greek and

---

[1]The thematic unity of this section has been clearly demonstrated by L. T. Johnson, 'James 3:13 – 4:10 and the Topos ΠΕΡΙ ΦΘΟΝΟΥ', *NovT* 25, 1983, pp. 327–347.

Hellenistic-Jewish moralists. These illustrations are of a type that would have been widely known among those with even a minimal acquaintance with Hellenistic culture. The picture of James that emerges is of a reasonably well-educated Jew who knows his Old Testament thoroughly and who is well acquainted with Hellenistic-Jewish culture, language and literature.

1. James approaches the subject of the tongue by means of a warning about the teaching office. *Teachers* (*didaskaloi*) played a prominent part in the life of the early church. Paul singles them out as exercising one of the three most prominent ministries in the church, along with apostles and prophets (1 Cor. 12:28; see also Acts 13:1; Rom. 12:7; Eph. 4:11). Somewhat comparable to the Jewish rabbi, the teacher in the early church was entrusted with the crucial task of transmitting Christian doctrine (see 2 Tim. 2:2). A certain authority and prestige naturally adhered to the teaching ministry. Particularly was this so in a society where few people could read and where people in the lower classes had few opportunities for advancement in status. It is not surprising, then, that Christians were attracted to the teaching ministry. Concern about believers flocking to this ministry for the wrong reasons probably lies behind James' warning: *Let not many of you become teachers*.

As a reinforcement of this warning, James points to another, less attractive, aspect of teaching: *we who teach shall be judged with greater strictness*. An alternative, more literal, translation of the Greek would be 'we shall receive a greater judgment', the word 'judgment' (*krima*) suggesting the idea of punishment or condemnation. Clearly, James cannot mean that Christian teachers will receive a more severe penalty than other Christians – few, indeed, would become teachers in that case! Probably we should understand him to be saying that the importance of the teaching ministry renders it liable to a closer scrutiny and that failure to discharge the ministry faithfully will bring a correspondingly more severe penalty. Jesus warned that 'to whom much is given, of him will much be required' (Lk. 12:48). Those who have been given the teaching 'gift' bear an awesome responsibility for their exercise of that gift in nurturing people in the faith. Paul was very much conscious of this responsibility. As he

bade farewell to the elders of the Ephesian church, he stressed
that he had been faithful to his task as a herald of the gospel: 'I
testify to you this day that I am innocent of the blood of all of you,
for I did not shrink from declaring to you the whole counsel of
God' (Acts 20:26–27). As an example of a failure to discharge this
responsibility we may cite the insincere, rapacious Jewish scribes
of whom Jesus said: 'They will receive the greater condemnation'
(Mk. 12:40). One who undertakes to lead others in the faith must
be careful that his own life reflects what he is teaching. His
greater knowledge brings with it a greater responsibility to live
according to that knowledge. James' intention is not to dissuade
those from teaching who, like himself, have the call and gifts to
teach. But he does want to impress upon his readers the seriousness of the ministry and to warn them that it must not be
entered into frivolously or for selfish reasons.

2. The teacher places himself in greater danger of judgment
because the main tool of his ministry is also the part of the body
most difficult to control: the tongue. To highlight the peculiar
danger of the tongue, James first acknowledges the prevalence of
sin: *we all make many mistakes*. The verb James uses (*ptaiō*) means
'to stumble' and is applied figuratively to spiritual failure both in
Judaism and the New Testament (*cf.* 2:10; Rom. 11:11; 2 Pet. 1:10).
It may suggest sins of a relatively minor, even inadvertent nature.
The emphasis is probably not on the number of sins (as the RSV
may suggest), but on the variety of sins; *cf.* NIV: 'we all stumble in
many ways'. In contrast to this, James says, is the one way in
which we all sin – with the tongue. James is not the first to single
out impure speech as a particularly widespread sin. Proverbs, for
instance, has a great deal to say about the importance of and
power of words (*cf.* 10:8, 11; 16:27–28; 18:7–8). Jesus ben Sirach,
like James, highlights sins of speech in conjunction with inadvertent sins: 'A person may make a slip without intending it. Who
has never sinned with his tongue?' (Ecclus. 19:16). James puts it
positively: the person who never 'stumbles' *in what he says* is
perfect, able to bridle the whole body also. So difficult is the mouth to
control, so given is it to utter the false, the biting, the slanderous
word, so prone to stay open when it were more profitably closed,
that the person who has it in control surely has the ability to

conquer other, less unruly, members of the body.

Since James continues to include himself in his strictures ('*we all make many mistakes*') he may also be continuing to think specifically of teachers in this verse. But the rest of the passage makes no reference to teachers, and James' warning about the tongue certainly has general application. Probably, then, James intends to include *all* his readers in the first person plural of verse 2. His warning to would-be teachers has suggested to his mind the problem of the tongue; and this is a problem for everyone in the church.

3. With this verse begins a series of illustrations that James uses with great effect in portraying the power and danger of the tongue (vv. 3–6a). None of these illustrations is original to James; he draws from familiar and widely used images to make his points.

According to AV, James introduces the first illustration, in verse 3, with 'Behold'. This reading, although supported by several recent commentators, is probably inferior to the conditional construction (*If*, 'when') adopted by most modern translations. The difference is a matter of one letter in Greek, and it is likely that early scribes substituted *ide* ('see', 'behold'), for *ei de* ('and if') as an assimilation to verse 4 (*idou*, 'behold'). While the image of the horse may have been suggested to James by his use of 'bridle' in verse 2, the use of the horse to illustrate the idea of something small controlling something large was not new. The fifth-century BC playwright Sophocles has one of his actors say 'I know that spirited horses are broken by the use of a small bit' (*Antigone*, 477). To be sure, James does not specifically mention the small size of the bit. But he probably intends this to be inferred since he *does* stress that bits, when inserted into horses' mouths, enable us to control *their whole bodies*.

4. The contrast between a small instrument and the large object it can control is made explicit in the second illustration. 'Take ships as an example' (NIV): though they are very large and are driven by strong winds, a very small instrument, the rudder, can turn them in whatever direction the steersman wishes. (NEB implies a slightly different interpretation – large ships can be directed even *against* strong winds by the rudder – but the difference is unimportant.) Once again, James has employed a very popular image. Aristotle specifically contrasted the small size of the rudder, turned by one man, with the 'huge mass' of the ship it controls (*Quaest. Mechan.* 5), and both man and God were often compared to a helmsman. Interestingly, one also finds several places in which the horse and its rider and the ship and its rudder are used together to illustrate various points.[1] Sometimes even fire (*cf.* v. 5) is included along with the horse and the ship.[2] The fact that the combination of images found in verses 3–5 is attested elsewhere may suggest that James is dependent on these sources. But such a hypothesis is probably not necessary. The illustrations are, after all, rather obvious, as the frequency of their occurrence suggests. They were probably 'in the air', as it were, so that James' use of them demonstrates nothing more than that he was acquainted with the wider culture around him.

Both illustrations in verses 2–4 focus on the *control* exercised by a person through a small object (the bit, the rudder) on a large body (the horse, the ship). A strict application of this imagery would suggest that the believer similarly uses the tongue to control 'the whole body' (v. 2), but it is difficult to understand how the tongue could directly control the body. Probably we should make the application a little differently: just as the bit determines the direction of the horse and the rudder the ship, so the tongue can determine the destiny of the individual. When the believer exercises careful control of the tongue, it can be presumed that he also is able to direct his whole life in its proper, divinely charted course: he is a 'perfect man' (v. 2). But when that tongue is not restrained, small though it is, the rest of the body is likely to be uncontrolled and undisciplined also.

5a. The first part of this verse concludes the opening section of James' discourse on the tongue by explicitly applying the illus-

[1]The combined imagery is often used to illustrate God's control of the cosmos (Pseudo-Aristotle, *Mund.* 6; frequently in Philo) and sometimes of man's derived authority over creation (Philo, *On the Creation*, 88). Man's mind, or higher nature, is also compared to the charioteer and helmsman, as that which must control the whole person (Philo, *On the Migration of Abraham*, 67; Strobaeus *Ecl.* 3.17.17; Plutarch *Quorm. adol. poet. aud. deb.* 33F). Dibelius gives a large sample of the relevant texts (pp. 185–190).
[2]See particularly Philo, *Allegorical Interpretation*, 3.223–224, in which mind is called the

trations of verses 3–4. The importance of the bit and the rudder, small though they may be, is comparable to the importance of the *little member*, the tongue: it *boasts of great things*. 'Boasting' is often in the New Testament a sinful activity, and manifests an arrogant presumptuousness before God. Here, however, 'boasting' is used without these negative connotations – the tongue *does* have considerable importance and it can legitimately boast about its power to determine a person's destiny. Phillips paraphrases, 'the human tongue is physically small, but what tremendous effects it can boast of!'

5b. This half-verse effects a transition from verses 3–5a, which focus on the disproportionate power of the tongue, to verse 6, which highlights the tongue's destructive potential. *How great a forest is set ablaze by a small fire!* A peculiarity of this translation is that the same Greek word (*hēlikos*) is given different, indeed opposite, meanings in its two occurrences: it is rendered both *how great* and *small*. The explanation is that the word 'expresses magnitude in either direction' (Hort) – immensity or minuteness. Used in the same sentence in this way, a certain antithetical symmetry is achieved.[1] As an image, the rapid destructive spread of fire was frequently used to convey a warning about the effect of unrestrained passions. The Old Testament compares the speech of a fool to 'a scorching fire' (Pr. 16:27) and Sirach says that the tongue 'will not be master over the godly, and they will not be burned in its flame' (Ecclus. 28:22). The word translated *forest* in RSV (*hylē*) could refer to the brush which covered so many Palestinian hills, and which, in that dry Mediterranean climate, could so easily and disastrously burst into flame.[2]

6. The identification of *the tongue* with *fire*, implicit in verse 5, is now stated and the destructive potential of the tongue is spelt out further. These points, made at the beginning and end of verse 6, are clear, but the middle part of the verse presents the reader of

---

'charioteer and helmsman of the soul' and irrationality, if it gains control, is said to set the mind on fire.

[1]*Cf.* also Philostratus, *Vit. Ap.* 2.11.2 – 'for it seems to me a super-human feat for such a tiny [*tēlikoud*] mite to manage so huge [*tēlikouto*] an animal'.

[2]L. E. Elliott-Binns, 'The Meaning of 'YLH in Jas. III.5', *NTS* 2, 1955, pp. 48–50; *cf.* also the note in Hort, pp. 104–107.

the Greek text with a notable difficulty. Including the first part of the verse, James uses five expressions in the nominative case with only one indicative verb. The interpreter or translator must decide how best to combine these words to make sense of the verse, and every combination has some difficulties. Because of this, many have suggested that the text must be emended, that we have to change the wording to make sense out of it. But conjectural emendation of the New Testament text, with its wealth of manuscript evidence, should always be a last, desperate, resort. We will therefore attempt to explain the text as it stands.

An initial problem is the meaning of the phrase *ho kosmos tēs adikias*, which immediately follows the statement *the tongue is a fire*. Taking *kosmos* to mean 'adornment' (*cf.* 1 Pet. 3:3), some think that James may be suggesting that the tongue 'adorns' unrighteousness, by using flowery language to make sin attractive. But this meaning of *kosmos* is poorly attested in the New Testament and is far from the obvious meaning of James' phrase. By translating *an unrighteous world*, the RSV appears to adopt a second option: that *kosmos* means 'sum total' or 'mass' (see BAGD, Pr. 17:6a [LXX only]). On this understanding, James emphasizes the great evil inherent in the tongue, a 'mass' or great body of unrighteousness. The problems with this view are that the meaning 'totality' for *kosmos* is poorly attested, the article before *kosmos* is not adequately explained, and the force of the verb *kathistatai* ('appoint', 'cause') is lost (RSV lamely translates *is*). The most natural translation of the phrase, which gives *kosmos* the same meaning it has in three of its other occurrences in James (1:27; 4:4), is 'the unrighteous world'. The phrase is then parallel to Luke 16:9, *mamōna tēs adikias* (= 'unrighteous mammon'), and uses 'world' in its well-attested New Testament sense – the fallen, rebellious, sinful world-system.

If we adopt this translation of the phrase *ho kosmos tēs adikias*, two different punctuations of the verse are possible: *a.* 'The tongue is a fire. It is appointed (or appoints itself) as the unrighteous world, which stains the whole body . . .' (*cf.* NEB). *b.* 'The tongue is a fire, the unrighteous world. It is appointed (or appoints itself) among our members as that which stains the whole body . . .' (*cf.* NASB). The latter, although it is supported by

Bengel and makes good sense, must probably be rejected because the feminine participle *hē spilousa* ('that which stains') is best taken as an attributive modifier of *glōssa* ('tongue') rather than as a predicate following the verb *kathistatai* ('appoint') (in the latter case, the neuter would have been expected). As the parentheses in the quotations above imply, there is one other ambiguity in the sentence: the meaning of the verb *kathistatai*. While it could be passive ('is appointed'), James uses the same verb in 4:4 with a reflexive, middle meaning: 'makes itself'.

What does it mean, then, to say that 'the tongue makes itself the unrighteous world in our members'? Presumably, James wants to suggest that the tongue contains within it the sins of the fallen world. As Calvin puts it, 'a slender portion of flesh contains the whole world of iniquity'. Jesus, it will be remembered, claimed that 'what comes out of the mouth' defiles a man and explained further that the mouth expressed the heart, in which are found 'evil thoughts, murder, adultery, fornication, theft, false witness, slander' (Mt. 15:11, 18–19). No other 'member' of the body, perhaps, wreaks so much havoc to the godly life.

Verse 6 concludes with a series of three participles that further describe the tongue. In *staining* (*spilousa*) *the whole body*, the tongue accomplishes what is just the reverse of 'pure religion': keeping oneself 'unstained (*aspilon*) from the world'. The sins committed with the tongue spread spiritual pollution to the whole person. With the second two participles, James returns to the imagery of fire to characterize, respectively, the extent and the source of the devastation wrought by the tongue. In saying that the tongue sets on fire *the cycle of nature*, James clearly intends to reiterate the magnitude of the tongue's destructive potential, but his precise meaning is unclear. The phrase, and others parallel to it, were used in the Orphic religion to describe the unending cycle of reincarnations from which deliverance was sought. But there is sufficient evidence to show that what had originally been a technical religious or philosophical expression had become 'popularized' and was used in James' day as a way of describing the course of human life, perhaps with an emphasis on the 'ups and downs' of life.[1] The point, then, is that the

---

[1] See the references and discussion in Dibelius, pp. 196–198.

tongue's fiery destructive power affects all of human existence, from beginning to end, and in all its circumstances. Where does this enormously destructive potential come from? From *hell*, says James. He uses the term *gehenna* here, reflecting again his acquaintance with Jesus' teaching, who used it often to describe the place of ultimate condemnation. The word is a transliteration of the Hebrew 'Valley of Hinnom', which had an evil reputation in the Old Testament and in the intertestamental period came to be used of the place of final judgment. The power of Satan himself, the chief denizen of hell, gives to the tongue its great destructive potential.

James does not elaborate the ways in which the destructive power of the tongue can make itself felt: but he undoubtedly would have thought of those sins of speech that are enumerated in Proverbs: thoughtless 'chattering' (10:8; *cf.* 12:18; 29:20); lying (*cf.* 12:19); arrogant boasting (18:12); gossiping (10:18). Think what enormous, sometimes irreversible, harm can be caused to people by unsubstantiated, often false, rumours. Such a rumour can be harder to stop than any forest fire (*cf.* v. 5). We know from bitter experience that the childhood taunt, 'Sticks and stones may break my bones, but words will never hurt me', reverses the truth of the matter. The wounds caused by sticks and stones heal; the wounds caused by words sometimes never heal.

7. The *For* (*gar*) introducing this verse suggests that verses 7–8 provide the basis for something that has been said in verse 6. Probably we should consider the stress on the untameable nature of the tongue as providing proof for the assertion that the tongue receives its power from hell. How else explain its peculiar insusceptibility to training, greater than any animal's? James' assertion of man's dominance over the animal world clearly alludes to the Genesis creation story. The fourfold division of the animal kingdom picks up the similar classification in Genesis 1:26.[1] And the peculiar repetition of the verb 'tame' in the perfect tense (*dedamastai*) may well reflect the dominion over creation which man was given in the beginning. Humankind, the 'species' (*physis*) of man, was given the power to subdue every 'species'

---

[1] *Cf.* Philo, *On the Special Laws*, 4. 110–116.

(*physis*) of the lower creation, and that power has been continually exercised. It is an interesting coincidence, and perhaps no more than that, that Philo compares man to the driver of a chariot (*cf.* Jas. 3:3), and the pilot of a ship (3:4) in stressing his dominion over creation.[1]

8. In the Greek of this verse, *the tongue* comes first for contrast: man may subdue animals, but *the tongue* no-one can tame. It is not clear what we should make of James' addition of *anthrōpōn* ('of men') to *oudeis* ('no-one') (*cf.* RSV, *no human being*). This may simply be a continuation of the stress on 'humankind' from verse 7. But Augustine suggested a more subtle interpretation: '. . . he does not say that no-one can tame the tongue, but no-one of men; so that when it is tamed we confess that this is brought about by the pity, the help, the grace of God.'[2]

The two descriptions of the tongue that complete the verse may be in apposition to *tongue* (RSV, – *a restless evil, full of deadly poison*) or be the predicates of a separate sentence (NIV, 'It is a restless evil, full of deadly poison'). *Restless* translates the same word (*akatastatos*) that James used in 1:8 to describe the 'double-minded man, *unstable* in all his ways'.[3] As a modifier of *evil*, it may suggest that the 'evil' is difficult to control – 'always liable to break out' (Phillips) – or that the evil involves 'instability and lack of single-mindedness' (Davids). The first interpretation would make this a natural complement of verse 8a; the second would prepare the way for the description of the 'double', contradictory, use of the tongue in verses 9ff. Probably the former should be accepted, because it yields a more natural meaning in combination with 'evil'. The final description of the tongue in this verse, *full of deadly poison*, reflects Old Testament teaching: evil men 'make their tongue sharp as a serpent's, and under their lips is the poison of vipers' (Ps. 140:3). The poison produced by the tongue 'destroys the neighbour' (Pr. 11:9) and brings the one who sins to ruin also (Pr. 10:8).

---

[1] *On the Creation*, 8.   [2] *de Nat. et Grat.*, c. 15; *cf.* Knowling, p. 78.
[3] And see Hermas, *Mandate*. 2.3: 'Slander is evil; it is a restless (*akatastaton*) demon, never at peace' (*cf.* Jas. 4:1). The word is also linked with sins of speech in Pr. 26:28, LXX.

9. As a final, climactic indictment of the tongue, James attributes to it that 'doubleness' which he so deplores. The inconsistent, unstable wavering of the double-minded man (1:7–8), which is manifested in an attitude of partiality (*cf.* 2:4) and a failure to produce justifying works (2:14–26), also comes to expression in the tongue. Like Bunyan's 'Talkative', who was 'a saint abroad and a devil at home', the double-minded man shows by the contradictory nature of his speech that his faith lacks focus and stability.

It is deplorable that the same instrument is used to *bless the Lord and Father* and to *curse men, who are made in the likeness of God*. The blessing of God was a prominent part of Jewish devotion. 'The Holy One, Blessed be He' is one of the most frequent descriptions of God in rabbinic literature and 'the eighteen benedictions', a liturgical formula used daily, concluded each of its parts with a blessing of God. Christians, of course, also blessed God in prayer (*cf.* Eph. 1:3; 1 Pet. 1:3). It is rare to designate God as *Lord and Father* (although see 1 Ch. 29:10; Is. 63:16), but it is doubtful whether James intends anything special by these titles. This activity of blessing, in which we praise and honour God, is cited by James as the highest, purest, most noble form of speech. The lowest, filthiest, most ignoble form of speech, on the other hand, is cursing. The word of the curse, which is the opposite of blessing (*cf.* Dt. 30:19), was seen to have great power in the ancient world. For to curse someone is not just to swear at them; it is to desire that they be cut off from God and experience eternal punishment. Jesus prohibited his disciples from cursing others; indeed, they were to 'bless those who curse you' (Lk. 6:28; *cf.* Rom. 12:14). What makes cursing particularly heinous is that the one whom we pronounce damned has been made in God's image (James' further allusion to Gn. 1:26 [*cf.* v. 7] is clear). The rabbis cautioned against cursing for the same reason: one should not say ' "Let my neighbour be put to shame" – for then you put to shame one who is in the image of God' (*Bereshith Rabba* 24, on Gn. 5:1).

10. The deceitful duality of the mouth, then, is clearly marked: from it come both blessing and cursing. James' interesting shift to *mouth* here, along with his use of the verb *exerchomai* ('come out'), strongly suggests that his words are dependent on Jesus' teaching regarding the defiling power of speech (cf. Mt. 15:11, 18–19). Like Jesus, James sees a person's speech as a barometer of his spirituality; it reveals what is in the heart. Jesus' warning must be taken with utter seriousness: 'I tell you, on the day of judgment men will render account for every careless word they utter; for by your words you will be justified, and by your words you will be condemned' (Mt. 12:36–37). The person who is double and inconsistent with regard to the things of God in his heart (*dipsychos*) will be double and inconsistent in his speech. The same theme is found in many Jewish works. According to The Testament of Benjamin 6:5, 'the good set of mind does not talk from both sides of its mouth: praises and curses, abuse and honour, calm and strife, hypocrisy and truth, poverty and wealth, but it has one disposition, uncontaminated and pure, towards all men'. This kind of doubleness in speech *ought not to be so*. Christians who have been transformed by the Spirit of God should manifest the wholeness and purity of the heart in consistency and purity of speech.

11. James asserts the incompatibility of a pure heart and impure speech with three illustrations. Each is cast in the form of a rhetorical question, expecting the answer 'no' – a favourite literary device in James. The importance of the *spring (pēgē)* in dry Palestine can hardly be over-estimated. On this source of water depended the very existence of many a village. One can imagine how critical it was that a fresh-water spring continue to produce *fresh*, sweet (*glykos*) water. To be sure, some streams and springs produced a mixture of fresh and salt water which was unusable. But James' point is that the same spring does not pour forth fresh water one minute and bitter, brackish water the next. Its water may be good, bad or indifferent, but it is consistent in producing the same kind of water. The tragedy of the tongue is precisely this inconsistency; its tendency to bless God one minute yet curse men the next. The word James uses to describe the useless water, *brackish (pikros, 'bitter')*, is not one normally used of water: it may be that he assimilates his description of the water to language associated with the tongue, whose speech is often said to be 'bitter' (Ps. 64:3; Pr. 5:4; Sirach 29:25; and *cf.* 3:14).

12. The image of the plant that produces according to its nature was a popular one in ancient literature. Epictetus, for instance, asked: 'How can a vine be moved to act, not like a vine, but like an olive, or again an olive to act, not like an olive, but like a vine? It is impossible, inconceivable.'[1] As a direct ancestor of James' imagery we naturally think of Jesus' teaching about the good tree producing good fruit, and vice versa: 'Are grapes gathered from thorns, or figs from thistles?' (Mt. 7:16). Nevertheless, James' language and teaching does not closely correspond to Jesus', so we may be justified in supposing that James picks up the imagery from the general culture. The point he makes is the same as that in verse 11: as the fig tree cannot produce olives or the grapevine figs, so the pure heart cannot produce false, bitter, harmful speech.

The final sentence returns to the image of salt and fresh water from verse 11, but is used now to make a negative point: *No more can salt water yield fresh*. The image is introduced awkwardly (*oute*, 'neither') and some manuscripts attempt to ease the construction by adding *houtōs*, 'similarly', before it. But, while a bit awkward, the sentence is perfectly understandable; the sense is captured well by the RSV. Another difficulty in the verse, which also has given rise to a textual variant, is the notion that salt water could produce fresh (some manuscripts add the word 'spring' after 'water'). We must suppose that the word *halykon* ('salt') stands here for a 'salt spring' rather than 'salt water' (see BAGD; NIV). In any case, James' warning is obvious: what is good at heart must produce good; what is evil at heart will inevitably produce evil. So the heart that is not right with God cannot help but produce ungodly speech. It should be mentioned that James' imagery (as that of Jesus in Mt. 7) must not be pressed beyond its intention. 'A man is after all not a tree'[2] and the automatic natural processes of plant life cannot be exactly compared to the willing, deciding processes of human life. But, whatever its limits, the imagery conveys an important warning: only a renewed heart can produce pure speech; and consistently (though not perfectly) pure speech is to be the product of the renewed heart.

---

[1] *Discourses*, 2.20. 18–19.   [2] H. Berkhof, *The Christian Faith* (Eerdmans, 1979), p. 452.

b. True wisdom brings peace (3:13–18)

What gives this section and the next its unity is the problem of jealousy (*zēlos*, 3:14, 16; 4:2) and the related ideas of 'selfish ambition' (3:14, 16), 'selfish desires' (4:2, 3) and arrogance (3:14). The first paragraph (3:13–18) describes this sinful attitude and sets it in contrast with the 'wisdom from above'. The second paragraph (4:1–3) describes the effects of this attitude: fighting, quarrels, murder, unanswered prayer. As we suggested earlier, the whole section is reminiscent of, and perhaps modelled on, a popular Hellenistic-Jewish moral tradition that traced social ills back to jealousy (*zēlos*) and envy (*phthonos*). Particularly close to James' teaching are some sections of The Testaments of the Twelve Patriarchs, a Jewish pseudepigraphical work most of which was written around 100 BC. In this book, slander (*katalalia*, Test. Gad 3:3), violence (*polemos*) and murder (Test. Simeon 4:5) are all connected to jealousy – and these are topics treated by James in 4:1–12. Moreover, the problem of 'double-mindedness' is frequently mentioned in the Testaments, striking another familiar chord for the reader of James (*cf.* 4:8). It is most unlikely that James has borrowed directly from the Testaments; our point is rather to suggest that James stands in the same stream of Hellenistic/Jewish moral tradition represented by the Testaments and that this circumstance may aid in our understanding of this section of his letter.

13. The question introducing this section – *Who is wise and understanding among you?* – is in fact a challenge: if you claim to be wise, demonstrate your wisdom in the works that true wisdom produces. Many commentators think that James' question is directed particularly to the teachers who were mentioned in verse 1. But neither *sophos* (*wise*, 'wise person') nor *epistēmōn* ('knowledgeable', 'full of understanding') is regularly used as a title for the teacher. They occur together several times in the Septuagint, once with reference to the qualities leaders should possess (Dt. 1:13, 15) but also with application to all of Israel (Dt. 4:6; Dn. 5:12 applies them to the prophet). Clearly James considers 'wisdom' a virtue available to all (1:5), and even 3:1 is not really directed to teachers, but to those who would *become* teachers. Therefore James' exhortation is better taken as directed generally to all believers, but especially to those who pride themselves on their superior understanding.

As Dibelius points out, James' exhortation to the 'wise person' reads awkwardly, because he has combined two ideas in it: wisdom is to produce works and wisdom is to be characterized by humility. The first idea reminds us strongly of James' earlier demand that faith manifest itself in works. True wisdom, like real faith, is a vital, practical quality that has as much (or more) to do with the way we live as with what we think or say. In this James is true to the Old Testament conception of wisdom as a way of life, the attitude and conduct typical of a godly person. But James is even more interested in the second idea mentioned above, the qualities that wisdom should manifest. *In the meekness of wisdom* is to be taken as qualifying the *works*; they are to be done 'in meekness' that characterizes, or springs from, 'wisdom' (taking the genitive as descriptive or as designating origin). *Meekness* (*praütēs*) was hardly a virtue to be sought after in the minds of most Greeks: it suggested a servile, ignoble debasement. But Jesus, who was himself 'meek' (Mt. 11:29), pronounced a blessing on those who were meek (Mt. 5:5). This Christian meekness involves a healthy understanding of our own unworthiness before God and a corresponding humility and lack of pride in our dealings with our fellow-men.

14. The opposite of meekness is *bitter jealousy and selfish ambition*. *Jealousy* (*zēlos*) is not, of course, always a bad thing; Phinehas is commended for his 'zeal' for the Lord's cause (Nu. 25:11–13) and Jesus himself was consumed by a similar zeal (Jn. 2:17). But true, unselfish zeal for the Lord lies all too close to a selfishly motivated, harsh and violent fanaticism. It is 'jealousy' or 'zeal' in this sense that Paul often condemns (Rom. 13:13; 2 Cor. 12:20; Gal. 5:20) and that James speaks of here. It is related to what we would call 'jealousy' in that such zeal is often selfishly motivated and involves envy and criticism of others. *Eritheia*, translated *selfish ambition*, is a comparatively rare word. It is tempting to define it with reference to the similar *eris* ('strife') which Paul uses three times in close conjunction with *zēlos*. But this derivation is unlikely. In its only pre-New Testament occurrences (in Aristotle), the word refers to the selfish ambition, the narrow partisan zeal of factional, greedy politicians. This meaning makes excellent sense here in James. Some who pride themselves on their wisdom and understanding are displaying a jealous, bitter partisanship that is the antithesis of the meekness produced by true wisdom.

People like this should certainly not *boast*. Several commentators (and *cf.* NEB) understand *the truth* to be the object of both 'boast' and 'lie against'. But it is simpler to take 'boast' absolutely and infer that its object is 'wisdom'. Being *false to the truth* will then designate the result of this unjustified boasting. GNB reflects this interpretation: 'don't sin against the truth by boasting of your wisdom'. To boast about wisdom when one is displaying jealousy and selfish ambition is, in effect, to give lie to the truth that wisdom must be associated with humility. It should be noted that, while the verse is couched in the form of a conditional sentence, it is not a true conditional relationship: the imperatives would be valid whether the condition were fulfilled or not.[1] James does not mean that it is *only* when bitter jealousy and selfish ambition exist that we should not boast and speak against the truth. It is always wrong.

15. In a semi-ironical way, James now contrasts the *wisdom* such as these jealous and contentious people have with the wisdom that *comes down from above*. This phrase has already been used once by James (1:17) to indicate divine origin. True wisdom, as Scripture makes plain, comes only from God: 'the LORD gives wisdom' (Pr. 2:6). That is why it can be had only by asking God (Jas. 1:5). The 'wisdom' that manifests itself in selfishness and envy has a quite different nature and origin. James describes it with three adjectives, each of which takes its meaning from its implied opposite. First, this wisdom is *earthly* instead of heavenly. *Earthly* (*epigeios*) can have an entirely neutral significance (*cf.* Jn. 3:12), but it easily takes on negative connotations, describing that which is transitory, weak and imperfect (see the contrast between 'earthly' and 'heavenly' bodies in 1 Cor. 15:40;

[1]See Moule, p. 152, on this.

cf. 2 Cor. 5:1). Its derogatory sense is obvious in Philippians 3:19, where Paul says that 'the enemies of the cross of Christ' have their minds 'set on earthly things'. Secondly, this wisdom is *unspiritual* rather than spiritual. The word used, *psychikos*, is the adjective derived from *psychē*, 'soul', and always has a negative nuance in the New Testament. It has to do with that part of man 'where human feeling and human reason reign supreme' (Knowling). In every other New Testament occurrence, the word is explicitly contrasted with 'spiritual' (1 Cor. 2:14; 15:44, 46; Jude 19). Thirdly, this wrong kind of wisdom is *devilish* (*daimoniōdēs*, lit. 'pertaining to demons'). This word occurs only here in the Greek Bible and may mean either that the wisdom is demonic in nature or, more probably, in origin. The wisdom that does not produce a good lifestyle (v. 13) is, in sum, characterized by 'the world, the flesh and the devil'. In each of these ways, it is the direct antithesis of 'the wisdom that comes from above' – heavenly in nature, spiritual in essence and divine in origin.

16. In this verse, James justifies his harsh verdict on false wisdom by describing the effects it produces. *Jealousy* (*zēlos*) and *selfish ambition* (*eritheia*) have already been singled out as characteristic of those who are making a false claim to wisdom (v. 14). Now James points out how egocentric, selfish attitudes inevitably lead to *disorder and every vile practice*. *Akatastasia* (*disorder*) is the noun form of the adjective James has used in 1:8 and 3:8 to characterize the 'double-minded' man and the 'double-speaking' tongue. The term connotes a restless, unsettled state. It is used in Luke's Gospel to describe the 'tumults', the uprisings and revolutions, that will typify the period preceding the *parousia* (Lk. 21:9). And Paul, pleading with the Corinthians to refrain from an unbridled, unorganized display of individual spiritual gifts in the assembly, reminds them that 'God is not a God of confusion (*akatastasis*) but of peace' (1 Cor. 14:33). 'Confusion', 'disorder' and 'tumults' will inevitably break out in the church where Christians, especially leaders, are more interested in pursuing their own ambitions or partisan causes than the edification of the body as a whole. What one ends up with is 'evil of every kind' (NEB). Where the hearts of individual Christians are wrong, an unlimited variety of sins will be found also.

17. James has described what *the wisdom from above* is *not* (v. 15); now he tells us what it *is*, with a series of seven adjectives. Or, more properly, he tells us what effects divine wisdom should produce – for almost all of these adjectives describe what wisdom does rather than what it is. It is again clear that James does not view *wisdom* as a series of correct propositional statements, but as a quality that motivates certain kinds of behaviour. James' description of *the wisdom from above* reminds us inevitably of Paul's description of 'the fruit of the Spirit' in Galatians 5:22–23. While there is little verbal resemblance, the emphasis in both texts is on humility, peaceableness and upright behaviour. What Paul says the Spirit produces, James says wisdom produces. This similarity, coupled with the fact that James never (except perhaps in 4:5; see below) mentions the Holy Spirit, may point to the equivalence of wisdom and spirit in James' thinking. Certainly, the two were frequently associated in Jewish literature.[1] However, we must be cautious in speaking of 'equivalence' – because what is produced by James' wisdom and what is produced by Paul's Spirit are similar does not mean that the two can be seen as equivalent concepts.

The first, and overarching, attribute of wisdom is *purity*. The word *pure* (*hagnos*) connotes moral blamelessness, such as the unsullied chastity of the virgin bride (*cf.* 2 Cor. 11:2). Wisdom which is free from any stain or blemish would be incapable of producing anything evil (*cf.* v. 16). James has arranged the following series of adjectives in such a way that a pleasing auditory effect is achieved. The first four (*peaceable, gentle, open to reason, full of mercy*) all begin with an 'e' sound – *eirenikē, epieikēs, eupeithēs, eleous* – and combine to produce an alliteration. The last two also involve an alliteration – this time with an 'a' sound – and, in addition, have an almost metrical, rhyming similarity – *adiakritos, anypokritos* (*cf.* also *agathōn*).

That the list begins with *peaceable* is completely appropriate, since James criticizes those who falsely claim to be wise for their contentiousness and the disputes they spawn (3:14; 4:1–2). According to the Old Testament also, wisdom produces peace

[1]See on this J. A. Kirk, 'The Meaning of Wisdom in James: Examination of a Hypothesis', *NTS* 16, 1969–1970, pp. 24–38, and the section on 'Wisdom' in the Introduction, pp. 52–53.

(Pr. 3:17) and Paul lists 'peace' as a fruit of the Spirit. Why is wisdom *peaceable*? Because it is also *gentle* and *open to reason*. To be *gentle* (*epieikēs*) is to be kind, willing to yield, unwilling 'to exact strict claims' (Hort). With such an attitude, the believer, motivated and empowered by wisdom, will follow in the footsteps of his Lord, who also was characterized by 'meekness and gentleness' (2 Cor. 10:1). The person who is *open to reason* (*eupeithēs*) is one, literally, who is 'easily persuaded' – not in the sense of a weak, credulous gullibility, but in the sense of a willing deference to others when unalterable theological or moral principles are not involved. Wisdom is also *full of mercy and good fruits*. James provides his own definition of 'mercy': it is that love for the neighbour that shows itself in action (2:8–13). It is not surprising, then, that James couples *mercy* so closely with *good fruits* – acts of mercy are those 'fruits' which genuine wisdom, like genuine faith, must produce.

The second to the last attribute, *adiakritos*, is the most difficult to define. It may mean 'impartial' (NIV; *cf.* AV, GNB), in the sense of not exhibiting prejudice; 'straightforward' (NEB), simple (*cf.* also RSV(?), *without uncertainty*); or 'unwavering' (NASB), not doubting or being divided. Either of the latter two suggestions makes good sense in light of the use of *diakrinō* (related to the word used here) in 1:6 and, possibly, 2:4 – and we have seen the importance which James gives to the need to be 'undivided', 'not of two minds'. On the other hand, James also stresses the incompatibility of Christianity and partiality (2:1–4) and mentions mercy in that context, as he does here. Probably the former meaning 'impartial' should be accepted.[1] Finally, the 'wisdom from above' is *without insincerity* – it is genuine, 'without show or pretence' (Mayor). In a society that tends to elevate intelligence and cleverness, Christians need to assert that the values James lists here are the truly enviable, enduring ones.

18. In this verse James singles out for special emphasis one attribute of wisdom – its peaceableness. This emphasis is no doubt the product of James' desire to eradicate the bitter, con-

---

[1] *Adiakritōs* (an adverb) is also used in the Testament of Zebulon 7:2 with reference to showing mercy. The context favours the translation 'without discrimination' (see Charlesworth, p. 806).

tentious quarrels and disputes that were rending the church (3:16; 4:1–2). The peace that genuine wisdom should produce was notably absent. While the connection to the preceding context through the stress on *peace* is therefore obvious (and note also the mention of 'fruit' in both v. 17 and v. 18), the verse as a whole fits a bit awkwardly in its present position. Dibelius was probably right in seeing it as an originally independent proverb. This circumstance helps to explain why the verse is somewhat difficult to understand. Most translations understand the verse as a statement about what peacemakers *produce*, taking the dative *tois poiousin* (*those who make*) as the agent (the one who does the action) of the passive verb *speiretai* (*sow*) (*cf.* RSV, NIV, NASB, NEB, GNB). The problem with this view is that the dative is not normally used in this way in the New Testament; it is more natural to translate it as a dative of advantage, in which case the verse promises 'the fruit of righteousness' as the reward '*for* those who make peace'. Nevertheless, a dative of agency is not unknown in the New Testament and this translation makes much better sense of the verse – peacemakers produce, in the atmosphere of peace they create, *the harvest* (fruit) *of righteousness*.

What is this 'fruit' of righteousness? The phrase is a familiar one in the Septuagint, where it means 'the fruit which *is* righteousness' (an epexegetic genitive). Laws argues that this fruit of righteousness may be nothing else than wisdom itself,[1] but there is not enough reason to make this identification. Others, noting the frequent association of righteousness and peace in the Old Testament, interpret the fruit of righteousness as peace. But it is unnecessary to introduce these more specific ideas. *Righteousness* in James 1:20 meant that conduct which is pleasing to God, and this is the 'fruit' intended here also. It includes all the virtues listed in verse 17 and is the opposite of 'every vile practice' (v. 16). This righteousness cannot be produced in the context of man's anger (1:20); but it *can* grow and flourish in the atmosphere of peace. Those who create such an atmosphere are assured by their Lord of their reward: 'Blessed are the peacemakers, for they shall be called sons of God' (Mt. 5:9).

[1] She links Pr. 11:30, where 'fruit of righteousness' is connected with the 'tree of life', and Pr. 3:17, whose 'wisdom' is associated with the 'tree of life' (p. 166).

c. Evil passions are the source of dissensions (4:1–3)

1. As he did in 3:13, James uses a question to introduce his next topic. In this case, the topic is one that arises naturally from the preceding discussion. James has suggested a connection between 'jealousy and selfish ambition' and 'disorder' (v. 16). Now he specifies more clearly what he means by 'disorder' and portrays the way it is produced by jealousy and by other desires. In place of 'disorder' we now read of *wars* (*polemoi*) and *fightings* (*machai*). As with our English words, both words were most often used to describe physical conflicts between individuals or nations. In a metaphorical sense, however, both words could describe violent verbal disputes. Paul, for instance, cautions Titus to avoid 'quarrels (*machai*) over the law' (Tit. 3:9); and in the Psalms of Solomon 12:3, slanderous lips are said to 'kindle strife' (*polemos*). Both words resemble their English counterparts. We, too, use 'fight', 'battle', 'war', *etc.*, for verbal disputes as well as armed conflicts (*e.g.*, 'the United Nations fought over the meaning of the treaty clause'; 'Churchill always loved a parliamentary battle'). The Christians to whom James wrote were obviously engaged in such verbal battles. And since disputes of this sort are almost always accompanied by harsh words, criticism and slander , the misuse of the tongue that James castigates (*cf.* 3:1–12; 4:11–12; 5:9) probably arose from these disputes.

It is deplorable that the Christian church has so often been characterized by such bitter controversies. The seventeenth-century Jewish philosopher Spinoza observed: 'I have often wondered that persons who make boast of professing the Christian religion – namely love, joy, peace, temperance, and charity to all men – should quarrel with such rancorous animosity, and display daily towards one another such bitter hatred, that this, rather than the virtues which they profess, is the readiest criteria of their faith.'[1] Some battles are, to be sure, worth fighting; but even then they must be fought without sacrificing Christian principles and virtues. We do not know what the disputes that James refers to were about.[2] At any rate, James seems to be

---

[1]*Tractatus Theologico-Politicus*, ch.6.
[2]Mussner (pp. 169, 188–189) suggests that the place of the Torah among Christians may

bothered more by the selfish spirit and bitterness of the quarrels than by the rights and wrongs of the various viewpoints. It is suggestive that James has used a word connoting political 'factions' (*eritheia*) in 3:14 and 16.

What is the source of these quarrels? James points his finger at the *passions that are at war in your members*. *Passions* translates the word *hēdonē*, a term that means simply 'pleasure', but which often carries the negative connotations of sinful, self-indulgent pleasure (we get our word 'hedonism' from it). It consistently has this negative meaning in the New Testament (Lk. 8:14; Tit. 3:3; 2 Pet. 2:13). The appropriateness of James' use of the term here is demonstrated by its description in 4 Maccabees 1:25–26: 'in pleasure (*hēdonē*) there exists even a malevolent tendency, which is the most complex of all the emotions. In the soul it is boastfulness, covetousness, thirst for honour, rivalry, malice; in the body, indiscriminate eating, gluttony, and solitary gormandizing'. James would have undoubtedly added to this list jealousy (see 4:2) and selfish ambition (see 3:16). The military imagery of the opening words of the verse is carried on in James' description of the passions as 'waging war in your members'. It is possible that he intends to suggest the conflict and tumult of the passions with one another within the individual, but it is better to assume that the object of the 'warring' is the person's higher nature, or soul, as in 1 Peter 2:11. The arguments and conflicts that were disrupting Christian fellowship could not be ascribed to righteous passion or justifiable zeal; it was selfish, indulgent desire that was responsible.

2a. That illicit desire was responsible for the disputes and conflicts plaguing the church is made even more explicit in this verse. James uses a different word for *desire* (*epithymeō*), but this is due simply to the fact that the verb *hēdomai* is rare. Clearly he means the same thing.[1] Just what James is saying about 'desire' and its results is a matter of dispute. The fundamental problem is to determine the relationship among the series of verbs in the first

---

have been the issue. But if so, it is surprising that James writes so unreflectingly about the law (1:25; 2:8–11; 4:11–12).

[1] The verb form corresponding to *hēdonē* is never used in the New Testament; and Tit. 3:3 shows how *hēdonē* and *epithymia* were often interchangeable.

half of the verse. NIV separates them into three separate sentences:

    a. 'You want something but don't get it.'
    b. 'You kill and covet, but you cannot have what you want.'
    c. 'You quarrel and fight' (*cf.* also AV).

This rendering takes the sequence of positive-negative verbs as key to the structure, so that each of the first two sentences describes a frustrated desire. An emphasis on frustrated desire would certainly make good sense in the light of verses 2b–3. But the rendering has against it the difficult subordinate position of 'you kill'. The second main alternative is represented in the RSV:

    a. You desire and do not have; so you kill.
    b. And you covet and cannot obtain; so you fight and wage war (*cf.* also NEB, NASB, GNB).

This structure places the emphasis on the fact that frustrated desire leads to violence, and it should be preferred because it matches closely a pattern of moral exhortation common in the Hellenistic world. This pattern, which has been richly illustrated by L. T. Johnson,[1] focuses on the way in which 'envy' (*phthonos*), 'jealousy' (*zēlos*) and related emotions inevitably lead to hostile acts, such as quarrels, wars and murder. One or two examples will suffice to illustrate the pattern. The Testament of Simeon (in The Testaments of the Twelve Patriarchs) is titled 'concerning envy' (*phthonos*). A central theme of the Testament is the way in which envy led Simeon to seize and almost murder his brother Joseph. Simeon warns his children that 'envy dominates the whole of man's mind' and 'keeps prodding him to destroy the one whom he envies' (3:2–3). Epictetus, a second-century AD moralist, implies an organic relation between envy and violence when he notes that Caesar can free people from 'wars and fightings' (*polemoi kai machai*) but not from 'envy' (*phthonos*).[2] In the New Testament, the chief priests' decision to deliver Jesus to Pilate is attributed to 'envy' (*phthonos*) (Mk. 15:10), while the persecution suffered by the early church is often attributed to 'jealousy' or 'zeal' (*zēlos*) (Acts 5:17; 13:45; Phil. 3:6). James'

---

[1] 'James 3:13 – 4:10', *NovT* 25, 1983, pp. 327–347.   [2] *Discourses*, III. 13.9.

teaching appears to fit perfectly into this well-known pattern. While he uses the root *zēlos* rather than *phthonos* (which is more often found in these traditions), the two were often interchangeable (1 Macc. 8:16; Testament of Simeon 1:6; 4:5) and *zēlos* is found in these traditions also. But if James is utilizing this pattern, it is clear that 'murder' and 'fight and wage war' must be the *results* of the attitude of jealousy, envy and covetousness described. This relationship is preserved in the RSV punctuation.

But is James seriously accusing his readers of murder? Indeed, it has been asserted that he is doing just that. Some recent Jewish-Christian converts among James' readers, it is alleged, may have been members of the radical Jewish Zealot movement, which advocated assassination of prominent Romans and their collaborators as a policy of terror. Perhaps James must warn them that such practices are totally incompatible with their new faith.[1] While such a scenario is not impossible, granted the socio-political situation in Palestine in James' day, it does not square well with James' clear indication that the problems he addresses were within the church (*cf.* 'among you' in 3:13; 4:1). More popular has been the suggestion that *phoneuete* (*you kill*) be emended to *phthoneite* ('you are envious'), but there is no textual justification for the change. Others suggest that 'murder' may connote attitude rather than action: 'you are murderously jealous' (Phillips; *cf.* Mt. 5:21–26; 1 Jn. 2:15). However, in the light of the tradition we have cited, it is simplest to take 'murder' straightforwardly and to regard it as that extreme to which frustrated desire, if not checked, may lead.[2] Things have not yet gone this far among James' readers. But 'fightings' and wars *are* already in evidence among them; and, if covetous zeal goes unrestrained, the danger of actual violence is real. With penetrating insight, then, James provides us with a powerful analysis of human conflict. Verbal argument, private violence or national conflict – the cause of them all can be traced back to the frustrated desire to

---

[1] See Ross, p. 45; M. Townsend, 'James 4:1–4: A Warning against Zealotry?' *ExpT* 87, 1976, pp. 211–213; R. P. Martin, 'The Life-Setting of the Epistle of James in the Light of Jewish History', *Biblical and Near Eastern Studies*, ed. G. A. Tuttle (Eerdmans, 1978), p. 100.

[2] Davids (pp. 158–159) notes that James accuses the rich of murdering the poor in 5:6 and that the biblical tradition characterized a failure to meet the needs of the poor as murder. However, 5:6 comes in a denunciation of those who are clearly outside the community, and is not parallel to 4:1–3.

want more than we have, to be envious of and covet what others have, whether it be their position or their possessions.

2b–3. Why is this desire 'to have' frustrated? Because of a failure to pray properly. *You do not have, because you do not ask.* Oh yes, *you ask,* James admits, but your asking is done *wrongly,* with selfish motives – and it is for this reason that *you do not receive.* Jesus had promised, 'Ask, and it will be given you' (Mt. 7:7). But clearly Jesus had in mind that asking which has as its focus and motive God's name, God's kingdom and God's will (Mt. 6:9–10) – not an asking that had the purpose of the indulgence of those 'pleasures' (*hēdonai*) that are at war with our souls (*cf.* v. 1). Hort comments: 'God bestows not gifts only, but the enjoyment of them: but the enjoyment which contributes to nothing beyond itself is not what He gives in answer to prayer; and petitions to Him which have no better end in view are not prayers.'

In the Greek text of verses 2b–3, an interesting phenomenon is encountered: the verb *ask, aiteō,* shifts in voice from middle to active and back to middle. Many attempts to find significance in this shift have been made. Mayor suggested that the active (v. 3a) denoted 'the word without the spirit of prayer', while Hort argued that the active suggests the asking of a person, while the middle connotes asking for something. In three of the four other New Testament instances where the same verb shifts voice, however, it is difficult to discern any difference in meaning.[1] Probably, then, we should see no difference in meaning in the two forms of the verb that James uses.

d. A summons to repentance (4:4–10)

In the preceding nine verses, James has analysed the sin of human jealousy. He has portrayed it as 'earthly, unspiritual and devilish' – the antithesis of that 'wisdom from above' that God gives to those who ask. He has described the horrendous con-

---

[1]Mt. 20:20–22; Mk. 6:22–25; Jn. 16:23–26; 1 Jn. 5:14–16. Only in the Markan text is there some possibility of distinguishing the active and middle (but even then, the commentators do not agree on what the difference is!). Note, further, Turner, *Syntax,* p. 55. Mussner (p. 179) and Davids (p. 160) suggest that the active may be due to assimilation to the form of Jesus' saying (Mt. 7:7)

sequences of unrestrained and unfulfilled jealousy and desire. Now he turns from analysis to exhortation. Calling his readers 'unfaithful creatures' (v. 4) and 'men of double mind' (v. 8), James warns them about flirtation with the world and its consequences for their relationship to God (v. 4). He reminds them of God's jealousy for his people and the availability of his grace (vv. 5–6). And on the basis of this, he urges his readers to repent (vv. 7–10). Throughout the section James depends heavily on the Old Testament, quoting it twice and reflecting its vocabulary and themes in every verse.

4. This dependence on the Old Testament is clearly seen in James' opening address of his readers. *Unfaithful creatures* translates *moichalides*, a feminine noun that means 'adulteresses' (*cf.* NASB). The difficulty of the feminine form is erased in some manuscripts that add the masculine 'adulterers' (*cf.* AV), but this is clearly a secondary attempt to get around the problem. Why then the feminine form? Some have thought that James intends it literally, that he is now turning his attention to women in the church who are unfaithful to their marital vows. But the context gives no indication of this. It is the Old Testament that provides the explanation for the address. As stressed especially in the prophets, God has joined himself with the people Israel by graciously electing them and bringing them into covenant relationship with himself. This relationship is frequently portrayed with marital imagery (Is. 54:1–6; Je. 2:2). Thus, when that relationship is jeopardized by Israel's dalliance with other gods, the situation can be labelled 'adultery'. 'As a faithless wife leaves her husband, so have you been faithless to me, O house of Israel, says the LORD' (Je. 3:20). It is in Hosea that this theme finds its most poignant expression. The prophet's marriage to an unfaithful harlot is used to mirror the unfaithfulness of Israel to the LORD. Israel 'has played the harlot' (2:5), deserting her 'first husband', the LORD, in order to pursue other 'lovers', Baal and other false gods (2:7). Yet the LORD promises to show mercy to his people; they will again call him 'my husband' (2:16), for the LORD promises, 'I will betroth you to me in faithfulness; and you shall know the LORD' (2:20). Jesus made use of this imagery, calling those who rejected him 'an adulterous generation' (Mt. 12:39;

16:4). As these references suggest, this tradition always pictured the LORD as the 'husband', Israel as the 'wife'.

James' use of 'adulteresses' thus serves to characterize his readers as the unfaithful people of God. By seeking *friendship with the world* they are, in effect, committing 'spiritual adultery', and making themselves enemies of God. In the light of the Old Testament background, this must mean not only a hostility of the believer towards God, but of God towards the believer. God must judge those who break their covenant vows to him. Certainly James' readers were not overtly disclaiming God and consciously deciding to follow the world instead. But their 'jealousy', 'selfish ambition' and 'unrestrained passion', exhibiting as they did 'earthly, unspiritual and devilish' attitudes (3:15), amounted to just that. God will brook no rival, and when the believer behaves in a way characteristic of the world, he demonstrates that, at that point, his allegiance is to the world rather than to God. By drawing out the ultimate consequences of worldly behaviour in this way, James seeks to prick the consciences of his readers and to stimulate their repentance. They need to recognize that their selfish, quarrelsome behaviour is a serious matter indeed.

5. The striking and forceful application of the Old Testament imagery of God as the spouse of his people is the key to understanding this verse. It explains the seriousness of any flirtation with the world by bringing to mind the jealousy of the Lord, which demands a total, unreserved, unwavering allegiance from the people with whom he has joined himself. In understanding the verse this way we follow the translation found in the RSV and NASB. This translation takes *pneuma* (*spirit*) as the object of the verb *epipothei* (*yearn*); understands *pros phthonon* as adverbial (*jealously*)[1] and assumes that the subject of this verb is God.[2]

However, this interpretation is by no means the only possible one. The most important alternative is represented by the NIV translation: 'the spirit he caused to live in us tends towards envy'

[1] *Cf.* A. T. Robertson. *A Grammar of the Greek New Testament in the Light of Historical Research* (Broadman Press, 1934), p. 626.

[2] An interpretation that may be considered a variation of this one takes *pneuma* as the subject of the verb, but views it as the Holy Spirit within the believer, who jealously yearns for the Christian (*cf.* JB).

(*cf*.also AV, NEB, GNB, Phillips). In this rendering, *pneuma* is understood as the subject of the verse, and is identified with the 'spirit' breathed into man by God at creation (Gn. 2:7). James would then be making a point about the human tendency to be envious and jealous. This interpretation can marshal some impressive supporting arguments. Linguistically, James' language is said to be more appropriate in a description of man's attitude than of God's. *Phthonos*, translated 'envy' in the NIV, always has a negative connotation in biblical Greek, and is naturally never used with reference to God. Moreover, as we have seen, *phthonos* is a key word in the tradition that James has used in 3:13 – 4:3, and in this tradition the word always describes a sinful human attitude. Similarly, the word *epipotheō* ('yearn', 'desire') is never used with reference to God in biblical Greek. Contextually, a reminder about the innate human propensity to sinful jealousy would make excellent sense. James' readers would need to recognize the strength of this desire in order to take the necessary steps to deal with it. And, finally, a statement about human sin would provide a natural contrast with the 'greater grace' of God highlighted in verse 6.

While these points are not without substance, none is decisive. Since *phthonos* and *zēlos* are sometimes interchangeable (*cf*. 1 Macc. 8:16; Testament of Simeon 4:5; Testament of Gad 7:2), and the latter was frequently used of the 'jealousy' of God, it is not impossible to ascribe *phthonos* to God. Moreover, *phthonos* was occasionally used by Greek writers of the jealousy of the Olympian gods. Therefore, while unusual, James' uses of *phthonos* with respect to God's desire for his people is by no means impossible. Perhaps he has chosen the word because he has used *zēlos* negatively in 3:13 – 4:3. On the other hand, James' use of *epipotheō* ('desire'), far from being a point against the RSV rendering, actually favours it. While not used elsewhere of God, it always has a positive connotation in the New Testament. Moreover, it is only with great difficulty that the word can be taken to mean 'tend towards', as the alternative interpretation requires. It is also natural to give both verbs in the sentence the same subject, in which case 'God' must be the understood subject of *katōkisen* ('make to dwell').

Ultimately, the appropriateness of a reference to God's jealousy for his people in this context outweighs the undoubted linguistic difficulty posed by *phthonos*. Verse 5 clearly substantiates a point made in verse 4. That this point is human susceptibility to jealousy fits awkwardly, at best, in this context. But to see in verse 5 a reminder of God's desire that his people be wholly and unreservedly his provides a beautifully appropriate substantiation of the warning against any flirtation with the attitudes and the values of the world in verse 4.

It is not clear whether James thinks of *the spirit which he has made to dwell in us* as the Holy Spirit given to believers (*cf.* NASB) or as God's creative spirit by which he has invigorated mankind (Gn. 2:7). In either case, the phrase reminds us that God has a claim on us by virtue of his work in our lives. More difficult is the question of the passage to which James alludes. As we have seen, James' words do not closely reproduce any Old Testament text. This has led many scholars to suppose that James is citing an apocryphal text.[1] But *scripture* (*graphē*) is limited to references to the canonical Old Testament in the New Testament, and we are probably justified in thinking that James has in mind the theme of God's jealousy as it is expressed in such verses as Exodus 20:5; 34:14; Zechariah 8:2 and others.[2]

6. The interpretation of verse 5 will determine the meaning of the mild contrast found in verse 6a: *But (de) he gives more grace*. If verse 5b is taken as a statement about the sinfulness of the human spirit, the *more* or 'greater' (*meizona*) *grace* will suggest the ability and willingness of God to overcome sinfulness: 'he gives us grace potent enough to meet this and every other evil spirit' (Phillips). If, however, verse 5b depicts the jealousy of God for us, verse 6a will emphasize that God's grace is completely adequate to meet the requirements imposed on us by that jealousy. Our God is 'a

---

[1] Some popular suggestions: Apocalypse of Moses 31; the lost Book of Eldad and Modad; an unknown book (see Adamson, pp. 170–171, for a list of suggestions).

[2] While *graphē* usually introduces a single text, it introduces an allusive reference in Jn. 7:37–39. Laws argues that James implies a reference to verses like Ps. 42:1 and 84:2, which speak of the soul's 'longing' (*epipotheō*) for the Lord. She punctuates the sentence as a question – 'Is pious longing the proper manner of the soul's desire?' – and suggests that these verses provide the answer (Laws, pp. 174–179; and, in greater detail, 'Does Scripture Speak in Vain? A Reconsideration of James IV.5', *NTS* 30, 1974, pp. 210–215. *Cf.* also Adamson, pp. 170–173. Schlatter [p. 249] had already mentioned Ps. 42:1 in connection with this verse). But the interpretation demands too allusive a scriptural reference.

consuming fire' and his demands on us may seem terrifying. But our God is also merciful, gracious, all-loving, and willingly supplies all that we need to meet his all-encompassing demands. As Augustine has said, 'God gives what he demands'.

There is, however, a requirement for the experience of this grace: humility. This is the force of the quotation from Proverbs 3:34 and it becomes the dominant motif in the commands in verses 7–10. God's gift of sustaining grace can be received only by those willing to admit their need and accept the gift. The *proud*, on the other hand, meet only resistance from God. This is a theme that sounds throughout the Old Testament (*cf.* Pss. 18:27; 34:18; 51:17; 72:4; 138:6; Is. 61:1; Zp. 3:11–12). It is worth noting that 'pride' (*hyperēphania*) is often associated with jealousy; perhaps James would want us to see here an implicit condemnation of these jealous and selfish people whom he has criticized in 3:13 – 4:3.

7–8a. The series of commands in verses 7–10 flow from the quotation of Proverbs 3:34: if God, indeed, gives grace to the humble, it is clearly man's responsibility to *submit to God*. This imperative stands almost as a 'heading' over the following series of commands, and is matched by the command to 'humble yourselves' which concludes the series in verse 10. This latter command picks up the word 'humble' from the quotation of Proverbs, thereby giving a strong coherence to the paragraph. Between these two basic commands are three couplets: *Resist the devil . . . Draw near to God* (vv. 7b–8a); *Cleanse your hands . . . purify your hearts* (v. 8b); *Be wretched . . . Let your laughter be turned to mourning . . .* (v. 9). The aorist tense is used throughout, perhaps suggesting that these attitudes are to be entered into while the previous sinful behaviour is discarded. The whole context, from verse 6 on, is strikingly similar to 1 Peter 5:5–9: a quotation of Proverbs 3:34 (v. 5b) is followed by commands to 'Humble yourselves . . . so that in due time he [God] may exalt you' (v. 6) and to resist the devil (v. 9). James and Peter seem to use independently a traditional teaching that connected Proverbs 3:34 with the need for humility and resistance of the devil.

While James has earlier stressed the person's own evil tendency as being responsible for sin (1:14), he recognizes here the role of a supra-personal evil being. The word *diabolos* is used in the Septuagint to translate *śṭn*, the Hebrew word which gives us the title 'Satan'. The two titles are thus identical in meaning (*cf.* Rev. 20:2), both suggesting that one of the devil's primary purposes is 'to separate God and man'.[1] This separation the Christian must *resist*. When he does, James promises that the devil *will flee from you*.[2] Whatever power Satan may have, the Christian can be absolutely certain that he has been given the ability to overcome that power.

Instead of succumbing to Satan's desire to separate us from God, we should *draw near* to him. God, James promises, graciously responds by drawing near to us in turn. It should, of course, be obvious that James is not here talking about salvation, but about the repentance of those who are already Christians. Those who sincerely repent and return to God will find him, like the father of the prodigal son, eager to receive back his erring children.

8b-9. How it is that we are to 'draw near to God' is spelt out by the commands in verses 8b-9. Together, these call for a sincere and radical repentance from the sinful ways that James has described in 3:13 – 4:3. The two commands in verse 8b are formulated in a perfectly balanced parallelism, the imperative in each clause being followed by its object, with a pejorative address to the readers completing the clause. A note of blunt vividness is given the two clauses in the Greek by the lack of any articles or possessive pronouns. And this bluntness is also expressed by James' strongly negative descriptions of his readers: *sinners, men of double mind*. These create quite a contrast to James' familiar and affectionate address, 'brethren', and serve to impress on his readers the seriousness of the sins that they are involved with.

Men of double mind translates the word *dipsychos* ('two-souled') which James earlier used to characterize the person whose faith is marked by doubting and instability (1:6–8). In the present context, the term brings forcibly to mind the 'doubleness' of the Christian who seeks to become 'a friend of the world' (v. 4). God

---

[1] W. Foerster, *TDNT* 2, p. 73.
[2] In addition to 1 Peter, this idea is found in pre-Christian Judaism; *cf.* Testament of Naphtali 8:4; Issachar 7:7.

and 'the world', the kingdom of Christ and the kingdom of Satan, the age to come and this evil age – the Christian is pulled and torn between them. To allow 'the world' to entice us away from a total, single-minded allegiance to God is to become people who are divided in loyalties, 'double-minded' and spiritually unstable. James' readers, by exhibiting a jealousy and selfishness typical of this world (*cf.* 3:15), by failing to act on what they hear and say (1:19 – 2:26), in their 'double' use of the tongue (3:9–10) and in their violent disputes with one another (4:1–2), are guilty of this 'double-minded' attitude. What is required of them is a repentance from both this external behaviour (*cleanse your hands*) and this internal attitude (*purify your hearts*). 'Cleansing' and 'purifying' stem from the Old Testament provisions for priestly purity in ministering the things of the Lord, but both had also come to be used of ethical purity. Also stemming from the Old Testament is the juxtaposition of *hands* and *heart* to denote both deed and disposition. The Psalmist required 'clean hands and a pure heart' for those who would stand before the LORD (Ps. 24:3–4); James asks the same of those who would 'draw near to God'.

If the language of 8b reflects priestly traditions, the severe commands of verse 9 echo the language of the prophets. They often used the language of mourning to describe the disasters accompanying the judgments of God; but they also used it to call for God's people to repent from sin. Thus, Joel, warning of the nearness of 'the day of the LORD', pictures the Lord as inviting his people to ' "return to me with all your heart, with fasting, with weeping, and with mourning . . ." ' (2:12). It is in this sense that James uses this language. He, too, was firmly convinced of 'the nearness of the Lord' (5:8), and he demands of his readers a deep heartfelt sorrow for sin that is the mark of true repentance – what Paul called a 'godly grief . . . that leads to salvation and brings no regret' (2 Cor. 7:10). This is also how we are to understand James' command that *laughter be turned to mourning* and *joy to dejection*. James is no killjoy, denying any place for laughter and joy in the Christian life. But 'laughter' in the Old Testament and Judaism is often the scornful laughter of the fool (Ec. 7:6; Ecclus. 27:13) who blithely refuses to take sin seriously. It is the mark of the one who prospers in this world, without regard to the world to come. For this reason Jesus warned: 'Woe to you that laugh now, for you

shall mourn and weep' (Lk. 6:25b). What men will do when
God's judgment overtakes them can be avoided if they mourn
and weep for sin now. Jesus also said: 'Blessed are those who
mourn, for they shall be comforted' (Mt. 5:4). Many people in
our day, both outside the church and within it, are marked by
a superficial joy and brittle laughter. They live the hedonist
philosophy, 'eat, drink and be merry, for tomorrow we die',
that ignores the terrifying reality of God's judgment. But even
the committed Christian can slip into a casual attitude towards
sin, perhaps presuming too much on God's forgiving and
merciful nature. It is to all such people that James issues his
plea for a radical, thoroughgoing repentance. Only such
repentance can produce true Christian joy – the joy that
overflows from the consciousness of sins forgiven.

10. James concludes his series of commands with a summarizing exhortation, *Humble yourselves*, that reflects the
promise of the Proverbs quotations in verse 6: God 'gives grace
to the humble'. To 'humble ourselves before the Lord' means
to recognize our own spiritual poverty, to acknowledge conse-
quently our desperate need of God's help and to submit to his
commanding will for all our lives. This humility is beautifully
exemplified in the tax-collector of Jesus' parable, who, deeply
conscious of his sin, called out to God for mercy. In response,
Jesus pronounces him justified, and summarizes: 'every one
who exalts himself will be humbled, but he who humbles
himself will be exalted' (Lk. 18:14). This saying (parallel to
others where humility before other people is the point: Mt.
23:12; Lk. 14:11) was taken up as a popular motto in the early
church (*cf.* 2 Cor. 11:7; 1 Pet. 5:6). It expresses the fundamentally
important principle that the enjoyment of spiritual vitality and
victory comes not through independent effort of our own but
through complete dependence on the Lord. To try to 'exalt
ourselves' by relying on our own abilities, or status, or money
brings only failure and condemnation – God 'humbles us'.
James has expressed this earlier in his letter when he encouraged the 'humble' poor Christian to boast in his 'exaltation'
and warned the rich Christian to boast in his 'humiliation'
(1:9–10).

e. A prohibition of critical speech (4:11–12)

The connection between this section and its context is not immediately clear. It may be that speaking evil of others is to be seen as a manifestation of the pride God resists (4:6) and which is to be avoided by humility before God (4:10). On the other hand, 'speaking evil' (*katalalia*) is often linked to 'jealousy' (*zēlos*) (2 Cor. 12:20; 1 Pet. 2:1), 'selfishness' (2 Cor. 12:20), quarrels (*polemas* in Psalms of Solomon 12:3) and pride (Testament of Gad 3:3), and is seen as a manifestation of double-mindedness (Hermas, *Similitude* 8.7.2; see *Mandate* 2). Finally, the prominence of 'the law' and 'judging' in verses 11–12 corresponds to the theme of 2:8–13. Just as Leviticus 19:18 (the 'love command') was quoted there, so Leviticus 19:16, which prohibits slander, may be in James' mind here; the shift from 'brother' to 'neighbour' in verse 12 makes this especially plausible. These several possibilities suggest that verses 11–12 should be seen as a basically independent section which picks up a number of James' favourite themes. But the prominence of the tradition that links 'speaking evil' to the sins of jealousy, quarrelling and pride, which have been the focus of 3:13 – 4:10, suggests that they belong generally to this larger discussion. Perhaps verses 11–12 should be seen as a brief 'reprise' of the larger discussion of sins of speech that opened the section (3:1–12).

11. After the harsh, denunciatory tone of address in 4:8, suited to a strong call for repentance, James returns here to the more familiar *brethren*. The word *katalaleō* (RSV *speak evil against*) means literally 'to speak against' and describes many kinds of harmful speech: questioning legitimate authority, as when the people of Israel 'spoke against God and against Moses' (Nu. 21:5); slandering someone in secret (Ps. 101:5); bringing incorrect accusations (1 Pet. 2:12; 3:16). The form of James' prohibition (*mē* with a present imperative) implies that his readers were speaking against each other in one or more of these ways, and needed to stop doing so. Perhaps the dissensions that were racking the church (3:13 – 4:3) provided the context for personal attack and slanderous accusations – even debates that focus on 'issues' generally descend to such personal abuse at some point.

James' justification for his prohibition is interesting: to speak against or to judge one's *brother* is to speak against or to judge *the law*. The *law* to which James refers could be the Old Testament law, especially since James may be depending on Leviticus 19:16 ('You shall not go up and down as a slanderer among your people, and you shall not stand forth against the life of your neighbour: I am the LORD'). But since 2:8 (*cf.* also 1:25; 2:12) shows that James considers the Levitical 'love command' to have been taken up into the law of the kingdom of God, we should probably identify *the law* here also with that wider body of teaching, focused especially on the teaching of Jesus, that James considers authoritative for Christians. How is it that 'judging' a fellow believer involves 'judging' this law? Since James contrasts 'judging the law' with 'doing the law', he apparently thinks that failure to do the law involves an implicit denial of the law's authority. However high and orthodox our view of God's law might be, a failure actually to do it says to the world that we do not *in fact* put much store by it. Again we see coming to the surface James' understanding of Christianity as something whose reality is to be tested by the measure of obedience.

12. Speaking evil of fellow Christians is wrong not only because it involves 'judging the law'; it is wrong also because it involves 'judging the neighbour'. And this critical, condemnatory judgment involves both disobedience of the demand that we love the neighbour *and* an arrogant presumption on the rights of God himself. For he is the *one lawgiver and judge* who alone has the ability to determine the eternal fate of his creatures (*cf.* also Mt. 10:28). Yet when we criticize and condemn others, we are in fact pronouncing our own verdict over their spirituality and destiny. This charge shows that James is not prohibiting the proper, and necessary, discrimination that every Christian should exercise. Nor is he forbidding the right of the community to exclude from its fellowship those it deems to be in flagrant disobedience to the standards of the faith, or to determine right and wrong among its members (1 Cor. 5 and 6). James' concern is with jealous, censorious speech by which we condemn others as being wrong in the sight of God. It is this sort of judging that Paul condemned among the Roman

Christians, who were apparently questioning the reality of one another's faith because of differing views on the applicability of some ritual laws (Rom. 14:1–13; cf. especially vv. 3–4 and 10–13). It is entirely possible that some situation like this was responsible for the problems James addresses. A bitter, selfish spirit (3:13–18) had given rise to quarrels and disputes about certain matters in the church (4:1–2). These disputes were apparently conducted, as they usually are, with a notable absence of restraint in the use of the tongue (3:1–12), including perhaps cursings (3:10) and denunciations (4:11–12) of one another. Such behaviour is nothing more than a manifestation of a worldly spirit (3:15; 4:1, 4). It must be replaced by 'the wisdom from above', with its meekness, reasonableness and peaceableness (3:17). This flirtation with the world must be seen to be incompatible with God's jealous desire to have his people's whole-hearted allegiance (4:4–5). Yet God is willing to turn and bestow his favour if sinful pride can give way to deep-felt repentance and sincere abasement before him (4:6–10).

V. IMPLICATIONS OF A CHRISTIAN WORLD-VIEW (4:13–5:11)

The fourth general grouping of James' exhortations has as its unifying theme the Christian perspective on the period of time in which the church lives. This perspective is the touchstone for each major topic in 4:13 – 5:11. 4:13–17 prohibits an arrogant, boastful attitude that neglects to take into account the transitoriness of this life. In 5:1–6 James pronounces judgment on rich oppressors because they have lived lives of self-centred luxury 'in the last days' – days that are quickly moving towards a climactic day of judgment. Christians, on the other hand, must exercise patience as they wait for this day to dawn, and should remain steadfast in their faith as they encounter trials (5:7–11).

a. A condemnation of arrogance (4:13–17)

Several expositors take this section closely with 4:11–12 or 4:1–12, singling out arrogance or worldliness as the unifying theme.

153

However, while the attitude of those who presume to stand in judgment of others may be labelled arrogant, James does not highlight this. And the identical introductions to 4:13–17 and 5:1–6 (*Come now*) strongly suggest that James saw them as closely linked. Moreover, these sections are associated also by the theme of wealth. To be sure, those described in 4:13–17 are not explicitly said to be rich, but the extensive travel plans mentioned in verse 13 implies that they were well-off, and their intention is to 'get gain'. Both paragraphs 4:13–17 and 5:1–6, then, criticize 'people of the world' for leaving God and his values out of their way of life. However, while the rich in 5:1–6 are unreservedly condemned, the businessmen in 4:13–17 are exhorted to change their attitudes. It is not their wealth that James criticizes, but their boastful arrogance. This suggests that the businessmen addressed in this paragraph are probably Christians. However, James' failure to address them as 'brethren' and the lack of overtly Christian presuppositions suggest that he may also have in mind people outside the church.

13. *Come now* (*age nyn*) is not used here as a true imperative, as its singular form (with plural *legontes*, 'saying', following) demonstrates. It is a form of address that is found elsewhere, particularly in 'popular' Greek style. Combined with *you who say*, it gives to James' language a rather brusque tone. These businessmen whom James addresses are characterized as deliberate and self-confident planners. They decide where they will go, when they will go, how long they will stay, and they are absolutely certain that they will gain profit from their venture. The picture James paints here would be familiar to his readers. The first century was a period of great commercial activity, and especially the Hellenistic cities of Palestine (the Decapolis, for instance) were heavily involved in commerce of various kinds. Many Jews were active in these business comings-and-goings; large numbers had settled in cities throughout the Mediterranean world for commercial reasons. It need hardly be said that the people James pictures are easily recognized also by the modern reader. The distance between cities may be greater, the means of transportation quicker and the business activities different, but in James' day, and ours, the 'bottom line' is the same – profit. As the following verses demonstrate, however, it is not the desire to make a profit that James criticizes. He is concerned rather about the exclusively this-worldly context in which the plans are made – a danger, it must be said, to which business people are particularly susceptible.

14. In laying their plans with reference only to this world, these business people have failed to reckon with a fundamental fact – the insubstantial and transitory nature of 'this world'. For such people as they are (a paraphrase of the indefinite relative *hoitines*) to plan so confidently is the height of foolishness. This, the main point of verse 14, is clear, although the precise way in which James expresses it is debated. The RSV (along with AV, NIV and NEB) divides the first part of the verse into two parts: a statement, *you do not know about tomorrow,* and a question, *What is your life?* Other versions combine these into a single statement: 'you do not know what your life will be like tomorrow' (NASB; *cf.* also GNB and the punctuation of the Nestle-Aland (26th edition) and United Bible Societies (3rd edition) Greek texts). The situation is complicated by the presence of several variant readings.[1] Without rehearsing all the arguments, the decisive consideration seems to be the placement of *poios* (*what*), which is most awkward if it is construed as the object of *epistasthe* (*know*).[2] It is more naturally taken as the introduction to a separate question, as in the RSV translation.

The answer to this question, then, is given in the last part of the verse, in which life is compared to *a mist* (*atmis*). This word could also be translated 'a puff of smoke' (GNB, Phillips; *cf.* Acts 2:19), and has some affinity with the 'vanities' of life that Ecclesiastes talks so much about. Whatever the exact meaning, James obviously intends to emphasize the extremely short duration of life. Illness, accidental death, or the return of Christ could cut short our lives just as quickly as the morning sun dissipates the mist or as a shift in wind direction blows away smoke. This

---

[1] See B. M. Metzger, *A Textual Commentary on the Greek New Testament* (United Bible Societies, 1971), pp. 683–684 and Ropes, pp. 278–279, for discussion of these variants.

[2] In the New Testament *poios* always occurs closely with a verb of knowing when it is its object. It is separated from it only by the subject of the verb (see Mt. 24:42 and 43; Lk. 9:55; 12:39; Rev. 3:3).

realistic reckoning with the brevity and uncertainty of life, and even the images used to describe it, are found frequently in Scripture. Proverbs 27:1 warns: 'Do not boast about tomorrow, for you do not know what a day may bring forth'. Job 7:7, 9, 16 and Psalm 39:5–6 describe life as a 'breath'. Particularly close to James' teaching are, as so often, some words of Jesus. In Luke 12:15, he warns the crowds about covetousness and reminds them that 'a man's life does not consist in the abundance of his possessions'. In a brief parable, he illustrated his point with a rich man, who, like James' businessman, made definite plans for acquiring more goods, but who was prevented from executing his plans by his death (Lk. 12:16–20). This passage contains several themes that James utilizes both here and in 5:1–6 and it is quite possible that it has furnished the stimulus for his own exhortations.

15. *Instead* of (*anti*) the self-confident, this-world-oriented attitude expressed in verse 13, the business people should qualify all of their plans and hopes with reference to the will of the Lord. What must be recognized is that this world is not a closed system; that an influence quite outside the material sphere ultimately determines the success and failure of plans – indeed, the very continuation of life itself. Such a conception is not, of course, specifically Christian. Any world-view that is not narrowly materialistic would naturally incorporate this perspective. Thus it is not surprising that the formula 'if God wills' or 'if the gods will' is widespread in pre-Christian Greek philosophy and religion.[1] The very generality of the phrase has led some commentators to suppose that James may have in view non-Christians in this paragraph. However, it should not be overlooked that James speaks of *the Lord* rather than 'God'; and although the reference is probably to God the Father rather than to Jesus, the implication of God's control of history through Christ is not far removed. Thus, however widespread the phrase may have been, James 'baptizes' it in service of a specifically biblical world-view of history and its sovereign ruler.

According to the best texts (which read the indicative *zēsomen*,

---

[1] Dibelius (pp. 233–234) cites a number of texts.

we shall live, rather than the subjunctive *zēsōmen*, 'if we live'), the will of the Lord is to be acknowledged as the condition under which the Christian is to view both his life itself and his specific plans.[1] This Paul did, as he frequently expressed his submission to the Lord's will in his plans for missionary work (Acts 18:21; Rom. 1:10, 1 Cor. 4:19; 16:7; *cf.* Heb. 6:3). However, as Calvin pertinently observes, Paul and the other apostles do not always *state* this condition; what was important was that 'they had it as a principle fixed in their minds, that they would do nothing without the permission of God'. What James encourages is not the constant verbalization of the formula *If the Lord wills*, which can easily become a glib and meaningless recitation, but a sincere appreciation for God's control of affairs and for his specific will for us.

16. James now traces the failure to take God into account in making plans to its root – arrogant pride. Most English translations suggest that 'arrogance' qualifies 'boasting' as describing the *manner* of the boasting (*cf.* NIV, 'boast and brag'; RSV, *you boast in your arrogance*). But when *in* (*en*) follows *boast* (*kauchaomai*) in the New Testament, it always signifies the object in which one boasts, and the plural 'arrogances', 'matters of arrogance' (*alazoneiais*) also supports this interpretation. Phillips perfectly captures the resultant meaning: 'you get a certain pride in yourself in planning your future with such confidence'. It is this 'pride of life', this arrogant sense of self-sufficiency and self-importance, that John deplores as characteristic of the world (1 Jn. 2:16; see also Rom. 1:30; 2 Tim. 3.4). People not only leave God out of account in planning their lives; it is the essence of sin that they brag about it as well – 'I' takes centre stage in place of God. This kind of boasting is *evil*, then, not because of the arrogant manner in which it is done; it is evil because the objects of the boasting are instances of arrogant disregard for God.

17. Commentators are nearly unanimous in viewing this verse as a traditional saying that circulated independently of this

---

[1]The *kai* preceding *zēsomen* may then be taken as equivalent to a Semitic *waw* introducing an apodosis (BDF, #442 [71]) or be construed with the second *kai* in a 'both . . . and' construction (Davids, p. 173).

context. Not only does the sudden shift to the third person suggest this, but the verse fits somewhat awkwardly in the paragraph. Nevertheless, James does connect it to the preceding verses with an *oun* ('therefore', omitted by RSV), thereby indicating that he sees some point of contact. Laws thinks that James may still have in mind Proverbs 3, from which he has quoted in 4:6. Verses 27–28 of that chapter prohibit any delay in doing good to the neighbour – and in the Septuagint this prohibition is based on the consideration that 'you do not know what the next day will bring forth'. With this Old Testament tradition in mind, then, James' criticism of one who fails to do good may be seen as a second implication of the transitoriness of life, stated in verse 14. It is doubtful, however, whether so allusive a reference provides a sufficient explanation. Another suggestion is that James is indirectly rebuking the merchants for failing to do good with their money. But however widespread this motif may have been, it fits poorly here, since James is not yet talking about riches *per se*. More probable is the supposition that James adds the saying as an encouragement to do what he has just commanded. He has told his readers *what is right*; if they now *fail to do it*, they are sinning. They cannot take refuge in the plea that they have done nothing positively wrong; as Scripture makes abundantly clear, sins of *omission* are as real and serious as sins of *commission*. The servant in Jesus' parable who fails to use the money he was entrusted with (Lk. 19:11–27); the 'goats' who failed to care for the outcasts of society (Mt. 25:31–46) – they are condemned for what they failed to do.[1] Another teaching of Jesus reminds us very forcibly of James' words here: 'that servant who knew his master's will, but did not make ready or act according to his will, shall receive a severe beating' (Lk. 12:47).

b. A condemnation of those who misuse wealth (5:1–6)

This section is closely related to 4:13–17 both in style – the two are introduced with the imperitival *age nyn, Come now* – and in content – a pursuit of wealth that disregards God and his purposes in history is condemned in both. But the prominence of the

[1] See the excursus in Tasker, pp. 106–108.

eschatological consummation ties 5:1–6 closely to 5:7–11 also. If 4:13–17 is directed both to the church and to the world, and 5:7–11 clearly to the church, 5:1–6 unmistakably addresses non-Christians. This is clear both from the many biblical and extra-biblical traditions concerning unrighteous wealth that James utilizes, and from James' failure to hold out any prospect of deliverance for those whom he condemns in this paragraph. The rich people pictured are clearly wealthy landowners, a class accused of economic exploitation and oppression from early times. In James' surroundings, we may think particularly of Palestinian Jewish landlords, who owned large estates and were often concerned only about how much profit could be gained from their lands. James proceeds to announce the condemnation of these rich landholders (v. 1) and justifies their condemnation on the grounds of their selfish hoarding of wealth (vv. 2–3), their defrauding of their workers (v. 4), their self-indulgent lifestyle (v. 5) and their oppression of 'the righteous' (v. 6).

Why does James preach this message of denunciation of non-Christians in a letter addressed to the church? Calvin appropriately isolates two main purposes: James '. . . has a regard to the faithful, that they, hearing of the miserable end of the rich, might not envy their fortune, and also that knowing that God would be the avenger of the wrongs they suffered, they might with a calm and resigned mind bear them'.[1]

1. James speaks in the tones of the Old Testament prophets. *Weep* (*klaiō*) and *howl* (*ololyzō*, an onomatopoeic word, sounding like what it describes) are frequently used by the prophets to describe the reaction of the wicked when the day of the LORD comes (*cf., e.g.*, Is. 13:6; 15:3; Am. 8:3). In fact, *ololyzō* is found only in the prophets in the Old Testament and always in the context of judgment. This background makes clear that *the miseries that are coming upon* the rich refer not to earthly, temporal suffering, but to the condemnation and punishment that God will mete out to them on the day of judgment.

James' denunciation of the rich picks up and develops a per-

[1]Calvin, p. 342. Wessel suggests, further, that the preaching may represent a prophetic attempt to reach non-Christians who were frequenting Christian assemblies (*ISBE*, 2, p. 965).

vasive biblical theme. God's concern for the poor is reflected in many of the Mosaic laws giving direction for life in the covenant. In Israel's later history, these laws were ignored and the poor were often oppressed and taken advantage of by wealthy, powerful Israelites. Hence, 'the rich' occasionally becomes a synonym for 'the unrighteous' in Wisdom traditions (cf. Pr. 10:15–16; 14:20), and many of the prophets were especially outspoken in their condemnation of rich oppressors (cf. Amos). This theme was very prominent in intertestamental Jewish literature (cf. especially 1 Enoch 94–105) and found a secure place within the New Testament. Jesus, especially in Luke's Gospel, has much to say about the dangers of wealth. In a saying particularly close to James' teaching, he pronounced a woe upon the rich and warned that their 'consolation' in this world would be replaced by 'mourning' and 'weeping' in the next (Lk. 6:24–25). Revelation 18:10–24 is a lengthy 'woe' directed to the 'merchants of the earth' who 'weep and mourn' over the devastation of 'the great city', Babylon. In all this, it is not always easy to determine the basis on which the rich are being judged. But although some traditions appear to condemn the rich merely because they are rich, in the New Testament, at least, condemnations of wealthy people are almost always attributed to a *misuse* of wealth. Certainly James' enumeration of the sins of the rich people that he condemns shows that this is the case here. It is particularly obvious that James does not intend to pronounce judgment on all rich people if, as we have argued, James 1:10 implies the presence of rich Christians among James' readers. The designation *you rich* in verse 1, therefore, essentially means, as so often in Scripture, the *unrighteous* rich. Having said this, it would be wrong to ignore the fact that 'the rich' and 'the unrighteous' are so easily associated; Scripture warns that wealth can be a particularly strong obstacle to Christian discipleship. Not for nothing did Jesus warn, 'It will be hard for a rich man to enter the kingdom of heaven' (Mt. 19:23). (See, further, the section 'Poverty and wealth' in the Introduction, pp. 53–55.)

2–3. The first indictment of the rich has to do with the worthlessness of the worldly goods that they have so carefully assimilated. James singles out three classes of material goods.

Riches (*ploutos*) is sometimes understood as a reference to crops, with *garments* and *gold and silver* then specifying the two other most common forms of wealth in the ancient world. But it is more likely to be a general summarizing term for any wealth; *rot* (*sēpō*) can refer to the decay or transitoriness of all forms of human endeavour (Ecclus. 14:19). The *moth-eaten* garments remind us strongly of Jesus' similar warning about the transitoriness of 'earthly treasures' that are consumed by moths (Mt. 6:20). James' reference to the *rusting* of gold and silver has sometimes been taken as an indication of his impoverished background since, of course, these precious metals cannot, in fact, rust. But the word *rust* (*ios*) was already being applied to gold and silver (Epistle of Jeremiah 10) and the image seems to have become a traditional way of designating the temporality of even the most precious metals (*cf.* also Ecclus. 29:10). All three statements, in fact, reflect the traditional Old Testament and Jewish teaching about the foolishness of placing reliance upon perishable material goods.

It is striking, however, that James uses the perfect tense in all three clauses to designate the perishing of these riches. Many commentators take these perfect tense verbs as 'prophetic' or 'proleptic' perfects: the destruction of these goods in the 'miseries' of the judgment is so certain that it can be described as already present. Ropes, however, protests that James' shift to the future tense when depicting the judgment in verse 3 ('their rust *will* be evidence against you and *will* eat your flesh') renders this suggestion implausible. It is probably better, then, to take the perfect tenses with their natural force, and to see them as emphasizing the present worthless state of the rich people's possessions. Probably this is to be understood figuratively, in the sense that the riches provide no spiritual benefit in the present nor do they give grounds for hope at the judgment.

Not only will wealth bring no long-lasting benefit – its 'decay' will testify against the rich at the judgment and bring a guilty verdict upon them: *eating the flesh like fire* is an image of God's judgment (Judith 16:17). The reason for this judgment may simply be because the rich have concentrated on the accumulation of earthly treasure to the exclusion of heavenly treasure, thereby plainly indicating where their 'heart' is (*cf.* Mt. 6:19–21). On the other hand, the hoarding of wealth by the rich is condemned (in at least one passage that James may have been familiar with) because it was put to no use in aiding the poor: 'Help a poor man for the commandment's sake, and because of his need do not send him away empty. Lose your silver for the sake of a brother or a friend, and do not let it rust under a stone and be lost. Lay up your treasure according to the commandments of the Most High, and it will profit you more than gold' (Ecclus. 29:9–11). The same sentiment is found in the Lucan version of Jesus' words about treasure: 'Sell your possessions, and give alms; provide yourselves with purses that do not grow old, with a treasure in the heavens that does not fail, where no thief approaches and no moth destroys' (Lk. 12:33). The hoarding of wealth is wrong not just because it demonstrates utterly false priorities; it is doubly sinful because it also deprives others of their very life.[1] This is another instance in which *failing* to do good is sin (4:17): 'God has not appointed gold for rust, nor garments for moths; but, on the contrary, he has designed them as aids and helps to human life' (Calvin). In this sense, James may intend the decay of the goods described in verses 2–3a to be understood, at least in part, literally: the actual evidence of disuse will stand as a witness against the rich.

James summarizes this first indictment of the rich at the end of verse 3: *You have laid up treasure for the last days. Ethēsaurisate* ('lay up treasure') may have as its object 'fire' or a word to be supplied, such as 'wrath' (*cf.* Rom. 2:5), but a more striking image is yielded if, as in Luke 12:21, the verb is taken absolutely: 'laying up treasure', the hoarding of material things in itself is what James condemns. It may be, as the RSV translation suggests, that this laying up of treasure is semi-ironical: the rich have assiduously 'stored up' for themselves, all right, but what they have stored up is the 'misery' that will be theirs when *the last days*, the time of judgment, arrive. But the preposition James uses before 'last days' (*en*) is more naturally translated 'in', and it is the pervasive belief of New Testament Christians that they were themselves living in *the last days* (Acts 2:17; 2 Tim. 3:1; Heb. 1:2; 2 Pet. 3:3 (?); 1 Jn. 2:18; Jude 18). The application of this expression to their own time testified to the early Christians' belief that they were living in

---

[1] *Cf.*, most clearly, Dibelius, p. 236; Davids, p. 176; and Tasker, pp. 110–111.

that era when God's promises were coming to fulfilment; an era of indefinite duration immediately preceding the climax of history. James shares this perspective, as his conviction about the nearness of the *parousia* makes clear (5:8). What James is saying, then, is that those who are avidly accumulating wealth in his day are particularly sinful, because they utterly disregard the demands made upon people by the display of God's grace in Christ, and especially foolish, because they ignore the many signs of the rapidly approaching judgment. Like the rich fool, they failed to reckon with sudden judgment (Lk. 12:15–21). 'It is in *the last days* that you are laying up treasure'! As those who live in these 'last days', we, too, should recognize in the grace of God already displayed and the judgment of God yet to come a powerful stimulus to share, not hoard, our wealth.

4. A second charge that James levels against the rich is more specific: they have defrauded[1] their workers of their pay. The circumstances pictured by James are very much true to life. First-century Palestine, before AD 70, witnessed an increasing concentration of land in the hands of a small group of very wealthy landowners. As a result, the smallholdings of many farmers were assimilated into these large estates, and these farmers were forced to earn their living by hiring themselves out to their rich landlords. Jesus' parable about the workers in the vineyard (Mt. 20:1–16) is cast against this familiar rural background, and it is significant that the workers expect their pay at the end of the day. Indeed, this was commanded in the law: 'You shall not oppress a hired servant who is poor and needy, whether he is one of your brethren or one of the sojourners who are in your land within your towns; you shall give him his hire on the day he earns it, before the sun goes down (for he is poor, and sets his heart upon it); lest he cry against you to the LORD, and it be sin in you' (Dt. 24:14–15). Such warnings are found elsewhere, for instance in Leviticus 19:13 (another possible instance of James' use of this chapter), and in Malachi 3:5 where, significantly, oppression of 'the hireling in his wages' is associated with

---

[1] Two early, excellent manuscripts (א and B) read the verb *aphystereō*, 'defraud', here, but the majority of manuscripts have *apostereō* 'withhold'. The difference in meaning is not great, since the latter certainly connotes an illegitimate, fraudulent action.

oppression of 'the widow and the orphan' (*cf*. Jas. 1:27). Prompt payment would have been very important for the labourer, who often got by at a barely subsistence level and who needed a steady income to provide 'daily bread' for himself and his family. In a society where credit was not readily available, the failure to pay workers promptly could jeopardize life itself.

James is convinced, however, that the rich will not get away with their sin. In a vivid image reminiscent of Cain's blood crying out to God (Gn. 4:10), James pictures the wages themselves 'crying out', making God aware of the sin and pleading for vindication (*cf*. Ps. 18:6). What the rich think they do in secret, and without danger of prosecution, is not hidden from *the Lord of hosts*. *Hosts* translates *Sabaōth* (*cf*. AV, NASB), which is itself the transliteration of a Hebrew word that means 'army'. The title *Lord of hosts* thus pictures God as the almighty, powerful leader of a great army. Sometimes this army is an earthly one, as when David expresses his confidence in the outcome of his fight by claiming to come 'in the name of the LORD of hosts, the God of the armies of Israel' (1 Sa. 17:45). More often it is the heavenly host that God is pictured as leading. It was 'the LORD of hosts' whom Isaiah saw in his famous vision (Is. 6), and the title became a favourite one of his. He uses it often in descriptions of the judgments that God will bring upon Israel and the nations and sometimes, as in Isaiah 5:9, this judgment is linked specifically to oppression of the poor. Therefore, when James affirms that the wrongdoing of the rich has become known to God, he makes clear that this God is holy, powerful and determined to judge those who infringe his commandments.

Because the accusation of withholding wages is a traditional description of the depravity of the rich, it has been suggested that James is not intending to describe conditions that actually existed in his day. But while it may be that the tradition has influenced James in singling out this particular sin, it is almost certain that the rich whom James chastises were actually guilty of this sin also.

5. The pursuit of a luxurious lifestyle that is selfish and unconcerned about others' needs is the third accusation brought against the rich. To be sure, James says simply that the rich *have* *lived on the earth in luxury and in pleasure,* but it is clear both from this context and from scriptural parallels that this description implies an uncaring self-indulgence. The verb *spatalaō* which James uses here is found elsewhere in Scripture only in 1 Timothy 5:6 and in Ezekiel 16:49 (LXX) where the people of Sodom are condemned for their 'prosperous ease' and for not aiding 'the poor and needy'. The force of the other verb James uses, *tryphaō*, can be appreciated in light of 2 Peter 2:13, which uses the cognate noun *tryphē* to denote the daytime 'revelling' in which depraved false teachers delight. Even the easily over-looked phrase *on the earth* bears clear negative connotations, suggesting a contrast between the pleasures the rich have enjoyed in this world and the torment that awaits them in eternity. An illuminating parallel is found in Abraham's words to the rich man 'who feasted sumptuously every day': 'Son, remember that you in your lifetime received your good things, and Lazarus in like manner evil things; but now he is comforted here, and you are in anguish' (Lk. 16:25).

It is in the light of this 'reversal of fortunes' scheme that we are to understand the last clause of verse 5: *you have fattened your hearts in a day of slaughter.* Some commentators take *day of slaughter* as a reference to any time when the poor suffer horribly while the rich are indulging themselves: 'You can live riotously while it goes badly for the pious' (Dibelius). But the popularity of the tradition that contrasts earthly luxury with future judgment, along with the parallel between 'you have fattened your hearts in a day of slaughter' and 'you have laid up treasure in the last days' (v. 3), suggests rather that *the day of slaughter* is a vivid description of the day of judgment. While not found in the Septuagint, the phrase has an equivalent in the Hebrew text of Isaiah 30:25 (v. 24, Heb.), where the day of the Lord is pictured. The pseudepigraphical 1 Enoch also uses the phrase to describe the judgment (90:4) and in a context that has many parallels to James 5:1–6. Moreover, the Bible often uses the imagery of a slaughter in battle to describe the day of judgment (*cf., e.g.,* Ezk. 7:14–23; Rev. 19:17–21). James' point then, as in verse 3, is that the rich are selfishly and ignorantly going about accumulating wealth for themselves and wastefully spending it on their own pleasures in the very day when God's judgment is imminently threatened.[1] The 'last days' have already begun; the judgment *could* break in at any time – yet the rich, instead of acting to avoid that judgment, are, by their selfish indulgence, incurring greater guilt. They are like cattle being fattened for the kill.

6. The final accusation against the rich is that they have *condemned* and *killed the righteous man*. Some have understood *the righteous man* to be Jesus, or even James 'the Just' himself (assuming, of course, that a later writer has used James' name), but it is far better to take the reference generically, as a way of describing the kind of man whom the rich persecute. This 'righteous man' is one who is 'poor and needy' and who trusts in God for his deliverance. He is often pictured as being persecuted by the wicked rich. In Wisdom 2:6–20, for instance, the desire of the wicked who live luxuriously in this life, with no thought for tomorrow, is to 'oppress the righteous poor man' (v. 10) and to 'condemn him to a shameful death' (v. 20). It is this widespread Jewish tradition (*cf.* also Pss. 10:8–9; 37:32) that James utilizes here to describe the excesses of the rich (*cf.* also Jas. 2:5–7). What does James mean when he says that the rich *have killed the righteous man*? This may refer to the practical outcome of the failure of the rich to share their possessions and to pay the wages of their workers: 'to take away a neighbour's living is to murder him; to deprive an employee of his wages is to shed blood' (Ecclus. 34:22). However, *condemn* (*katadikazō*) is a judicial term, and suggests rather that the rich are using, and perhaps perverting, the legal processes available to them to accumulate property and to gain wealth. Such activities had long been practised in Israel, and were roundly condemned by the prophets (*cf.* Am. 2:6; 5:12; Mi. 2:2, 6–9; 3:1–3, 9–12; 6:9–16).

As does the RSV, virtually all modern translations (NASB, NIV, NEB, JB, GNB, Phillips) take the last clause of the paragraph as a

---

[1]A. Feuillet has argued that this day of judgment may be not the final, end-of-history judgment, but the judgment that fell on Jerusalem and the Jews in the Roman conquest of AD 70. He contends that this was an early Christian conception of the *parousia* found also in Matthew 24 ('Le sens du mot Parousie dans l'Evangile de Matthieu – comparison entre Matth. xxiv et Jac. v, 1–11', *The Background of the New Testament and its Eschatology*, ed. W. D. Davies and D. Daube [Cambridge University Press, 1964], pp. 261–288). Quite apart from the question of the relation of AD 70 to the *parousia*, Feuillet's interpretation is too specific for the context.

statement: *he does not resist you*. Presumably this would be understood as a reference to the non-resistance of the poor, afflicted
righteous (*cf.* Mt. 5:39; Rom. 12:14): the oppression of the rich is
all the more heinous in that their victims refuse, or are unable, to
retaliate. However, it is possible to translate the clause as a
question, expecting the answer 'yes': 'does he not resist you?'
The subject of the verb could then be God (*cf.* the Twentieth
Century New Testament) or Christ, and the reference be to the
future judgment: 'will not God stand against you?' Alternatively,
the subject of the question could be 'the righteous man' and the
reference be to the attempts of the righteous to 'oppose the
actions' of the rich in this life (as in Wisdom 2:12); to the pleas for
vindication that the righteous, though perhaps dead, continue to
utter (*cf.* Rev. 6:9–11); or to the witness of the righteous against
the rich at the judgment. Of these, the first and generally accepted interpretation makes best sense. Although it has been criticized as being anticlimactic, the simple assertion that the righteous man is not resisting his rich oppressor 'brings the section to
an end on a note of majestic pathos' (Tasker).

c. An encouragement to endure patiently (5:7–11)

Psalm 37 is a marvellous song of encouragement directed to the
righteous. They are described as 'poor and needy' (v. 14) and as
suffering persecution at the hand of the wicked (vv. 12–15,
32–33). They are tempted to be envious of the prosperity and
well-being of the wicked (vv. 1, 7) and, somewhat paradoxically,
also to be impatient for the wicked to receive judgment. In this
situation, the psalmist encourages the righteous to 'be still before
the LORD' (v. 7); to 'refrain from anger' (v. 8), for God will
certainly vindicate the righteous and destroy the wicked (vv.
34–40). James writes to righteous people, mainly poor, who were
suffering from similar circumstances. His advice is the same as
the psalmist's: 'be patient', for the 'coming of the Lord', when the
wicked will be judged (5:1–6) and the righteous delivered, 'is
near'.

7. The transition from denunciation of rich non-Christians to
encouragement of believers is signalled by James' return to his

familiar address: *brethren. Therefore (oun)* shows that this encouragement is based on the prophetic condemnation of wicked, rich oppressors in 5:1–6: since God will punish these oppressors, the believers need to wait patiently for that time. *Patience* is clearly the key idea in this paragraph. It is expressed with the root *makrothym-* four times (vv. 7 (twice), 8, 10) and with the root *hypomon-* twice (v. 11). The latter root has figured prominently in chapter 1, where James encouraged his readers to 'endure' the trials they were experiencing. The two roots are often distinguished, *makrothym-* usually being used to indicate the long-suffering, loving attitude we are to have towards others (1 Cor. 13:4; Eph. 4:2; 1 Thes. 5:14), while *hypomon-* generally denotes the strong, determined attitude with which we are to face difficult circumstances (2 Thes. 1:4). However, no sharp difference in meaning can be found in this paragraph: the *makrothymia* of the prophets (v. 10) does not appear to differ from the *hypomonē* of Job (v. 11). A similar overlap in meaning can be observed in the Testament of Joseph 2:7, where Joseph, after successfully fighting against the temptation of Potiphar's wife, says 'perseverance (*makrothymia*) is a powerful medicine and endurance (*hypomonē*) provides many good things' (see also Col. 1:11). Nevertheless, *makrothymia* retains a more specific sense in verses 7–8, where it describes not fortitude in trials, but a patient, expectant waiting on the Lord.

Specifically, James encourages patience *until the coming of the Lord. Until (heōs)* has a 'pregnant' sense here, suggesting the idea of a goal as well as a time period: 'exercise patience as you wait for, and look for, the coming of the Lord'. *Parousia,* 'presence' or *coming,* became a technical term in the early church for the expected return of Jesus in glory to judge the wicked (Mt. 24:37, 39; 2 Thes. 2:8) and deliver the saints (1 Cor. 15:23; 1 Thes. 2:19; 3:13; 4:15; 5:23). This tradition strongly suggests that *the Lord* here is Jesus rather than God the Father (though *cf.* 2 Pet. 3:12).

As an example of patience, James cites *the farmer* who must patiently wait for the earth to produce *the precious fruit* on which his livelihood depends. Although the word *rain* is not actually used in this text (some manuscripts add it; others have 'fruit'), the reference of *the early and the late* is certainly to the rains that fell on Palestine in the late Autumn and early Spring and which were so vital for agriculture (*cf.* Dt. 11:14).[1] While it is possible that the image, being a traditional Old Testament phrase, says nothing about the provenance of the letter, it is more probable that James uses the language because it fits the circumstances of his readers.

8. As the farmer waits patiently for the seed to sprout and the crops to mature, believers must wait patiently for the Lord to return to deliver them and to judge their oppressors. And while they wait, they need to *establish* (*stērizō*) their hearts. Paul gave the same exhortation to the Thessalonians as they awaited the *parousia* (1 Thes. 3:13; *cf.* 2 Thes. 2:17) and the author to the Hebrews commended the 'strengthening of the heart by grace' as an antidote to false teaching (Heb. 13:9). What is commanded, then, is a firm adherence to the faith in the midst of temptations and trials. As they wait patiently for their Lord to return, believers need to fortify themselves for the struggle against sin and with difficult circumstances.

It may be asked if this advice is relevant to us, since James bases it on the 'nearness' of the Lord. Many scholars think that James' conviction that the Lord was near was a 'mistake', a mistake that he shared with many early Christians and perhaps with Jesus himself. Were this so, the legitimacy of the course of action James here suggests would be called into serious question: of what value would such advice be when the basic understanding of the course of history on which it is based is mistaken? The accusation that James has erred on this matter rests on the supposition that James believed that the *parousia* must *necessarily* occur within a very brief period of time. But there is no reason to think that this was the case. The early Christians' conviction that the *parousia* was 'near', or 'imminent', meant that they fully believed that it *could* transpire within a very short period of time – not that it *had to*. They, like Jesus, knew neither 'the day nor the hour' (Mk. 13:32), but they acted, and taught others to act, as if their generation could be the last. Almost twenty centuries later, we live in exactly the same situation: our own decade could be the

[1]Actually, three-quarters of the average rainfall in Palestine falls in December-February, but it is the rain at the beginning and end of the growing season that is critical. See Denis Baly, *The Geography of the Bible* (Harper & Row, 1974), pp. 50–51.

last in human history. And James' advice to us is the same as it was to his first-century readers: *be patient, establish your hearts!*

9. At first glance, this verse does not have much in common with its context, beyond sharing an emphasis on the imminence of judgment. However, grumbling against others is surely one temptation that accompanies the pressure of difficult circumstances. How often do we find ourselves taking out the frustrations of a difficult day on our close friends and family members! Refraining from this kind of complaining and grumbling can be seen as one aspect of patience itself: patience is linked with 'forbearing one another' in love in Ephesians 4:2 and is contrasted with retaliation in 1 Thessalonians 5:14–15. The word *stenazō, grumble* or 'groan', is usually used absolutely; only here in biblical Greek does it have an object (*against one another*). The meaning may be that believers should not grumble to others *about* their difficulties, or that believers should not blame others *for* their difficulties (*cf.* NEB). It is entirely possible, however, that both ideas are involved.

As he has done in 4:11–12, James connects speaking against others with judgment. There, however, he likened critical speech to judgment; here he warns that criticism of one another places a person in danger of judgment. This warning is similar to, and may be influenced by, Jesus' well-known prohibition: 'Judge not, that you be not judged' (Mt. 7:1). To reinforce his warning, James reminds his readers again that this judgment is imminent: *the Judge is standing at the doors.* In the light of 4:12 ('there is one judge'), it is plausible to think that the judge here is God the Father. However, the parallelism between this statement and the references to the *parousia* in verses 7–8 make it more plausible to identify Christ as the judge (see Mt. 24:33; Rev. 3:10). Davids' concluding comment on this verse bears repeating: 'The nearness of the eschatological day is not just an impetus to look forward to the judgment of "sinners" . . ., but it is also a warning to examine one's behavior so that when the one whose footsteps are nearing finally knocks on the door, one may be prepared to open . . . . The coming Lord is also the judge of the Christian.'

10. The somewhat parenthetical nature of verse 9 is suggested by the fact that verses 10–11 hark back to the exhortation to patience in verses 7–8. These verses cite the prophets and Job as examples of patience and endurance under affliction. The rehearsal of great feats of fortitude under persecution was a staple of many intertestamental books (*cf.* 2 Maccabees) and is found in the New Testament also (*cf.* Heb. 11). Jesus encouraged his disciples to face persecution boldly, 'for so men persecuted the prophets who were before you' (Mt. 5:12). Specifically, James says, the prophets are an example of *suffering and patience.* If the RSV is correct in translating *kakopatheia* as *suffering,* this phrase is best taken as a hendiadys, according to which the one word modifies the other: 'patience in the face of suffering' (NIV; *cf.* NEB, GNB). On the other hand, there is good reason to translate *kakopatheia* 'endurance of suffering' (*cf.* the RSV translation of the cognate verb in 2 Tim. 4:5). With this meaning *kakopatheia* would denote the *fact* that the prophets endured affliction; *patience* (*makrothymia*) would describe the *manner* in which they endured it. The fact that these prophets *spoke in the name of the Lord* is added to make clear that the suffering endured by them was a result not of wrongdoing, but specifically of their faithful adherence to the will of God.

11. The first sentence of this verse summarizes the main point of verses 10–11: those who faithfully endure suffering are 'called blessed'. The author of 4 Maccabees begins his account by 'calling blessed' those martyrs who exhibited 'endurance' (*hypomonē*) in the face of persecution (1:10). Similarly, Jesus had bestowed a blessing on those who 'are persecuted for righteousness' sake' (Mt. 5:10). 'To be blessed' is not, of course, the same as being *happy* (despite the tendency of modern versions so to translate): 'happiness' normally suggests a subjective, emotional reaction; 'blessing' is the objective, unalterable approval and reward of God. As the prophets received this reward because they were faithful in tribulation, so, says James, did *Job.* Many have wondered at James' allusion to Job as a model of faithful endurance of suffering; particularly since the AV translated 'the patience of Job'. Yet even when we translate, more accurately, *the steadfastness* or 'perseverance' of Job, the illustration seems to be less than appropriate. Did not Job grumble about his circumstances,

171

self-righteously proclaim his innocence and generally question God's way with him? The seeming incompatibility between the canonical portrait of Job and James' description of him has led some to think that James is dependent on the apocryphal Testament of Job, where Job is presented in a much more positive light. Yet there is still a sense in which the Job of the Old Testament can be seen as a great example of steadfastness. For although Job did complain bitterly about God's treatment of him, he never abandoned his faith; in the midst of his incomprehension, he clung to God and continued to hope in him (cf. Jb. 1:21; 2:10; 16:19–21; 19:25–27). As Barclay says, 'Job's is no grovelling, passive, unquestioning submission; Job struggled and questioned, and sometimes even defied, but the flame of faith was never extinguished in his heart'.[1]

In addition to 'the steadfastness of Job', James' readers have also heard of *the purpose of the Lord*. This phrase has been subject to a great variety of interpretations. Some translate *telos* as *purpose* (like the RSV and JB) and understand it as a reference to the ultimate purpose of God *behind* Job's sufferings (cf. Jb. 42:5–6). However, *telos* can also mean 'end' or 'outcome' (so most English versions). The reference may then be to the *parousia* – the 'end' that the Lord brings about – or to the death and resurrection of Christ – the 'end' and 'seal' of the Lord's life. However, it makes best sense to take the phrase as a reference to the end or outcome of Job's situation, which the Lord eventually brought about: *e.g.*, the restoration of his family and fortune (Jb. 42:13). This interpretation fits with the parallels to James' phrase (Testament of Gad 7:4 and Testament of Benjamin 4:1; *cf.* Heb. 13:7), provides a concrete example of the 'blessing' mentioned earlier, and explains the final clause: Job's 'end' shows that the Lord is indeed *compassionate and merciful*. This also matches the overall message of the book of Job, one of whose purposes is to show how Job's faithfulness was rewarded in the end. Certainly, James does not mean that patience in suffering will always be rewarded by material prosperity; too many examples, in the Old Testament (Jeremiah!) and the New, prove this wrong. But he does seek to encourage our faithful, patient endurance of affliction by remind-

[1] W. Barclay, *Letters of James and Peter* (Daily Study Bible; Saint Andrew Press, ²1960), pp. 147–148.

ing us of the blessing that we receive for such faithfulness from our merciful and compassionate God.

VI. CONCLUDING EXHORTATIONS (5:12–20)

a. Oaths (5:12)

12. Although this verse stands essentially on its own, the introductory *above all* does appear to suggest some connection with the previous context. Certainly James cannot mean that taking oaths is a worse sin than others he has mentioned in the epistle (murder, adultery, worldliness). Perhaps, however, the reference is only to the immediate context, and he intends to highlight the irreverent use of God's name as a sin more serious than others that may be committed in time of distress (vv. 7–11) – especially, perhaps, in comparison to the other sins of speech, *e.g.* grumbling against other people (v. 9), mentioned in the context. Such a connection seems to be rather artificial, however, and it is better to see *above all* simply as drawing particular attention to this exhortation (*cf.* 1 Pet. 4:8). It may be also that the phrase is intended to signal the final section of the letter (Paul uses *to loipon*, 'finally', in this way in several of his letters).

The *swearing* that James here prohibits is not 'dirty' language as such, but the invoking of God's name, or substitutes for it, to guarantee the truth of what we say. In the Old Testament, God is frequently presented as guaranteeing the fulfilment of his promises with an oath. The law does not prohibit oaths, but demands that a person be true to any oath he has sworn (*cf.* Lv. 19:12 – yet another instance in which James includes a topic also mentioned in that chapter). Concern about the devaluation of oaths because of their indiscriminate use and the tendency to try to avoid fulfilling them by swearing by 'less sacred' things (*cf.* Mt. 23:16–22) led to warnings against using them too often (*cf.* Ecclus. 23:9, 11; Philo, *On the Decalogue* 84–95). Jesus, it appears, went even further than this, when he commanded his disciples not to swear 'at all' (Mt. 5:34). Jesus' teaching in Matthew 5:34–37 is particularly important in understanding James' teaching, because it looks as if James is consciously reproducing that

173

tradition. The similarity between the two passages is clearly seen when they are set side by side:

Matthew 5:34–37	James 5:12
'Do not swear at all,	'Do not swear,
either by heaven . . .	either by heaven
or by the earth . . .	or by earth
or by Jerusalem . . .	or with any other oath,
Do not swear by your head . . .	
Let what you say be simply "Yes" or "No";	but let your yes be yes and your no be no,
anything more than this comes from evil	that you may not fall under condemnation

It is often argued that Matthews and James diverge on one crucial point: Matthew suggests a 'substitute oath' – 'yes, yes' and 'no, no' (the RSV translation is a bit misleading here; a literal translation would read 'let your word be Yes, yes, No, no'), while James simply prohibits all oaths. But it is more likely that Jesus in Matthew is saying the same thing as James: our truthfulness should be so consistent and dependable that we need no oath to support it: a simple 'yes' or 'no' should suffice. 'Our mere word should be as utterly trustworthy as a signed document, legally correct and complete' (Mitton).

The question remains whether Jesus and James intended to prohibit *all* oaths. At the time of the Reformation, many in the Anabaptist tradition believed this was the case and refused by consequence to take oaths in the courtroom or anywhere else – a belief that many sincere Christians continue to hold. However, it is questionable whether either Jesus or James intended to address the issue of official oaths, oaths that responsible authorities ask us to take. What both have in mind seem to be *voluntary* oaths. Even with these, it is argued, the intention is not to forbid *any* oath, but only oaths that would have the intention of avoiding absolute truthfulness. This would seem to be the problem that Jesus addressed (*cf.* Mt. 23:16–22) and the evidence from Paul's epistles show that he, for one, continued to use oaths (Rom. 1:9; 2 Cor. 1:23; 11:11; Gal. 1:20; Phil. 1:8; 1 Thes. 2:5, 10). Nevertheless, caution is required. The repetition of Jesus' teaching by James, where the polemical context of Matthew 5 is lacking, warns us against assuming that the prohibition of oaths was related only to that false teaching. And it may be questioned whether Paul's 'witness' formula really fits into the category of an oath or not. It is possible that Jesus and James do intend to prohibit any voluntary oath.

b. Prayer and healing (5:13–18)

James, like so many other New Testament letter writers, concludes his homily with an encouragement to pray. Prayer is clearly the topic of this paragraph, being mentioned in every verse. James commends it to the individual believer, in the very different kinds of circumstances that he may face (vv. 13–14) and to the community as well (v. 16a). And he encourages such prayer by underscoring the powerful effects of prayer that flow from a righteous heart (vv. 16b–18). Some relationship to verse 12 may be perceived through the common theme of speaking with reference to God (bad speech, v. 12; and good, vv. 13–18), but James does nothing to suggest this connection. It is more plausible to think that James wants to commend prayer as a great source of strength for the affliction that the readers are experiencing (see the use of *kakopatheia* in both v. 10 and v. 13). Essentially, however, the paragraph is an independent entity.

13. 'Pray at all times', Paul commanded (Eph. 6:18; 1 Thes. 5:17). James, similarly, exhorts the believers to pray in whatever situation they may find themselves. They are to pray when *suffering*. *Kakopatheia*, the same word James has used in verse 10 with reference to the prophets, is a general term that denotes the experience of all sorts of afflictions and trials. Paul used the verbal form of this word to describe his imprisonment and exhorted Timothy to be willing to undergo this same kind of suffering (2 Tim. 2:9; 4:5). The prayer believers are to offer in such circumstances is not necessarily for deliverance from the trial, but for the strength to endure it faithfully. The believer is also to pray when he is *cheerful*. *Euthymeō* refers not to outward circumstances, but to the cheerfulness and happiness of heart that one can have whether in good times or in bad. It was this sense of well-being that Paul encouraged his fellow travellers to have even though their ship was in imminent danger of destruction (Acts 27:22, 25). When our hearts are comforted, it is all too easy to forget that this contentment comes ultimately only from God. Thus, perhaps even more than when suffering, we must be reminded in times of happiness of our glad obligation to acknowledge God's supreme role in our lives. We are to do this, James says, *singing praise*. The word he uses, *psallō*, is easily recognized as related to our English 'psalm'. Taken from a Greek word that designated a kind of harp, the word was used in the Septuagint to describe certain types of songs, especially songs of praise. This singing in praise was closely related to prayer (*cf.* 1 Cor. 14:15); indeed, it can be regarded as a form of prayer.

14. A third circumstance in which prayer is to figure prominently is now specifically mentioned: *illness*. In this case, however, the believer who is ill is not commanded to pray, but to summon *the elders of the church* so that they might *pray over him*. *Elders* are mentioned in the book of Acts in connection with the church in Jerusalem (11:30; 15:2; 21:18) and the churches founded through Paul (14:23; 20:17). Although in his letters Paul refers to elders by name only in 1 Timothy (5:17) and Titus (1:5), 'overseer' (or 'bishop'), mentioned in the plural in Philippians 1:1 and in the (probably generic) singular in 1 Timothy 3:1, is probably a different title for the same office. Both Peter (1 Pet. 5:1) and James assume the existence of *elders* in the church, showing that the office must have been a widespread one in the early church. It is possible, though not certain, that the office was taken over from the synagogue. From the prominent role of the elders in Acts and the description of the office in the Pastoral epistles, it can be inferred that the elders were those spiritually mature men who were given responsibility for the spiritual oversight of individual, local congregations. Since the Ephesian elders were to 'shepherd', or 'pastor' their flock (Acts 20:28), and 'pastors' are never mentioned along with elders, it is probable that the function of what we know as the 'pastor' or 'minister' was carried out by the elders. Hence, it is natural that the believer who is suffering from illness should summon the elders.

When the elders come, they are to pray *over* (*epi*) the one who is sick. Only here in biblical Greek is *proseuchomai* (*pray*) followed by *epi*: it may simply indicate physical position, but could possibly imply that hands were also laid *on* the sick person (see Mt. 19:13). This prayer is to be accompanied by *anointing with oil* – probably at the same time as the praying (viewing the aorist participle, with most commentators, as contemporaneous), but also possibly as a preliminary to the prayer.

This anointing is to be carried out *in the name of the Lord*, signifying the divine authority with which the anointing is done (see Acts 3:6, 16; 4:7, 10). But what is the purpose of this anointing with oil? The practice is mentioned only one other time in the New Testament: Mark tells us that the twelve 'cast out many demons, and anointed with oil many that were sick and healed them' (6:13). Unfortunately no more explanation of the practice is given there than here in James. In general, there are two main possibilities for the purpose of the anointing.

First, it may have a *practical* purpose. Oil was widely used in the ancient world as a medicine. In Jesus' parable, he tells us that the Samaritan who stopped to help the man who had been robbed and beaten 'went to him and bound up his wounds, pouring on oil and wine' (Lk. 10:34). Other ancient sources attest to its helpfulness in curing everything from toothache to paralysis (the famous second-century physician Galen recommended oil as 'the best of all remedies for paralysis', *Mod. Temp.*, 2). What James may be saying, then, is that the elders should come to the bedside of the sick armed with both spiritual and natural resources – with prayer and with medicine. Both are administered with the Lord's authority and both together can be used by him in healing the sick.[1] The difficulty with this view is twofold. First, evidence that anointing with oil was used for *any* medical problem is not found – and why mention only one (albeit widespread) remedy when many different illnesses would be encountered? Secondly, why should the elders of the church do the anointing if its purpose were solely medical? Surely others would have done this already were it an appropriate remedy for the complaint.

As a different kind of practical purpose, others suggest that the anointing may have been intended as an outward, physical

[1]See, especially, J. Wilkinson, *Health and Healing: Studies in New Testament Principles and Practices* (The Handsel Press, 1980), p. 153; *cf.* also Ross, p. 79; Burdick, p. 204.

177

expression of concern and as a means to stimulate the faith of the sick person.[1] Jesus sometimes used physical 'props' in his healings, apparently with just such a purpose. But when Jesus did so, the physical action was specifically appropriate to the illness, such as rubbing the eyes of a blind man (Mk. 8:23–26) and placing his finger in the ears of a deaf man (Mk. 7:33). There is simply no evidence that anointing with oil was generally used with such a purpose.

It is probable, then, that anointing with oil has a *religious* purpose. This second main explanation of the practice can be further subdivided into two types, according to whether the anointing is seen to have sacramental or merely symbolic significance. A sacramental understanding of this practice arose early in the history of the church. On the basis of this text the early Greek church practised what they called the *'euchelaion'* (a combination of the words *euchē*, 'prayer', and *elaion*, 'oil', both used in this text), which had the purpose of strengthening the body and soul of the sick. The Western church continued this practice for many centuries, as well as using oil for anointing on other occasions. Later, the Roman church gave to the priest the exclusive right to perform this ceremony and developed the sacrament of 'extreme unction'. This sacrament has the purpose of removing any remnant of sin and of strengthening the soul of the dying (healing is considered only a possibility). The Council of Trent (XIV, 1) found this sacrament 'insinuated' in Mark 6:13 and 'promulgated' in James 5:14. Clearly this developed sacrament has little basis in James' text: he recommends anointing for any illness and associates it with healing rather than with preparation for death. Nevertheless, the oil could be considered to have a sacramental function in that it acted as a 'vehicle of divine power'.[2] Much as partaking of the Lord's Supper conveys to the believing partici-

---

[1]Tasker, p. 131; Mitton, p. 191; D. R. Hayden, 'Calling the Elder to Pray', *BibSac* 138, 1981, p. 265.

[2]Davids, p. 193; *cf.* also Calvin, pp. 355–356; Dibelius, pp. 252–254. There is evidence that oil was considered to have a spiritual value (Life of Adam and Eve 36) and to aid in exorcising demons (Testament of Solomon 18:34). That the oil here had the purpose of exorcism, the illness being viewed as demon-inspired, is argued by Dibelius, p. 252 and W. Brunotte, *NIDNTT* 1, p. 121. But anointing with oil is never done in conjunction with exorcisms in the New Testament; Mk 6:13, indeed, distinguishes between anointing the sick and casting out demons.

pant a strengthening in grace, so anointing may be mandated by God as a physical element through which he works the grace of healing in the sick believer. One's attitude towards this view will depend considerably on one's view of the 'sacrament' in general. But it may also be asked whether a practice mentioned only once in the New Testament (although *cf.* Mk. 6:13) can possess the importance which this view gives to anointing.

It is best, then, to think of the anointing with oil as a symbolic action. Anointing frequently symbolizes the consecration of persons or things for God's use and service in the Old Testament. And while *chriō* is usually used in these texts, James has probably chosen *aleiphō* because of the phsyical action involved (see Additional Note on *aleiphō* and *chriō*, below). As the elders prayed, they would anoint the sick person in order to symbolize that that person was being 'set apart' for God's special attention and care. While Calvin, Luther and other expositors think that the practice of anointing, along with the power to heal, was meant to be confined to the apostolic age, it is doubtful that such a restriction can be maintained. James' recommendation that regular church officers carry out the practice would seem to imply its permanent validity in the church. On the other hand, the fact that anointing a sick person is mentioned only here in the New Testament epistles, and that many healings were accomplished without anointing, shows that the practice is not a necessary accompaniment to the prayer for healing. Elders who pray for the sick *may* do it, and James clearly recommends the practice; but they do not *have* to do so.

Additional Note: *aleiphō* and *chriō* (5:14)

Scripture employs two Greek words to mean 'anoint': *chriō* and *aleiphō*. James' choice of the latter word in verse 14 may help our understanding of his allusive reference to 'anointing with oil'.

Aleiphō is used only twenty times in the Septuagint. Ezekiel is the only author to use it to mean 'rub whitewash' on walls (seven times, all translating Heb. *ṭûḥ*). The word frequently refers to the rubbing of oil on the face or body with a beautifying or hygienic purpose (nine times, usually with Heb. *sûk*). Four times, however, the verb has a ceremonial significance. The precise meaning of Genesis 31:13 is unclear, but in Exodus 40:15 (twice) and Numbers 3:3, *aleiphō* denotes the ceremonial anointing of the priests, whereby they were set apart for the service of God.

It is this last-named meaning that is the regular meaning of *chriō* in the Septuagint. In most of its seventy-eight occurrences, it designates the 'consecration' of priests, sanctuary furnishings or the king of Israel. Only three times does it refer to a cosmetic treatment. Significantly, neither word is used with reference to medicinal purposes in the Septuagint.

The same general picture is maintained in the New Testament. *Chriō* always has a metaphorical meaning, designating God's special setting aside of Jesus for his ministry (Lk. 4:18 [= Is. 61:1]; Acts 4:27; 10:38; Heb. 1:9 [= Ps. 45:7]), or the consecration of Paul to his (2 Cor. 1:21). As in the Septuagint, *aleiphō* most often designates a cosmetic or hygienic anointing (Mt. 6:17; Mk. 16:1; Lk. 7:38, 46 (twice); Jn. 11:2; 12:3). It is possible, however, that the word has some symbolic overtones in the account of Jesus' anointing (Jn. 11:2; 12:3).

The significance of this data for James 5:14 is not entirely clear. On the one hand, it can be argued that *chriō* is the word that more frequently has religious or symbolic overtones and that James would probably have chosen this word had he intended any such significance. On the other hand, however, neither word is used in Scripture with a medicinal meaning (leaving aside for the moment Mk. 6:13 and Jas. 5:14). In Luke 10:34, where oil (*elaion*) clearly has a medicinal use, the verb *epicheō*, 'put on', is used. Therefore it is probably because *aleiphō* is the New Testament word that describes the physical act of anointing that James has chosen to use it here; *chriō* never refers to physical anointing in the New Testament.

But while James clearly describes a physical action, it is not necessary to eliminate all symbolic significance from the action. As we have seen, *aleiphō* is used equivalently to *chriō* in the Septuagint with reference to the consecrating of priests (Ex. 40:15; *cf. chriō* in 40:13; Nu. 3:3). (Josephus can also use *aleiphō* with symbolic meaning, parallel to *chriō*; compare *Antiquities* 6.165 with 6.157.) It is best, then, to view James' anointing as a physical action with symbolic significance. Since the symbolism of 'anointing' is usually associated with the setting apart or consecrating of someone or something for God, we are probably to understand this as the symbolism intended in the action. As the elders pray for the sick person, they also set that person apart for God's special attention.

15. While anointing with oil, because of its uncertain meaning, not unnaturally attracts a good deal of attention, we must remember that it is *prayer* that is James' main concern in these verses. This is reflected in James' ascribing the anticipated healing to the elders' *prayer*, not to the anointing. Their prayer is denoted with an unusual word, *euchē*, which connotes a strong, fervent wish or petition (see the use of the verb *euchomai* in Acts 26:29; 27:29; Rom. 9:3). But it is not the fervency or the frequency of the prayer that renders it effective – it is *faith*. *Faith* in 1:6–8, where James also discusses the efficacy of prayer, refers to a whole-hearted unwavering commitment to God. Since it is the elders who offer this prayer, it is clear that it is also their faith that is intended here. James describes two results of *the prayer of faith*: the sick person will *be saved* and *the Lord will raise him up*. *Save* (*sōzō*) usually refers in the New Testament to deliverance from spiritual death, and some scholars think that this may be James' meaning here also. In fact, they suggest that all of verses 14–16a may be about restoration to spiritual health rather than physical health. But James' language is too definite to allow this interpretation; he is clearly thinking, at least primarily, of physical healing (see the Additional Note on Healing, pp. 183–187). The word *sōzō* is certainly appropriate as a description of restoration to health and is used in this way frequently in the Gospels. Similarly, *raise up* (*egeirō*) is used to describe the renewed physical vigour of those who have been healed (Mt. 9:6; Mk. 1:31; Acts 3:7). Thus the picture is of the elders praying 'over' the 'sick man' in his bed and the Lord intervening to *raise him up* from that bed.

James' introduction of the topic of *sin* at this point is no doubt occasioned by the widespread belief that sickness was caused by sin. But James' *and if* (*kan*) makes it clear that he does not believe that sickness is necessarily the result of sin, and in this, of course, he is following the teaching of Jesus (*cf*. Jn. 9:2–3). On the other hand, the New Testament makes clear that sickness and death can be caused by sin (Mk. 2:1–12; 1 Cor. 5:5(?); 11:27–30), and it is this eventuality that James provides for at this point. This is not to be explained along the lines of modern discoveries regarding the relationship of psychological and physical illness. It is sin, not emotional instability or psychological disorder, that James links to sickness.

James introduces no qualification to the promises in this verse: the prayer of faith *will* save the sick person, his sins *will* be forgiven. Does this mean that a prayer for healing that is offered in faith will infallibly be effectual? As we have seen, some have suggested that this is the case, but have confined these miraculous cures to the apostolic age. But there is nothing in the text to suggest such a restriction. A more helpful observation is to note James' specific reminder that the prayer must be a *prayer of faith.* This faith, while certainly including the notion of confidence in God's ability to answer, also involves absolute confidence in the perfection of God's will. A true prayer of faith, then, always includes within it a tacit acknowledgment of God's sovereignty in all matters; that it is *God's* will that must be done. And it is clear that it is by no means always God's will to heal those who are ill (*cf.* 2 Cor. 12:7–9). Therefore, the 'faith' that is the indispensable condition for our prayers for healing to be answered – this faith being the gift of God – can be truly present only when it is God's will to heal (see Additional Note on Healing, pp. 183–187).

16a. As a consequence (*oun*) of the promise that God responds to prayer (vv. 14–15a) and forgives sin (v. 15b), believers should be committed to confessing their sins to one another and praying for one another. Mutual confession of sins, which James encourages as a habitual practice (this is suggested by the present tense of the imperative), is greatly beneficial to the spiritual vitality of a church. This was seen at the time of the 'Methodist' movement in eighteenth-century England. The suggested 'rule' for the small meetings of believers that spiritually fuelled that movement had at its head the encouragement to mutual confession and prayer from James 5:16a.

What kind of *sins* are to be confessed? It may be that James thinks only of those sins which have brought harm to others (*cf.* Mt. 5:25–26). But the end of the sentence makes it probable that specifically those sins which may have caused illness are intended. *That you may be healed* expresses the purpose of mutual confession and prayer. Many take this 'healing' to be spiritual in nature, or perhaps a general healing, including both the physical and spiritual spheres. In this case, verse 16a is to be seen as a general deduction drawn from the specific situation of verses 14–15. But it is better to take this sentence as a concluding exhortation to the discussion of physical illness. This is because the verb *heal* (*iaomai*) is consistently applied to physical afflictions. To be sure, it is used in the Septuagint to describe the 'healing' of sin or faithlessness (*cf.* Dt. 30:3; Is. 6:10; 53:5; Je. 3:22), but in these contexts it is usually the case that sin has already been explicitly compared to a 'wound'. In the New Testament *iaomai* is used with spiritual application only in quotations from these Old Testament texts. Therefore, since the purpose of this confession and prayer is physical healing, it is best to understand the confession as involving any sins which may hinder that healing and the prayers to be specifically for the cure of bodily afflictions. It is striking that, while in verse 14 the elders are to pray for the healing, here the whole church body is to be involved in prayer for healing. As Davids says, James 'consciously generalizes, making the specific case of 5:14–15 into a general principle of preventive medicine . . .'. This verse also demonstrates that the power to heal is invested in prayer, not the elder. And while it is appropriate that those charged with the spiritual oversight of the community should be called to intercede for those seriously ill, James makes clear that *all* believers have the privilege and responsibility to pray for healing.

Additional Note on Healing

James 5:14–16 is the only passage in the New Testament epistles that directly addresses the question of physical healing. It is therefore appropriate to add some further comments on the text and to reflect further on the matter of healing. There are several issues to be considered.

a. Physical vs. spiritual healing. As we have seen, some argue that the text does not have to do with physical healing at all, but with spiritual restoration. They point out that *astheneō* in verse 14 can mean 'spiritually weak' (1 Cor. 8:11; 2 Cor. 13:3), as can *kamnō*, used in verse 15 (*cf.* Heb. 12:3). And *save* (*sōzō*), *raise* (*egeirō*) and *heal* (*iaomai*) are all used to describe restoration to spiritual vitality. Coming in a context in which the dangers of spiritual lethargy and slackness are all too real (*cf.* 5:7–11), an exhortation to the elders to pray for those downtrodden and weak in faith would be entirely appropriate.[1] While all this is true, James' language makes it impossible to eliminate the physical dimension. First, while *astheneō can* denote spiritual weakness, this meaning is usually made clear by a qualifier (*cf.* Rom. 14:2, 'in faith'; 1 Cor. 8:7, 'in conscience') or the context. Moreover, in the material that is most relevant to James, the Gospels, *astheneō* almost always refers to illness. The same is true for *kamnō*. And *iaomai*, when not used in an Old Testament quotation, always refers in the New Testament to physical healing. Beyond this, it is significant that the only other mention of 'anointing with oil' in the New Testament comes in a description of physical healing (Mk. 6:13).

Granted that physical healing is in view, then, is it possible that spiritual restoration is also involved? Many think that this is the case in verse 16a; others that the 'salvation' in verse 15 may be purposely broad so as to include both the physical and spiritual dimension. Thus, even if the prayer of faith does not bring healing, it may bring salvation from sin. But this idea does not fit well in the text. For one thing, salvation is never seen to be the result of prayer in the New Testament. For another, giving two different, though related, meanings to 'save' and 'raise up' violates a cardinal principle of semantics: never give a word more meaning than the context requires. A physical restoration is all that the context requires; and we should be wary of adding an unnecessary reference to spiritual deliverance. Several elements of the text require a reference to physical healing; everything in the text makes sense as a description of physical healing. Probably, then, the meaning of the text should be confined to physical healing.

b. Who heals? James' answer to this question is clear: '*the Lord will raise him up*'. Nowhere does the New Testament suggest

---

[1]See, for this general approach, M. Meinertz, 'Die Krankensalbung Jak. 5, 14f', *Biblische Zeitschrift* 20, 1932, pp. 23–36; C. Amerding, 'Is any among you afflicted? A Study of James 5:13–20', *BibSac* 95, 1938, pp. 195–201; C. Pickar, 'Is anyone sick among you?', *CBQ* 7, 1945, pp. 165–174; D. R. Hayden, 'Calling the Elder to Pray', pp. 258–286.

any other answer. When the apostles 'healed' people, they made it clear that they did so only through the power and the authority of the Lord Jesus (Acts 4:7–12). Paul spoke of a 'gift' of healing (1 Cor. 12:9, 28), but this gift, as all others, was empowered by and directed by the Spirit who gave the gift. It is interesting, however, that while Paul speaks of a gift of healing, James speaks only of elders who pray for healing. Were there none who had the gift of healing in James' churches? Is the power to heal confined by James to certain ecclesiastical office-holders? These questions are difficult to answer, and involve us in the larger question of the relationship between 'charismatic' and 'organized' ministries in the New Testament. Briefly, however, it would seem that early churches differed in the extent to which certain gifts were manifest. Indeed, the Corinthian church seems to be something of an exception in the New Testament, since only here do we read of such 'spectacular' gifts as 'healings' and 'miracles' (contrast Rom. 12:6–8 and Eph. 4:11). Church 'organization' must not be regarded as depreciating or ignoring gifts, but as a helpful means of recognizing and manifesting gifts for the edification of the church. Elders were those spiritual leaders who were recognized for their maturity in the faith. Therefore it is natural that they, with their deep and rich experience, should be called on to pray for healing. They, above all, should be able to discern the will of the Lord and to pray with the faith that recognizes and receives God's gift of healing. At the same time, James makes clear that the church at large is to pray for healing (v. 16a). Therefore, while not denying that some in the church may have the gift of healing, James encourages all Christians, and especially those charged with pastoral oversight, to be active in prayer for healing.

c. On what basis does God heal? Perhaps no greater challenge to faith occurs than that which comes when fervent, diligent prayer for our own, or others', healing is not answered. Several persistent questions arise in such situations.

Was it the sin of the sick person that prevented healing? There is no doubt that this can sometimes be the case. Paul specifically says that some of the Corinthian Christians have fallen ill and died because of their abuse of the Lord's Supper (1 Cor. 11:30). In times of illness it is appropriate to examine our spiritual lives to see if anything is amiss; and to encourage, with pastoral love, others to do the same. Confession of sin, says James, can lead to healing (v. 16). On the other hand, James also makes it clear that not *all* sickness is caused by sin (see the comments on v. 15). The idea that there must be a one-to-one correspondence between sin and sickness is clearly rejected in Scripture (*cf.* Job; Jn. 9:2–3). Therefore it is not always, and perhaps even not usually, a specific sin that causes prayers for healing to go unanswered.

Was it a lack of faith that prevented healing? Did I, or those praying for me, not *believe* sufficiently deeply? As we have seen, James clearly specifies that it is 'the prayer of *faith*' that God responds to. He does indeed seem to imply, then, that it is a lack of faith that will get in the way of God's healing work. But we must carefully note what is meant by this. The faith exercised in prayer is faith in the God who sovereignly accomplishes his will. When we pray, our faith will necessarily include this recognition, explicit or implicit, of the overruling providential purposes of God. Perhaps, at times, we are given insight into that will in specific circumstances and we pray with absolute confidence in God's plan to answer as we ask. But surely these cases are very rare – more rare even than our subjective, emotional desires would lead us to suspect. A prayer for healing, then, must usually be qualified by a recognition that God's will in the matter is supreme. And it is clear in the New Testament that God does *not* always will to heal the believer. Paul's own prayer for his healing, offered three times, was not answered; God had a purpose in allowing the 'thorn in the flesh', that 'messenger of Satan', to remain (2 Cor. 12:7–9). What we are suggesting, then, is that the faith with which we pray is always faith in the God whose will is supreme and best; only sometimes does this faith include assurance that a particular request is within that will. This is exactly the qualification that is needed to understand Jesus' own promise: 'if you ask anything in my name, I will do it' (Jn. 14:14). To ask 'in Jesus' name' means not simply to utter his name, but to take into account his will. Only those requests offered 'in that will' are granted. Prayer for healing offered in the confidence that God will answer that prayer *does* bring healing; but only when it is God's will to heal will that faith, itself a gift of God, be present. Such faith cannot be 'manufactured', however gifted, insistent, or righteous we are. In this life, we shall not, most of the time, be able to know whether God's will is to heal; we shall not always be able to sense whether that 'faith' that gets what is asked for is present. When our sincere, fervent prayers for healing go unanswered, therefore, it is not our lack of faith that is at fault; the context in which such faith could be present was absent.

16b. James' reminder of the great power of prayer in the last part of verse 16 provides a basis for the exhortations to pray, which he has given in verses 13–16a. The power possessed by prayer is not limited to 'super saints'; the *righteous man* simply designates one who is whole-heartedly committed to God and sincerely seeking to do his will. James employs a third word for *prayer* here (*deēsis*), but he apparently uses it without any difference in meaning from the other two words for prayer used in this paragraph (*cf. proseuchomai* in vv. 13, 14, 17–18; *euchomai* in vv. 15–16a). To emphasize the efficacy of prayer, James has added to the word 'be strong' (*has power*) two qualifiers: prayer is strong 'in much', 'to *great* degree' (*poly*) and 'in its working', *in its effects* (*energoumenē*). This last word, a participle, could be either passive or middle. If passive, we should translate 'prayer is very powerful when it is energized (by God or the Spirit)'. Thus there would be introduced a specific qualification on the effectiveness of prayer from the standpoint of the will of God. However, the participle is more likely to be middle (as most of the modern translations presume), with the meaning 'prayer is very powerful in its working, or in its effect'.[1]

17–18. As an example of a righteous man whose prayers had great effect James cites *Elijah*. The prophet, whose exploits were so spectacular and manner of 'death' so remarkable, was one of the most popular of all figures among Jews. He was celebrated for his powerful miracles and his prophetic denunciations of sin. Most of all, however, he was looked for as the helper in time of need whose coming would pave the way for the Messianic age

[1] The passive meaning was argued for by Mayor in a long discussion in which he sought to show that most of the New Testament occurrences of this form are passive (pp. 177–179; *cf.* also Davids, p. 197). But Adamson, who replies to Mayor, seems to be more convincing: the New Testament examples are all better interpreted as middles (pp. 205–210; *cf.* also Moule, p. 26).

(Mal. 4:5–6; Ecclus. 48:1–10; Mk. 9:12; Lk. 1:17). But it is not Elijah's special prophetic endowment or unique place in history that interests James, but the fact that, though he was *a man of like nature with ourselves*, his prayer had *great power in its effects*. James highlights the fervency of Elijah's prayer with the use of a Semitic influenced 'cognate' construction: literally, 'in prayer he prayed'. He wants his readers to recognize that this power of prayer is available to all who are sincerely following the Lord – not just to a special few.

The situation James describes is recorded in 1 Kings 17 – 18. The drought was proclaimed by God through Elijah as a means of punishing Ahab and Israel for their idolatry. Although the Old Testament does not state that Elijah prayed for the drought, 1 Kings 8:42 does picture him praying for the drought to end, and it is a legitimate inference to think that he prayed for its onset also. Similarly, we should probably take the three and half years specified by James (*cf.* also Lk. 4:25) as a more specific figure for the rounded-off 'three years' in 1 Kings 18:1. Perhaps the figure 'three and a half' was suggested by its symbolic associations with a period of judgment (Dn. 7:25; *cf.* Rev. 11:12; 12:14). But in the light of the fact that the Old Testament never specifically mentions Elijah's prayer for the drought, why has James chosen this as his example – particularly since other examples of his praying were much better-known (that fire would consume the sacrifice on Mount Carmel) or appropriate to James' context (raising the widow's son to life)? Perhaps James intends us to see in the deadness of the land brought back to life an analogy to the illness of the believer restored to health (Davids). On the other hand, evidence exists of a tradition that associated the drought with Elijah's praying (Ecclus. 48:2–3; 2 Esdras 7:109) and it is probable that James has chosen this simply as a familiar illustration.

c. A closing summons to action (5:19–20)

19–20. James closes his letter not with the greetings and benediction typical of epistolary endings, but with a summons to action. In this, his letter is typical of other more 'formal' New Testament letters that read almost like sermons (*cf.* 1 John especially). For a last time James addresses his *brethren*. He has spoken to them in his letter about many problems: sinful speech, disobedience, unconcern about others, worldliness, quarrelling, arrogance. Now he encourages every believer to take the initiative in bringing any who have 'wandered from the truth' in any of these ways back into fellowship with God and the community.

The truth does not refer here to Christian doctrine in the narrow sense, but more broadly to all that is involved in the gospel. This truth is something that is to be 'done' as well as believed (*cf.* Ps. 51:6; Gal. 5:7; 1 Jn. 1:6). And for James, of course, correct doctrine cannot be separated from correct behaviour. What the mind thinks, and the mouth confesses, the body must do – anything less is worldly, sinful 'double-mindedness'. The word translated *wanders* (*planaō*; from which the word 'planet', a heavenly 'wanderer', is taken) should not be restricted – as the English word could be – to an inadvertent or unconscious departure from 'the truth'; it was widely used to describe any deviation from the 'way of righteousness', whether wilful or not. Peter refers to his readers generally as those who 'were straying like sheep' (1 Pet. 2:25; see also Wisdom 5:6 and 2 Pet. 2:15).

The believer who sees his brother wandering from the fold should seek with all his power to *bring him back*. *Bring back* (*epistrephō*) can be used to describe an initial turning to God for salvation (Acts 14:15; 15:19; 26:18; 1 Thes. 1:9) but it also, as here, can refer to the turning *back* to the faith from which one has strayed (Mk. 4:12 [=Is. 6:10]; Lk. 1:16; 22:32). In verse 20, this straying is described as *the error of his way*, a phrase that could be translated 'his wandering way', in order to show that 'error' (*planē*) is cognate to 'wander' (*planaō*) in verse 19. The believer who succeeds in rescuing such a 'sinner' from 'the error of his way' should know what has thereby been accomplished: his soul has been saved from death and *a multitude of sins* has been *covered*.

But *whose* soul and *whose* sin? The Greek is completely ambiguous at this point, allowing either phrase to be applied to the one who has sinned or the one who has converted the sinner. However, the soul which has been saved from death is almost certainly the soul of the one who has sinned. *Death* refers to eschatological punishment in James (*cf.* 1:21), and only the one who has 'wandered away' is in danger of this judgment. In keeping with many other biblical texts, James pictures 'death' as the final destination on the path which the sinner has determined to take: when he is turned back from that journey, he has saved his life (see Ezk. 18:27; Rom. 6:23). It is more difficult to know whether the sins which are covered are the sinner's, the converter's, or both. The words are an allusion to Proverbs 10:12, where hate, which 'stirs up strife', is contrasted with love, that 'covers all offences'. The 'covering' here seems to be the overlooking of slights and offences against us in the interest of preserving peace. This meaning is unlikely in James, however, and 1 Peter 4:8 shows that the phrase had become a traditional one to designate God's forgiveness of sins (cf. Ps. 32:1). The notion that our efforts to bring others to repentance will bring benefit to our own spiritual standing is certainly biblical. The Lord promises Ezekiel that he 'will save his life' if he is faithful in warning his people of their danger of judgment (Ezk. 3:21); and Paul tells Timothy that he will 'save both himself and his hearers' if he takes heed to himself and his teaching (1 Tim. 4:16). The blessing given to the faithful believers must not, of course, be construed as a reward for his efforts. But the idea that God will treat us as we have treated others is inescapable in Scripture (Mt. 6:14–15; 18:23–35) and explicitly mentioned by James (2:12–13). Therefore James may well be encouraging his readers to seek actively the conversion of those who are straying by reminding them that their efforts will be met by God's approval and blessing. On the other hand, the sequence of thought in the verse makes it a little awkward to refer the covering of sins to a person different from the one whose salvation has been described. Furthermore, Scripture often associates salvation with the covering, the complete blotting out of sins, so that the two phrases could be parallel descriptions of the blessing attained by the sinner who is brought back. Probably this latter interpretation should be accepted, although the former is by no means impossible.

If James is indeed something of a sermon in epistolary form, these last two verses are an appropriate closing summons to action. Not only should the readers of James 'do' the words he has written; they should be deeply concerned to see that others 'do' them also. It is by sharing with James the conviction that there is indeed an eternal death, to which the way of sin leads, that we shall be motivated to deal with sin in our lives and in the lives of others.